HUMAN QUESTIONS AND COSMIC ANSWERS

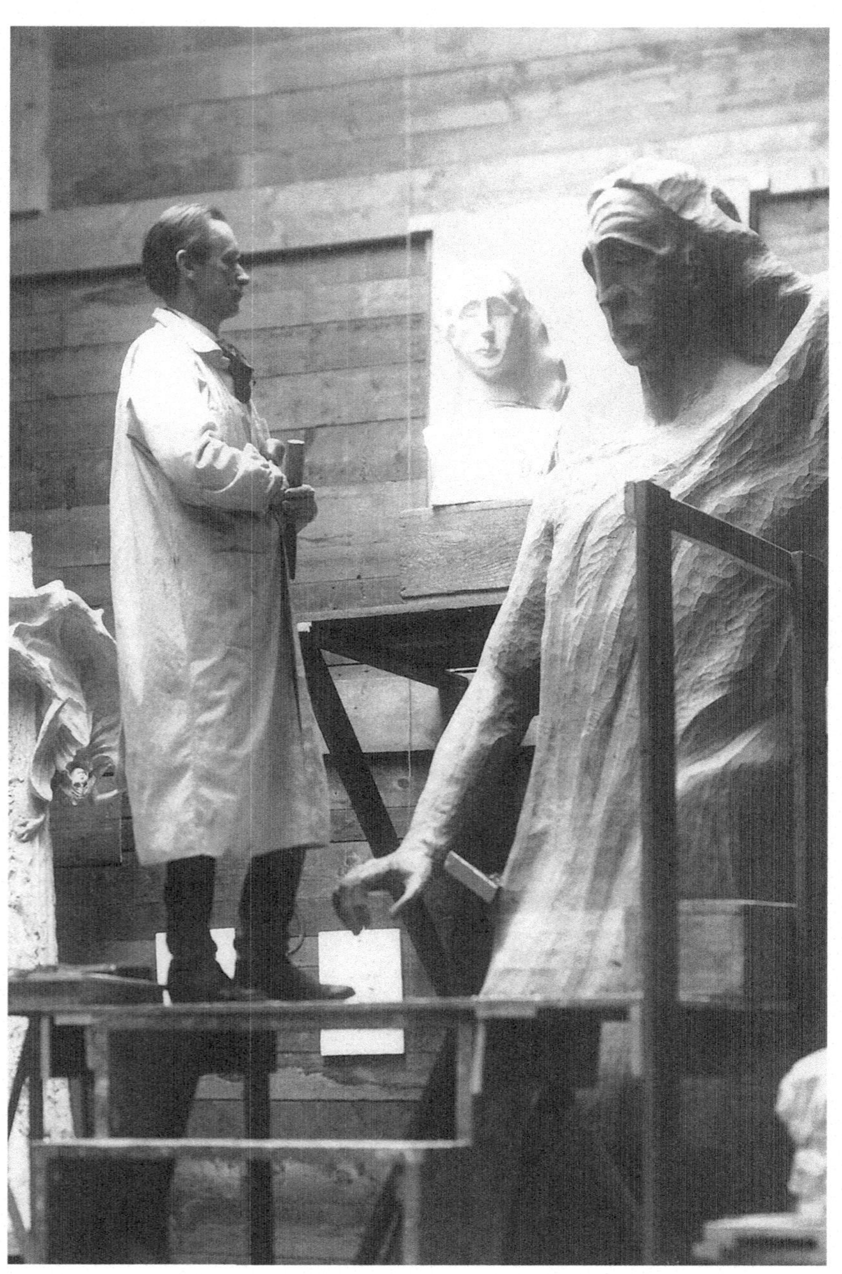

HUMAN QUESTIONS AND COSMIC ANSWERS

Thirteen lectures given in Dornach between 24
June and 22 July 1922

TRANSLATED AND INTRODUCED BY
ELIZABETH MARSHALL

RUDOLF STEINER

RUDOLF STEINER PRESS

CW 213

Rudolf Steiner Press
Hillside House, The Square
Forest Row, RH18 5ES

www.rudolfsteinerpress.com

Published by Rudolf Steiner Press 2024

Originally published in German under the title *Menschenfragen und Weltenantworten* (volume 213 in the *Rudolf Steiner Gesamtausgabe* or Collected Works) by Rudolf Steiner Verlag, Dornach. Based on shorthand notes that were not reviewed or revised by the speaker. This authorized translation is based on the second revised German edition (1987), edited by W. Dettwyler und R. Friedenthal

Published by permission of the Rudolf Steiner Nachlassverwaltung, Dornach

© Rudolf Steiner Nachlassverwaltung, Dornach, Rudolf Steiner Verlag 1987

This translation © Rudolf Steiner Press 2024

All rights reserved. No part of this publication may be reproduced, stored in a retrieval system, or transmitted, in any form or by any means, electronic, mechanical, photocopying or otherwise, without the prior permission of the publishers

A catalogue record for this book is available from the British Library

ISBN 978 1 85584 668 5

Cover by Morgan Creative
Typeset by Symbiosys Technologies, Visakhapatnam, India
Printed and bound by 4Edge Ltd., Essex

Contents

Introduction

THIS volume consists of a number of lectures given by Rudolf Steiner between 24 June and 22 July 1922 in Dornach. The subject matter varies from a description of the dimensions as they relate to the various members of the human organization, the state of European culture in the nineteenth and early twentieth centuries, the destruction by the Roman church of pagan and gnostic temples and rituals between the second and sixth centuries, and much, much more. Amongst all this is a strikingly compassionate look at the lives of Franz Brentano and Friedrich Nietzsche. Thus it is not possible to pick out an overarching theme to examine here in more detail. But there are several points which do rather present themselves for consideration and I will take a short look at them here, without however any claim to have even touched on all the possibilities offered in these lectures.

What particularly attracts the reader's attention is Rudolf Steiner's recurring appeal to us to open our hearts to the suffering of Franz Brentano and Friedrich Nietzsche. Both of these great men, as Rudolf Steiner himself calls them, foundered on their inability to reach the spiritual world. In Lecture Eight, Steiner says: '…the culture of the times had crushed the human soul, as we have seen in the example of Franz Brentano.'

Both Brentano and Nietzsche were great men in the sense that both were deep thinkers of great integrity, unable—as did other more superficial thinkers—to gloss over the abyss deepening between increasingly materialistic science and the need of their souls for the spiritual. Tragically they lived just before the advent of anthroposophy and the revealing and exploring of the wisdom of the Mysteries through Rudolf Steiner. So both were doomed to shipwreck on the rocks of nineteenth century materialism—the one suffering the constant agony of the soul hungering for the spiritual, the other descending into profound distress and ultimately madness.

In contrast we have the most blessed luck to live in times when the Mysteries have been and are being revealed and to actually have come into contact with this great work. I think we are inclined not to be sufficiently aware of the enormity of this situation, tending often to take for granted what has been offered us through Rudolf Steiner and his life's work. I know I have this tendency and it is important for me to consider what my life would have been like had I been born a century earlier. This is what Steiner is urging us to do. When we wake up to this realization, then we will be on our way to developing that quality we most need for the spiritual path: the quality of gratitude.

Another theme touched on repeatedly in these pages is the development of consciousness since the earliest human era. Beginning with the ancient initiates, Rudolf Steiner shows us how we have descended in consciousness from the etheric and astral worlds into the material/physical, from the intuitive/imaginative to the intellectual. The ancient initiates knew first-hand the healing properties of the plants and minerals, their relationship to the heavens and the cosmos. They knew of the interdependency of all creation, how we cannot understand a plant without knowing of its roots in the earth and its striving for the sunlight. We cannot understand a human thigh bone without knowing of the forces of gravity and their direction in relation to the earth. We cannot understand the human being without understanding the cosmos, the planets, the constellations and the zodiac.

Again Steiner emphasizes the inner state of mind of the ancient initiates. They approached the cosmos with the most profound respect, preparing and cleansing themselves before they turned in deepest reverence towards the recipient of their petitions, whether the sun, Mars or Jupiter, for example. Having asked their questions they then waited, sometimes many, many years, all the while cultivating within themselves an attitude of receptiveness and devotion, ready to accept the answers the cosmos would give them. They did not expect an answer immediately or think they could find it on their own at their writing desk or in their laboratory. They knew they must immerse themselves with reverence in the cosmos, in the spirits of the cosmos, to be able to understand the world and to understand themselves.

A third important aspect in these lectures is the question of what we have achieved through the development of thinking. Rudolf Steiner says that we have learnt 'to think like Ahriman'. The Scholastics, who developed Aristotelian thinking for the age of the intellectual soul, always recoiled in the last instance from Ahriman—as if burnt. Right up until Brentano, thinkers recoiled from Ahriman. Brentano himself recoiled from Ahriman. In the nineteenth century, rational thinking connected completely with Ahriman, especially in the theory of the atoms which was developed at that time. The danger, however, is that just as the attitude of the ancient initiates determined their ability to receive cosmic answers to their questions, so the attitude of thinking that the earth consists of atoms determines the actual existence of the earth. If we think the earth is made of atoms, there is the very real danger that it will actually end up consisting of atoms.

With these three examples I hope to have illustrated at least briefly how Steiner is pointing out to us that our own attitude, our own thinking, feeling and will affect reality, create reality. So too when we read these lectures, much depends on our attitude, our way of approaching what is said, as to whether we can really profit from them and how profoundly they can touch us. This is obviously true of all Steiner's work. When we realize how deeply Brentano and Nietzsche suffered through their inability to realize the spiritual world, when we see how devotedly the ancients prepared themselves for receiving knowledge of the cosmos, and when we are aware of how our own consciousness and beliefs shape and influence reality, then we will be able to approach such a work with the necessary humility and respect, without forfeiting our autonomy. Then it is possible for true learning, true spiritual science to be conveyed from the heart of one human being to another.

Elizabeth Marshall
Berlin, 8 August 2024

First Lecture

DORNACH, 24 JUNE 1922

T ODAY I will be dealing with some aspects which may seem quite remote from the practical considerations of anthroposophy, but which nevertheless must form the basis for many ideas which we can then elaborate in more intimate discussions.

When we speak of the physical human being on the one hand and the soul-spiritual on the other, then we are faced with a cognitive issue, a problem related to human intelligence. Human beings can conceptualize the physical with relative ease. We have as a template the physical body as revealed through the senses. It belongs to what confronts us on all sides as part of our environment, without us becoming active ourselves, at least with regard to our consciousness. However, it is a different matter when we speak of the soul-spiritual. The soul-spiritual is such that anyone who is sufficiently unprejudiced is clearly aware that it exists. Humanity has always included names, words, phrases, idioms for the soul-spiritual in the various languages and the fact alone that these names, words and phrases exist in language shows that for the unbiased consciousness there is something pointing the human being in the direction of the soul-spiritual.

However, difficulties immediately arise when we try to relate the physical world to the soul-spiritual world. This attempt to link the two is particularly problematic for those who think about such things in, let us say, a philosophical mode. They know that the physical is spread out in space. They can even make representations of the physical in space. And human beings can develop the relevant concepts comparatively easily, since we can use what space with its three dimensions offers us to conceptualize the physical. But we cannot find the spiritual itself anywhere in space.

People who see themselves as not at all materialistic, but who in reality are, want to see the soul-spiritual in space and end up with the usual spiritualistic fallacies.[1] These spiritualistic fallacies are materialistic fallacies: they are attempts to bring the soul-spiritual into space. But apart from that human beings are aware of their own soul-spirit. They know how the soul-spiritual functions because they can say to themselves that, when for example they want to make a movement in space, the thought they have is transferred into action by the will. The movement is in space; but an unbiased person cannot say that the thought is in space. Thus, huge problems have developed for philosophical thinking. We can ask: How can a person's soul-spirit, to which the I also belongs, act on the physical which is in space? How can something non-spatial affect space?

Various theories have been developed which all suffer more or less from the problem of bringing the non-spatial soul-spiritual into line with the spatial physical. They say the soul-spiritual acts through the will on the physical. But so far nobody has been able to explain with ordinary consciousness how the thought flows into the will and how the will, which is itself of the spirit, manages to appear in external movement, in outer activity.

On the other hand, the processes engendered in the physical body, in the senses, through the physical world, are spatial. By transforming into the soul-spiritual they become non-spatial. Through their ordinary consciousness human beings are not able to explain how the spatial, physical which takes place in the sense organs affects the non-spatial, namely the soul-spiritual.

Recently the term I have often remarked on has been used: psychophysical parallelism. Basically, this is just conceding that no one knows what to say about the relationship of the physical with the soul-spiritual. For example, they say: The human being walks, they move their legs, they change from one place to another in space. All this represents something spatial, something physical.

Simultaneously when something happens in the body, something happens in the soul-spiritual, something to do with thinking, feeling and willing. We only know, they say, that when something happens on the physical level in space, then something also happens on the soul-spiritual level. However, we cannot explain how the one affects the other. Psychophysical parallelism[2] means that when a physical process occurs, a psychic or soul process also takes place. But they cannot get beyond this, one could almost say, most fascinating secret, that the two processes occur parallel to one another. There is no notion of how they act on each other. This is what happens when people try to develop a concept about the existence, the presence of the soul-spiritual.

In the nineteenth century, when peoples' opinions were very much permeated by materialism, the following question arose among the materialists: Where in space are the souls who have left their bodies? And there were even people who attempted to refute spiritualism as an impossibility, since so many people are dying or have died already that the whole of space has not the capacity to provide room for all these souls of the dead. This ridiculous notion was often put forward in the nineteenth century. People said, human beings cannot be immortal as then all the space in the cosmos would be full of these immortal souls. All these ideas show us what difficulties arise when we consider the relationship between the physical which is clearly spread out in space and the soul-spiritual which we cannot locate spatially.

Gradually intellectual thinking began to put the physical and the soul-spiritual abruptly next to each other. For modern consciousness they are in juxtaposition, with no transition between the two. In fact, in the way people have come to think of the physical on the one hand and the soul-spiritual on the other there is no possibility of finding a connection. People think nowadays of the physical in such a way that it cannot accommodate the soul-spiritual and of the soul-spiritual as being so abruptly separated from the physical/spatial that the whole non-spatial soul-spiritual has no possibility of affecting it. However, this idea of antithetical states has only developed gradually. We have to base our ideas on a completely different approach, one which can only develop by listening to what anthroposophical spiritual science has to say. Anthroposophical spiritual science should first look at volition. Firstly, an unbiased view will show that a person's will follows all their movements and that the movements that a person performs in space by moving themselves, but also the movements taking place inside them in the course of their bodily functions, all a person's activity here in the physical world, is three-dimensional. An unbiased person cannot doubt this. All these movements are accompanied by volition; hence the will has to be able to go wherever there are three dimensions. There can be no doubt about this.

Therefore, when we speak of the will as soul-spiritual, there can be no question that this will, despite being soul-spiritual in nature, is also three-dimensional, it has a three-dimensional gestalt. We simply have to think as follows: when through our volition we move a hand, for example, the will moves closely with the arm and the hand into all those positions that they adopt in space. The will accompanies whatever movement a limb is making. Therefore we can refer to the will as that aspect of the soul which can take on a three-dimensional form.

A further question is whether all of the soul can adopt a three-dimensional gestalt. Here we go from the will to the world of feeling, so that initially when a person thinks about these things with their ordinary consciousness they would say: When for example a needle is stuck into the right side of my face, I can feel it; on the left side the same. With ordinary consciousness they could think that feeling extends over their whole body. And then they would speak of feeling as being three-dimensional in the same sense as the will.

However, here they have succumbed to an illusion. It is not as they think. In fact, they need to take into account how a person can experience themselves and then to continue from these experiences. What we are considering today will be quite subtle, but without such subtleties we cannot really understand spiritual science.

Now think about what happens when you touch your left hand with your right hand. You have a perception of yourself. Just as you would sense an external object, so now when you touch your right hand with your left, you sense yourself, let us say, through the medium of each finger.

This becomes even clearer when you think about the fact that you have two eyes and that when you look at an object with both eyes, you have to exert your will. Usually, we do not think about this exertion of the will. To illustrate: you have to look at an object very close to you, so that it emerges more strongly than usual, so you turn the left eye to the right and the right to the left, and you focus on the object by bringing the lines of sight into contact with one another in a way similar to what you did when you touched the right hand with the left, when you so to speak, touched yourself.

So, you can see that it is important for human beings, for their orientation in the world, to relate the left to the right, to bring left and right into line with each other.

Now ordinary consciousness does not usually go any further than to become aware of the importance of this basic fact through the touching of the hands or the intersection of the lines of vision; but we can pursue this chain of thought further.

Let us assume that we are being pricked by a pin on the right side of the body: we sense, we feel the sting. However, by pointing to the body's surface we cannot really say where we feel the pinprick. This is because if all the separate parts of the organism were not in a vital interrelationship with one another, mutually affecting each other, then our human-physical-soul-being would not be what it is. This means that even when we are not touching the left hand with the right one so as to feel the left hand through the right one, or even when our organism is being pricked by a pin on the right side, there

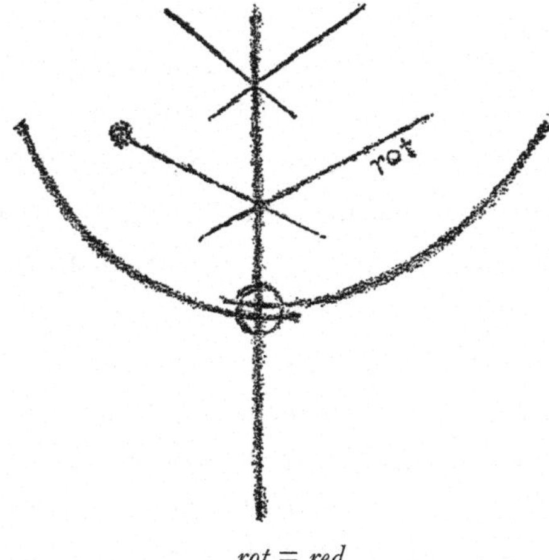

rot = red

is always a conduit between the right-hand side and the symmetrical plane of the body and the left side of the body must relate to the right side in order to create a sensation or a feeling.

It is relatively easy to say that when I have here the symmetrical plane, seen from anterior to posterior, then the right hand touches the left and the feeling in both hands, in each hand through the other, takes place in the symmetrical plane.

This is quite obvious and it is relatively easy to speak of crossing the line of sight of the eyes. However, when we are being stung on the right side there is always a pathway [red] where the left side of the body crosses with the right side in these conduits; otherwise, no sensations would arise. The fact that we are built symmetrically, that we have a right side and a left one, plays an extremely important part in the pathways of our sensations and feelings. As a result, we always relate what is happening on the right side to the left, so that something always reaches over invisibly from the left so as to converge with what is flowing over from the right side.

Only in this way does feeling develop. Feeling never develops in three-dimensional space; it always takes place on a plane. In reality the realm of feeling is not spread out in three dimensions, but is in fact two-dimensional. We human beings experience feelings only on that level which, if we were to develop it into a sectional plane, would split a person into two symmetrical halves.

The life of feelings is actually like a painting done on canvas, which is, however, not just painted from the one side but also from the other. Imagine that I take a canvas and paint it from right to left and then from left to right, then I jumble up what I have painted from the front and from the back, meaning from right to left and left to right. And the resulting painting is only two dimensional. All that is three-dimensional has been so to speak projected onto two dimensions.

You could also develop this idea in another way. Imagine you were able to throw shadow images of objects from the right and others from the left on to a flat surface. Thus, you would have shadow images of objects from the right and others from the left on the flat surface of the wall. This is what our feeling realm is like.

It is not three-dimensional, but two-dimensional. The human being is basically a painter working from two sides, not feeling out into space, but drafting all the feeling impressions that they encounter in space onto the flat surface of a painting in shadow images, in pictures, by means of their three-dimensional will, which is the painter. The feeling life of the human being is a painting drawn through their body in two-dimensions, but painted from both sides. This means that when we look for the transition in the human soul from feeling to willing, we have to go from the three-dimensional to the two-dimensional.

However, this means that the soul expressing itself in feeling has a different relationship to the spatial than if we just say it is non-spatial. The plane has two dimensions, but is not spatial. You could call the blackboard a plane, but in reality, it is a body, since it has depth. A plane is indeed in space, but is not itself spatial; space must always have three dimensions. And only the will can move into this three-dimensional space. Feeling does not go into the three dimensions of space. It is two-dimensional. However, it does have a relationship to space, just as a shadow image has a relationship to space.

I want to point out to you an extremely significant fact, which since people are not inclined to look at the peculiarities of their emotional life with their ordinary consciousness, is not so easy to comprehend. The realm of feeling is always permeated with that of the will. Just think that if you really have been stung on the right side of the body, as I spoke about before, you do not immediately separate the feeling from the will. Without a doubt you would not just accept the sting patiently, but would grasp the place on the body where you had been stung, meaning that with your will you move into three-dimensional space, and apart from that you would have a defensive reaction which does not reveal itself externally, but only in various small, intimate movements of the blood and of the breathing. What we do when we are stung by a mosquito and touch the place externally is only the crassest reaction. We usually take no notice of the finer defensive responses, which take place in the movement of the blood and the breathing and other internal reactions. So, we do not separate what the will does from the feeling content. The feeling content is too diffident. We can only manage this in very attentive meditation. However, if you could exclude from feeling everything belonging to the will, you would contract from left and from right and would become the plane in the middle. Then when you are the plane in the middle and as an artist, so to speak, you paint your experience on this plane, then you will begin to grasp why the realm of feeling is so very different from normal experience.

We can experience this two-dimensional aspect of feeling, but we have to experience it meditatively. We need to have the whole shadowy existence of feelings in comparison with more robust experiences in three-dimensional space. We have to prepare ourselves for this. But if we do so we can experience it. And then we come closer to this truth that feeling is a two-dimensional process. And then thinking can be quite simply characterized, if we admit to ourselves with an unbiased mind how impossible it is to assert that a thought exists in space. A thought is really nowhere in space. But it must have some relationship to space, since the brain is without doubt when not the tool, at least the basis of thinking. Without a brain we cannot think. However, if thinking is a process based on the activity of the brain, but has nothing to do with space, then we would have the curious fact that someone can think well at the age of twelve and then their head subsequently grows out of what it was when they were twelve; then they would also have grown out of thinking. This is not the case. By growing we do not leave thinking behind. This alone shows that when we grow, our thinking is also in space.

Now just as we can feel the emotional realm of experiencing feelings for ourselves, by coming into our symmetrical plane, we can experience thinking as having only the vertical dimension. Thinking is one-dimensional, a linear process in human beings. So, we have to say that the will proves to be three-dimensional, feeling two-dimensional and thinking one-dimensional.

So you see, when we differentiate space, we come to a less abrupt transition than does the intellect. We come to a gradual transition. Mere intellect says: the physical is spread out in three-dimensional space, the soul-spiritual is not spread out at all, so that it is impossible to find a relationship between what is spread out in space and what is not spread out at all. However, if we notice that the will is three-dimensional, then we can find the will everywhere in the three-dimensional world. If we know that feeling is two-dimensional, then in moving from three dimensions to two, we arrive at something which depicts relationships, but is no longer spatial, since the plane itself with only two dimensions is not spatial. Feelings are *in* space however and not completely beyond it.

Then when we move from feeling to thinking, we go from two dimensions to one dimension and hence not completely beyond space. We are moving slowly from the spatial to the non-spatial. I have often said that the tragedy of materialism lies in the fact that it is matter itself in its three-dimensionality which materialists are unable to understand. They think they have understood it, but it is just precisely matter which they do not understand. In the nineteenth century various significant phenomena appeared which nowadays we are unable to decipher with our ordinary consciousness. Think for instance of the deep impression Schopenhauer's philosophical system made on the intellectuals of the time: 'The world as will and idea'. According to this the idea is unreal, only the will is real. So how did *Schopenhauer*[3] have the idea that the world consists only of will? This is because he was consumed by materialism! In the world in which matter spreads out in three dimensions, there is only the will. Whoever wants to find feelings in this world has to find the

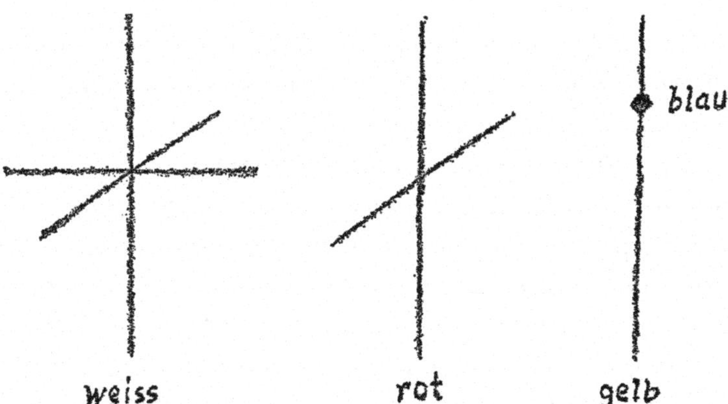

weiss = white, rot = red, gelb = yellow, blau = blue

relationship between a three-dimensional object and a two-dimensional shadow image. In feelings we experience the shadow images of what the will lives in three dimensions. And what we experience in thinking are one-dimensional structures. So that it is only when we go beyond dimensions that we arrive at our I. This has no dimension, is just a point. So we can say: we go from the three-dimensional [white], to the two-dimensional [red], to the one-dimensional [yellow] and to the point [blue].

Staying with the three-dimensional, our will is in there. Feeling and thinking are also in there but not spread out in the three dimensions. When we leave out the third dimension and just have two dimensions, we have the shadow of external existence, where the soul-spiritual spreads out and lives in feelings. We are already leaving the spatial. When we come to thinking, we are leaving it further and with the I we go even further beyond the spatial. In a sense we are gradually being led beyond space. And we can see that it is meaningless to speak of the soul-spiritual and the physical merely as opposites. It makes no sense, because if we want to discover the relationship between the soul-spiritual and the physical we have to ask the following: How do things that are spread out in three-dimensional space, for example our bodies, relate to the soul as a will-being? How does the physical aspect of the human being relate to the soul as a feeling being? The physical relates to the soul as a will-being like a sponge soaking up water; it is steeped on all sides, in all dimensions, in the will.

The physical relates to feeling like an object casting its shadow on a wall. And when we want to go from feelings to thinking, then we have to become an idiosyncratic artist, who paints onto a line what otherwise exists as two dimensions in a painting.

Now ask yourself the following question—this is of course a quite demanding process for inner contemplation—but imagine you are standing in front of let us say *The Last Supper* by Leonardo da Vinci. What you are initially looking at is the surface. First you consider the two-dimensional. Obviously, we have to disregard the thickness of the paint, but what you see as the painting is two-dimensional. Now I imagine a line drawn in the middle from top to bottom and this

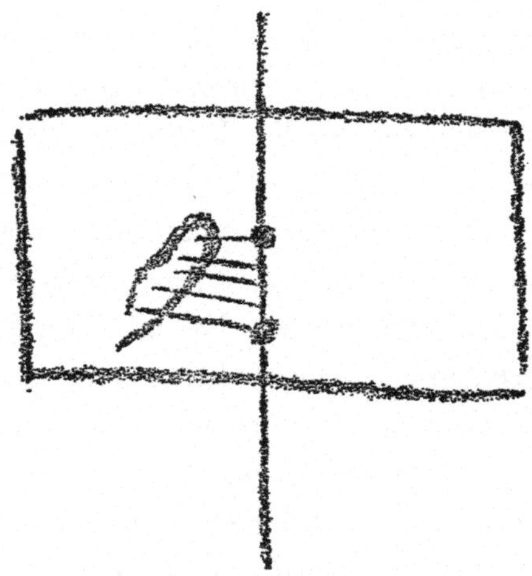

line represents a one-dimensional being. This one-dimensional being has a certain quality, let us say that it is not indifferent to Judas over here [see diagram above]; this being has a certain relationship to the presence of Judas. It is as follows: where Judas's head is bent down, they feel more, where Judas is turned away, they feel less. And for all the other figures the feelings of this one-dimensional being vary according to whether they are wearing blue robes or yellow. This one-dimensional being has feelings towards all that is going on to the left and to the right. This means that everything in this painting is being felt by this one-dimensional being.

This is how our thinking really is. Our thinking is such a one-dimensional being and only experiences the rest of our being as it does the painting, by dividing us into two, into a right-sided and a left-sided being, and through this detour through the painting it can relate to the three-dimensional world of the will.

Now if we want to get an idea of our soul-spiritual, insofar as it is a willing, feeling, thinking being without the I, we should not imagine it as a kind of cloud, but rather we have to go through an inner process. We want to get a schematic idea of the soul-spiritual. In a sense we have to look at it: it appears at first as a cloud. However, this is only the will-being. It constantly tends towards contraction: then it becomes a feeling being. At first, we see a cloud of light, then a cloud of light which creates a plane in its middle and through this it can feel itself. And this plane in turn tries to become a line. So, we have to imagine: cloud, plane, line as a living structure which constantly wants to be a cloud, but tries to contract itself into a plane and to become a line. If you imagine a line becoming a plane, then a plane becoming a three-dimensional cloud, cloud, plane, line—line, plane, cloud and so on, then you have a schematic idea of what your soul in its innermost being, in its innermost essence really is. You cannot get by with an idea which remains static. No static idea can express what the soul is. You need an idea which itself is creating an inner process, a process in which the soul is playing with the dimensions of space: it makes the third dimension disappear and loses the will, lets the second dimension disappear and loses feeling and it loses thinking when it lets the first dimension disappear. Then we have arrived at the point. Then we can go on to the I.

This is why it is so difficult. People want to see the soul, but they are only used to developing ideas rooted in space. They then develop ideas of the soul which are also spatial, however rarefied. But in space you only have the will. We should develop an idea of the soul by imagining a cloud, then constantly pressing the cloud together until we imagine it as one-dimensional. Without creating a thinking which is mobile in itself, we cannot have any idea of the soul-spiritual. Someone who wants to imagine the soul-spiritual and creates the same image in two consecutive moments, has only imagined the will. We should not imagine the soul-spiritual as the same idea

(monomorphic) in two consecutive moments. We have to become flexible internally; not so that we go from one point in space to another, but from one dimension to another. This is what is so difficult for modern consciousness. This has even led to well-meaning people—well-meaning in relation to spiritual ideas—attempting to overcome the three dimensions. They arrive at a fourth dimension. This is quite cute, going from three to four dimensions. As long as we stick to mathematics, the ideas we can develop from there are all correct. However, when we come to reality it is no longer right, since in reality when we think of the fourth dimension, it cancels the third dimension out. The third dimension disappears through the fourth, the second through the fifth and the first through the sixth: then we are back at the point.

In fact, when we move from the third to the fourth dimension we enter into the spiritual and by leaving out a dimension, not by adding one, we come more and more into the spiritual. And through ideas such as this we gain insight into the human gestalt.

For an artistic sensibility is it not in a way brutal to regard human beings as we do when we look at them as beings standing in the world in all three dimensions? Obviously, we look at them like this, but it is not the only aspect. We have a general feeling of the left and right sides of the body as being essentially symmetrical. And by concentrating the human being in the midplane we go beyond the three dimensions. We have moved on to the midplane; and from here we have quite a clear idea of the one dimension in which human beings are growing. This transition from three to two to one dimension is often used by artists. If we cultivated this artistic view of human beings then we would be able to find the transition to the soul level more easily. We would never regard a being who is not symmetrically structured as capable of coherent feelings.

If you look at a starfish, which is not symmetrically formed, but five-pointed, you could of course have no feelings towards it; but if you put it to yourself on the emotional level, you could never say that it had a coherent feeling. The starfish is completely incapable of relating the right side to the left, of encompassing the right with the left, but must always relate the one arm to one other, or to two, or to three, or to all four other ones. This is why what we call feeling does not exist at all in a starfish.

Now I ask you to follow me carefully with this more intimate train of thought: what is this phenomenon we call feeling? What we call feeling comes from the right side, comes from the left side and rests in the middle. We go through the world by resting in the world with our feeling. The starfish cannot do this. It cannot relate what affects it from the world [red arrow] symmetrically to something else. It can relate it [red] to one or two or three or four of the other arms but it will always be something more powerful [yellow].

Thus, the starfish does not have this resting feeling, because when it focuses on the one side, then according to its structure, it will experience the following: you are sending out this ray [yellow arrow]. When it feels that part, it is as if there were something shooting out of it. It has no feeling at rest. It has the feeling of shooting something out. It feels as if it were radiating out into the world.

rot = red, gelb = yellow

If you develop your feeling to a fine degree, you will be able to experience this when you look at a starfish. Take any one arm and relate it to the whole starfish, then you will see in your imagination that the whole starfish is beginning to move in the direction of this one arm as if it were moving, streaming light. This is the same with all animals that are not symmetrically structured, that have no real symmetry axis or centre line.

If, instead of giving themselves over to the mere intellectual by dint of having developed into an intellectual being, people would pay more attention to this finer way of feeling, then they could feel their way into the world on a much more subtle level.

This is true too of the plant world, true of all that surrounds us. Real self-awareness carries us more and more into the inner world of all phenomena.

I would like to elaborate further tomorrow and in the coming days based on what I have explained in a more obscure way today.

Second Lecture

DORNACH, 25 JUNE 1922

Yesterday I attempted to show in a rather obscure way how we can find the transition from the spatial-physical, including human corporeality, to what can be thought of as spiritual, in that three dimensions are reduced in a sense to two or one dimensions and to a point. Now today I want to contrast yesterday's observations to some extent with a more cosmic point of view, which should show you how we can also develop ideas relating the world that forms our environment to the soul-spiritual. For modern consciousness it is completely impossible to view the material world surrounding us in a way that the soul-spiritual in human beings has a direct relationship to it. We have to explain this cognitively, if the modern person is not to say they cannot understand why anthroposophy alleges that the soul-spiritual, meaning the I and the astral body, leave the physical and ether bodies and are then outside of them. Where are they? asks that person, whose understanding is grounded in modern materialistic consciousness. A modern person is incapable of thinking that the soul is to be found somewhere in space. At most they are able to think that air is somewhere in space, that space is filled with light; but that the soul-spiritual is somewhere in space, this they cannot think. And from this impossibility it is but a short path to the other: that this modern person, who has grown up with a materialistic awareness, is incapable of imagining where the soul-spiritual goes when it leaves the human body at death.

Of course, the modern person claims to be able to believe these things. However, at that moment when they have to use their own faculty of thought they immediately get into various conflicts. These conflicts cease when we try to understand spiritual science. But the ideas we then have to absorb are so unfamiliar for contemporary human beings that they can only approach them slowly and gradually. Therefore, it is good to begin with the facts of soul-spiritual life, facts that nowadays are little known in the outside world.

As we all know, what humanity has today as venerable, old, traditional beliefs that have flowed into the various religions, can be traced back to an age-old knowledge; we know that in ancient times there were sacred mystery sites, which were churches, schools and centres for the arts in one and from where there originated all that has spread out among the mass of the people as knowledge, but also as impulses determining people's actions.

In these mystery schools there were so-called initiates, who had achieved a higher awareness through having undergone specific processes. Through the trials they had experienced they had gained a certain relationship to the world through which they could learn about world processes, world developments in whichever area they were interested in.

In external history we only find a degenerate kind of notion of world processes. You have all read about how in Greek temples, oracle sites, they made use of certain personalities, a kind of medium, who through exposure to vapours arising from the earth would fall into what nowadays people, who have only a dilettantish idea of the spiritual, would call a trance; this sort of trance is a spurious kind of hocus pocus which does not reveal the truth or any aspect of reality. However, in those times when the ancient paths of relating to the world had already degenerated, people took refuge in these oracles. And they accepted what was revealed in these trance-like states as revelations, so as to understand what the intentions of the real spiritual powers were, those divine-spiritual powers which are really behind all that happens in the world. They then acted in accordance with the revelations of the oracles.

However, these oracles were not the originals. Those were something very different. At the time people sought refuge in the oracles, the old faculties that initiates had cultivated in the mysteries were lost and the oracles had resorted to external procedures. I would like to describe to you one of these procedures through which in very ancient times the initiates of the mysteries listened to the secrets of the world, the secrets of the intentions of the divine spiritual beings, which are behind all natural phenomena.

Such initiates prepared their whole person over a long period of time to pay careful attention to life processes and they could put themselves into a certain emotional state at the time of the rising sun. This was an exercise that the ancient initiates practised repeatedly: putting themselves into a very receptive, spiritually receptive state at dawn, towards the rising sun. Particularly the dawn, the rising sun should evoke in these old initiates a reverential soul state, permeated by feelings of devotion. We cannot imagine today what such a state these initiates achieved in the face of the rising sun was like—if they were properly prepared then it was part devotion, part thirst for knowledge. I think we can only catch a glimpse of such feelings towards the external world—and this is more than a century ago—when we read the beautiful descriptions that *Johann Gottfried Herder*,[4] that fine poet and writer, gave of the dawn; not as a more modern, more trivial writer would have done, but from the dawn as a symbol for all awakenings, awakenings not just in nature but in the human soul. In a way this evokes in the human soul itself a kind of dawn, as if the sun is rising internally. Herder described this wonderfully as he attempted to show how the poetic mood had once made itself felt in human development and how this poetic mood could originate with what people could experience at dawn in the face of the rising sun.

The secrets of the dawn and of the rising sun were felt even more intensively by people like *Jacob Boehme*,[5] whose first work, as you know, is *Aurora or the Dawning of the Day in the East*. And the words such as those in Goethe's *Faust*[6] are not unrelated to the mysteries of the dawn: 'Disciple, up! Untiring, hasten. To bathe thy breast in morning red!' The further we go back in the history of human development, the more wonderful we find the moods of the human soul at the first rays of the morning sun, which are in a sense carrying in on their waves the vital, active light of the world. The ancient initiates in the mystery schools had prepared themselves so that they could send out from their hearts into the expanses of the world their most serious, most holy questions to the world spirits during the dawn. They said to themselves: When the sun sends out the first ray of light to the earth, this offers the best way for human questions to flow out to the expanses of the cosmos. And so in a sense these initiates radiated their questions, the riddles of their hearts and of humanity, out in to the wide expanses of the world. And then they did not approach the answer in a trivial or banal way, as we would do today in our physical sciences, but put themselves into a mood in which they said: Now we have transmitted our riddles and questions to the cosmic expanses; now they rest in the bosom of the world, the gods will receive our riddles and questions.

I am only describing here. We can think what we like about these things, but once they existed and this was how things were done. Then the initiates waited and during the night hours they prepared their hearts to be receptive. This in turn was not a mood in which questions were raised, but a responsive one in which they opened their hearts to a receptive and devotional mood. And they brought their devotion to the full moon shining down upon them. And then they felt: now we are receiving the answers from the universe.

In the old mysteries this was a very common process. At a certain point in time, they offered their questions as a covenant with the world by sending them out and then they received the answers, which at the full moon, in the light of the full moon were sent to earth by the gods.

This is how people used to communicate with the world. They were not so arrogant as to pose a question in their heads and then to look for the answer immediately, as do philosophers today, or so arrogant as to think that they could sit down with a blank piece of paper and work out the great riddles of humanity on their own. In fact, these old initiates believed that they should communicate with the divine spiritual powers which flow in and through the world about the questions and answers relating to the riddles of the world. They did this because they knew that outside in the world are not only the content of physical, sense perceptions, but also flowing in and through everything is the spiritual. And when the ray of sun touches me, I can send out to it the substance of my will.

This secret is wholly lost in human research. It was once real knowledge, actual human insight. One of the last people in Europe to have a not really clear, but still lively tradition in these things and who was also prepared to fight was *Julian the Apostate.*[7] He was incautious enough to still take these things seriously and thus succumbed to his opponents.

The modern human being would sketch—this is only a rough diagram, but it is just to show what the issue is—the earth and the sun (there would of course have to be a much greater distance between them) so that the sun sends its rays down to the earth. The old initiate would have said: This is just physical, the spiritual aspect is that people are living on the earth and there they develop their will [red] and while the sun's rays come down to the earth, human beings can send their will in the direction of the sun, up into the universe [arrows].

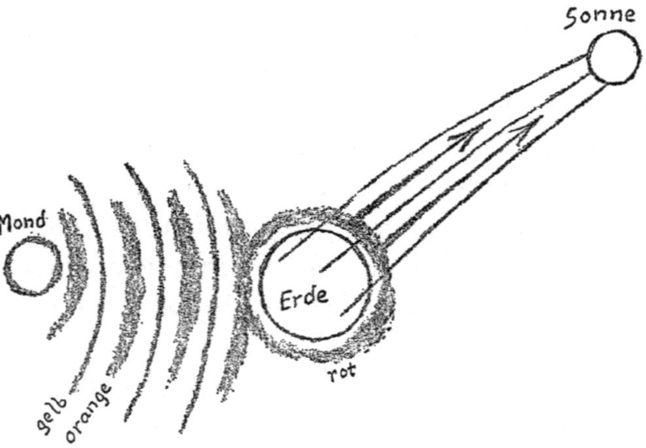

Mond = moon, Erde = earth, Sonne = sun, gelb = yellow,
orange = orange, rot = red

The old initiates sent their questions out into the cosmos in a sense on the crest of these waves of will, which flowed out from the earth to the sun. And when a modern person says that on the other side is the moon which sends its light down onto the earth [yellow], the old initiate says that is just the physical; in truth thoughts come down to the earth on these waves of moonlight [orange]. So the old initiates consigned their questions to the waves of will flowing from the earth to the sun and received the answers from the waves of thought flowing from the moon to the earth. Modern scientists know only one side of this. They see only the physical aspect of the sun and the moon. However, the old initiates said: While the sun is constantly sending its light to the earth, the earth is constantly sending waves of will out into the universe, the will of all the people living on the earth. And when the human being stands in the moonlight, then waves of thought are being sent to them from the cosmos.

Human organization has changed. The seeker of supersensible knowledge could not do this today. Human understanding is coarser now than it was in those days. Of course, today too our waves of will flow out into the cosmos. However, human beings do not care about these questions passionately enough for the waves of will to take them out into the universe. Today we humans have become too intellectualistic and the intellect cools all these questions down. We have little idea of the huge thirst for knowledge which people had with regard to the most sacred riddles of existence. We are no longer so thirsty for knowledge; in fact, we are just curious and want to know everything immediately without having to engage with the world. And at most we have lovers romancing in the moonlight; scholars would think it a terrible superstition to receive the answers to the burning riddles of existence through the light of the moon.

People see the world as despiritualized. No one knows anything about the spirit flowing all through the world, or when someone speaks about this, it is in a vague, pantheistic manner and not in the specific way of someone who knows of the relationship of the human will to the sun's rays, or that of human thought forms to the light of the moon.

However, in modern initiation we can learn to communicate with the cosmos and with the spirit of the world. But modern initiation does this differently. You can find exercises to prepare for initiation in my book *Knowledge of the Higher Worlds—How is it Achieved?* These exercises are all meant to help people of today find answers, not however by turning over the questions in their minds and giving the answers with their minds as modern arrogance demands. This only results in clever ideas, but cleverness does not lead to a real answer to the riddles of existence. By just turning things over in the mind people cut themselves off from the world. If we want answers from the world, we necessarily have to go beyond ourselves. We have to relate to the world. Thus, modern initiates must pose their questions and then have patience, when there is no immediate answer. Modern initiates gradually learn not to just look at the outer world to satisfy their curiosity through the impressions made on their eyes, ears and other senses. Of course, they also receive sense impressions from outside, but by looking at the flowers, the sun, the moon, the stars, other people, plants, animals and so on, by focusing their senses on all that is around them and letting all these external sense impressions flow through them, they send a stream from themselves out towards all this. And this is the stream signifying the riddles of existence. Someone sees a lovely flower. They look at it, but not just passively; they focus on for example the yellow. They let the yellow affect them. At the same time, they send a question towards the yellow and they let this riddle of existence immerse itself in the yellow of the flower, or in the colours of the rising sun.

It is not that they give up all the questions of their hearts to a certain impression, such as the rising sun, but they pour them out into all their sense impressions. Now if they then expected to receive the answers from these sense impressions themselves, that would be as if the old initiates had sent out their questions to the rising sun and then expected to receive the answers from it instead of from the full moon after having waited a while.

Such an old initiate had to wait at least fourteen days: they put their questions to the rising sun during the new moon and then they received the answer at full moon. No modern philosopher would wait that long, for then—at least in the days when they printed things more quickly[8]—the book would have had to be at the printers.

So, we must be patient. When we consign our questions to the impressions of the senses, when we immerse them in the phenomena, then we should not expect that these sense impressions will reveal anything to us and we have to wait, sometimes longer, until what we have given over to the world comes up from inside as the answer. We will be able to do this, if we have taken enough time to prepare.

You can rest assured that when you give your questions over to the world, you will receive responses that are purely coincidental, that give people a certain egoistic satisfaction, but which are not real answers. You must immerse your riddles in the flower, in the ocean, in the firmament, in the stars, in everything that comes to you as an impression; you immerse your riddles in all this and then you have to wait until the answers emerge from inside you. You cannot just wait for 14 days, you cannot even, as the old initiates did, determine the time. You must wait until the right moment has come when the outside has become the inside and the answer comes up from inside you.

Therein lies the art of spiritual research into the world, in being able to wait, in not thinking that the answer will emerge quickly. However, we will not receive answers if we do not pose questions. If you ask someone who has actually gained knowledge in the sense of modern initiation, then they will tell you: I was perhaps 35 years old when I had certain heartfelt questions about life; at the time I consigned these questions to some special outer impressions and when I turned 50 the answers emerged from inside me.

Today we have to immerse in the flow of time what we want to develop as a dialogue with the cosmos, just as the old initiates immersed their questions in the depths of space, so they could be reborn out of that space: the sun-like from the moon-like. And the cosmic must reappear, must be reborn out of the human soul after a time which the cosmic powers determine themselves, so that our task is to sense correctly when a real answer from the gods appears inside us and not just a human response to the questions we have posed.

Thus, in a sense what constituted the old initiation reappears in a different form. But you see what is important here. You see that, when human beings want to approach the great riddles of existence, then all depends on them being able to find a soul-spiritual connection to the soul-spiritual powers in the cosmos, not being hermits, wanting to resolve everything by themselves egoistically, but by being able to wait until the cosmos responds to what they themselves have sent out into the cosmos as riddles of existence.

Now you see, the fact is that when we have learnt to send out soul themes into the cosmos and to receive responses in return, then we are much better prepared to understand birth and death. When someone begins to understand how the soul flows out to the sun in the element of will, like a counter-current to the rays of the sun, how it flows out into all that we receive as impressions of the outside world, they are beginning to understand how the soul-spiritual flows out into the world on the waves of the spiritual in the cosmos, when the physical human being goes through death. And when they have learnt how they receive their best thoughts from the cosmos when they return, when they emerge inside them, as is the case with modern human beings, so they also learn to understand how the spiritual flows back from the moon-like, from the semblance of the world; it is from the moon-like in their own organism that the thoughts emerge.

We learn to realistically evaluate these transitory phenomena, found in between the physical-cosmic and the cosmic-spiritual. The modern human being, schooled only in a materialistic awareness, describes things merely on a physical level. They say: There are solar eclipses, whereby the moon comes between the earth and the sun so that the sun's rays are blocked and the sun is eclipsed. This is the next best physical explanation. When there is a light over there and here is an eye and I put my hand between them then the light is eclipsed—a purely spatial explanation. This is where modern consciousness comes to a standstill. However, we have to gain insight into such phenomena, which despite appearing rather infrequently, do have their spiritual aspect.

When there is a solar eclipse then something different happens to those parts of the earth affected by it than happens when there is no solar eclipse. When we know that the rays of the sun make their way to us and our will radiates up towards the sun, then we can imagine how such a solar eclipse can have a certain influence on the rays of the will, which are spiritual. The moon blocks the light rays—that is a purely physical process. The rays of the will cannot be blocked by the physical matter of the moon. They radiate out in to the darkness and there is a time, albeit a short time, when what is will-like on the earth flows out into space in a different way than it does when there is no solar eclipse. Normally the physical aspect of the sun's light connects to the rays of will being sent out. In this case the rays of the will flow out unhindered into the cosmos in a cone of light. The old initiates knew that in such a case all the unbridled will, the untamed instincts and drives that human beings hold in themselves flow out into the universe. And they taught their students that normally what the evil will of human beings radiates out into the cosmos is in a sense burned up by the sun's rays, so that it only harms humans themselves and does no damage in the cosmos. When, however, there is a solar eclipse then there is the chance that all the evil of the earth spreads out into the cosmic heavens. This is a physical phenomenon which has a quite clear spiritual aspect.

And when there is a lunar eclipse, modern consciousness says that the earth is between the sun and the moon, therefore we see the shadow of the earth on the moon. This is a physical explanation. Again, the old initiates knew that behind this is the spiritual, that when the moon is eclipsed, thoughts flow down through the darkness and that they have a more intimate connection to the human unconscious than to the conscious. These ancient initiates often spoke in parables to their students, so I will translate this into modern language: romantic people go for walks in the light of the full moon and those who aspire to receiving from the universe not the good thoughts, but those of the devil, they go out at eclipses of the moon.

So here we have again the spiritual aspect of a physical event. We cannot approach these things in the old way, that would only lead to superstition. But we have to aim at seeing the spiritual in particularly important world events. Because in reality when in each year eclipses of the sun and moon repeat themselves, this is in a sense like opposing 'safety valves'. Safety valves are installed to avoid damage; they open at certain times so as to let out steam for example. The valves which appear as the cosmic phenomena of solar and lunar eclipses exist so that in the case of a solar eclipse, the evil that has spread over the earth can be carried out in luciferic fashion into the cosmos to wreak more havoc there, whereas in the case of a lunar eclipse people who absolutely want to be possessed by evil thoughts can receive them from the cosmos. Those involved are not fully conscious of this, but nevertheless it is real, as real as the attraction of a magnet is for certain iron filings. These are forces at work in the universe, just like those we study today in the clinic or in the chemistry or physics laboratory.

Human beings will not be able to overcome the forces of decadence until they have the courage and the good sense to grasp the power of the spiritual. Then humanity will begin to have true ideas about life and death. And deeply immersed as it is in darkness, humanity needs these true ideas about birth and death. Also, we must learn the meaning of the sun, which sends us light. When the sun sends us light, in a sense it frees up the space around us for the path of the souls of the dead which must make their way out into the cosmos.

When the sun sends its light down to the earth, the earth sends its souls out into the cosmos. When people die, they radiate out into the vastness. Out there in the vastness they go through changes. Then spiritually formed they return through the moon sphere and again take up a physical body provided for them by the stream of physical heredity. Not until we really feel these things can we have a proper connection to the cosmos.

Nowadays we study astronomy, spectral analysis and so on. We learn how the sun's rays penetrate down to the earth and we think we know all there is to know. We learn how the sun's rays fall on to the moon and are reflected back onto the earth and physically we can then see moonlight. This preoccupies our minds. But this rational knowledge has little meaning. Rational knowledge separates humanity from the cosmos, it does not vitalize our souls. We can only come alive in our souls when we attain a real soul-spiritual connection to the cosmos. We can only attain this by saying again to ourselves for example: someone has died, their soul is shining towards the sun and flows out into the cosmos along the path of the sun's rays, until it arrives at where space ends, where the three dimensions stop being the three dimensions, where they become the plane. There processes take place beyond space and beyond time. Then after a while the soul returns from the opposite direction, from where the light of the moon flows down to us, unites with a physical human body and comes down again to the earth.

We humans must learn to say: Oh sun, the souls of the dead rise up towards you; Oh moonlight, on your waves young souls move into earthly life. When we learn to feel how natural phenomena are permeated with the spiritual, then there will be knowledge on earth that is also religion, then there will be knowledge that is also devoutness. Knowledge that is only concerned with the material cannot ever become religion. And religion only based on faith and not on knowledge can never unite harmoniously with the insight humanity gains from the cosmos. Today people recite the old prayers, but if you say to them there is profound wisdom in the old prayers, as I did for example in that small volume about the Lord's Prayer,[9] then these clever people say that is all in your imagination, all fantasy. It is not fantasy! It comes from a deep insight in to the fact that these prayers, given to humanity in the tradition from ancient times on, were formulated out of a profound knowledge of cosmic relationships. However, then we have to go beyond our own knowledge to attain what will enable a kind of religious connection to all the various phenomena of the universe. We must be able to say: Oh sun, you shine your light on me; along those trails that your light blazes from you, oh sun, to me on the earth, the souls of people who die flow out into the cosmos. Oh moonlight, you shine gently down on the earth, but on the waves of your gentle light souls come down from out of the cosmos into their earthly existence.

In this way we can find the connection between what shines outside in the world and what lives and works within humanity itself. And we will never again say thoughtlessly: Outside is the physical universe with all its substances and we do not know what the human soul will do when it separates from the body in this purely material cosmos. We will know that when the sun's rays blaze down through space, they are working with the rays of the human will, which find their way along the trails its light has prepared. And we will recognize that the moon is not sending out its gentle wavelike light to no purpose, but that in these waves of gentle moonlight the spiritual is flowing through space. Someone who can look at things in this way is not able to remain indifferent to what we can experience through the plant and its behaviour seen in the morning when the young morning sunlight shines upon it. The plant behaves in a specific manner at that time; the sap, rising in the capillaries, flows into the blossom- or leaf-like structures. Here the powers of the sun which flow into the plant make way for the will-forces of the earth. And it is not only the sap flowing through the plants, as our present-day scientists describe it, but the will-forces located deep in the earth flowing through the plant from the roots to the flower. In the evenings when the leaves roll themselves up and close, when the sun's rays no longer offer a path to the streaming of the will flowing up from the earth, then the plant becomes passive, its life is on hold. However, it is now exposed to the gentle moonlight. This gentle moonlight affects not only lovers, but the passive plant as well: what flows down to earth with the moonlight as world thinking is active in the passive plant.

Thus, we learn to view the plant as an interwoven net of earth willing and world thinking. We can examine each plant form as to how far it is woven together from earth-will and world thoughts. And when we learn to recognize how healing forces stream out of the spirit into world thoughts and earth-will, then we can understand the healing powers of the plant and we can recognize the plant as herbal medicine. But we can only really recognize the plant as herbal medicine through an intimate knowledge of the cosmos.

This is something we have to relearn. And there is more to relearn. Look at the human head—it is a recreation of the earth itself. Initially it is formed in the human embryo. It is a recreation of the earth and the rest is pieced on later in a sense. When light shines on the human head as for example when the sun shines, then what is similar to earth-will in the human head is beamed out particularly strongly into the universe.

Let us now look at the roots of a plant, which contain earth-will quite intensively; we know that the roots are not exposed to sunlight, but they are exposed quite strongly to the moonlight, which while only shining relatively faintly on the earth, still manages to penetrate its surface and reach the roots of the plant. When we expose the plant to light by burning the roots and gathering the ash to make a powder, then through cosmic processes we can understand how the powder from the root of one plant or another can influence the head, which is similar in the power of its will to that of the earth. It is a question of being able to fathom out in everything, be it the smallest piece or the largest mass of matter, its connection to the spiritual. Then we will be able to do what today is only possible in mathematics: we will be able to apply what we have first understood purely spiritually to the whole of nature.

Today we are no further than thinking a cube consists of six faces. We can think this for ourselves; it is just a thought picture. If we look at salt, quite ordinary table salt, nature shows us the cube. Here what we think, the spiritual, coincides with what is outside in matter. But I ask you, what do people today know about how much in the roots of the plant is spiritual will-forces, world-thought forces, earth-thought forces and will-forces? And yet it is the same process which today we can only carry out in an abstract manner when we have the idea of the cube and then recognize it in sodium chloride, in table salt.

What we can only do today with mathematics is what we have to do with everything the human soul can conceive of. Mathematics does not create a devout feeling in many people. Such a thoughtful person as *Novalis* was able to find a devotional mood even in mathematics,[10] which he saw as a grand and beautiful poem. Not many people can do that. Generally, we will not find many people who become religious through mathematics. However, when we go further, when we explore the spiritual in human beings and carry it out into the world—where it already exists, but we need to recognize it—then science will be transformed into religious feeling, then we will really create the harmonization of religion and science. This, my dear friends, is what I wanted to say to you today from my heart.

Third Lecture

DORNACH, 30 JUNE 1922

I WOULD just like to draw your attention with a few words to what I discussed here last Sunday. It was about the relationship of the human being to the world inasmuch as I spoke about the unfolding of the human will, how it finds its way out into the vastness of the world along the lines of light which shine down from the sun to the earth. So that we can say that something from earthly humanity, the unfolding of the will, is radiating out into space counter to the direction of the light. In contrast the thought-like descends to the earth in a sense with the waves of moonlight. We could go on to show that what spreads out when the human body disintegrates has a will-like character and flows out into the cosmos counter to the flow of light and how the human being returns again to earthly existence on the stream of the thought element along the lines of light and all that emanates from the moon.

Now of course for this idea of the will element, the light element, the thought element and the element of moonlight, as well as for what I will say in this vein today, we have to realize that when we speak of these things and use the idea of a world edifice as an illustration, we only mean it as an illustration. You should not imagine that in all I have said here the physical sun and the physical moon are anything other than symbols for what happens spiritually. We can describe the actual relationship as follows.

I would like to portray this historically, although I could do it differently. I would like to make it clear for you what descriptions, such as the one I am about to make, mean exactly. You know that more materialistic orientated thinking sees the origins of our universe in a kind of cosmic cloud; this means that through this thinking bound to the material, people have the idea that our cosmos as far as we can grasp it, our solar system has developed out of a kind of cloud nebula [white] which then formed a ball and contracted into what is now the solar system.

Weiss = white

Now after all you have heard in the course of our studies of anthroposophy, it will be quite clear to you that this cannot be the whole picture. Regardless of how you modify this materialistic description of the origins of the universe with various forces or similar, this cannot be the whole truth, since whatever the nebula cloud of the Kant-Laplace hypothesis or some other theory contains and what can then develop according to the laws of aerodynamics could never lead to the formation of what lives on the earth as animal and human souls, not even of plants and their growth.

When we make such an interpretation then we are dealing with an abstraction, even if it is a materialistic abstraction. It has to be clear that the spiritual is inherent in what materialistic thinking sees as the primeval cloud [see diagram, page 32, red on the left] and that this primeval cloud is only the outer, material expression of the spiritual. Therefore, if it is to be a full description, the existence and weaving of the spiritual must also be included. So when we look at the primeval cloud of Kant-Laplace, we have to complete it by thinking of it as the body of something soul-spiritual, a soul-spiritual, however, which does not have a unified nature as does the human being, that is manifold, multiform, but still something soul-spiritual.

The observations and hypotheses of mere materialistic thinking do not go further back than this primeval cloud. Now let us imagine that not we but other beings, beings from the future, would develop ideas about the origins of the universe in which they live, or will live, based on this materialistic thinking. This is not a question of whether what I am now saying is real or not, it is just to illustrate my train of thought. So we assume that beings in the distant future view this Kant-Laplace cloud as the beginning of the universe. Where would it then be on a timescale? In order that the idea can become clear, when such future beings look back, they must assume that our earth, our solar system, had long perished, space had become in a sense free and in this free space they would have to postulate the Kant-Laplace cloud of a future world. For as long as our solar system exists, we obviously cannot assume that there is a Kant-Laplace cloud in the same space. I will construct the example so that these beings who are developing a materialistic theory of the future locate their Kant-Laplace primeval cloud in place of our solar system. According to what we have said, the soul-spiritual must also be in this Kant-Laplace cloud of the future. It would just have to be the physical form of a cosmic soul-spiritual. Where would this soul-spiritual come from? What lies behind it? I will draw a schematic diagram.

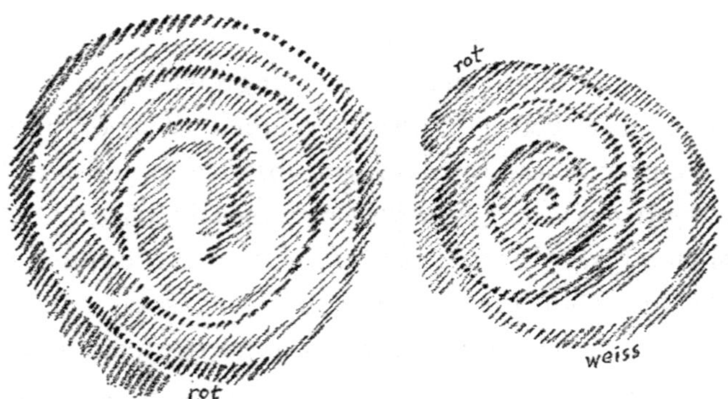

rot = red, weiss = white

This [diagram, left] would be the soul-spiritual-physical of our Kant-Laplace primeval cloud; and then in the future there would be the Kant-Laplace primeval cloud of the future beings I was talking about [right]. This Kant-Laplace nebula would contain the soul-spiritual [red]. Where would this come from? Now if this Kant-Laplace primeval cloud [right] were where our own solar system had been, then it would have developed; it would have enclosed a cosmic soul-spiritual. This soul-spiritual would be what was left over from the solar system we were living in. So we would live our solar system, as we have it now, to its end. It would then disperse into the cosmos. The soul-spiritual would remain and would then embody itself in the new Kant- Laplace primeval nebula. In other words what I have described here [diagram, right] would depict the development of Jupiter. But the soul-spiritual within this Jupiter development would be what had been prepared during the existence of humanity on the earth. Equally we would be able to go back beyond the Kant-Laplace primeval cloud of the earth to the soul-spiritual contained within it. And that was prepared by the beings who existed in the moon phase.

Thus when you look at our present solar system, then it is in a certain sense the outer embodiment of what has disappeared from the old moon existence, or what has transformed itself from the old moon existence to that of the earth. In turn, what we are sending out into the cosmos is preparing the Jupiter existence. Hence when we look at the external solar system, in reality we always have something that is the work of an earlier phase of existence.

Therefore when I am speaking of the light that shines down upon us from the physical sun, then I am talking about something that comes to us from the past. And when I speak of the will-streams which flow counter to the light rays, then I am talking about something which is preparing the future. So that the cosmic clockwork—I call it that so as to have an expression for what is happening spiritually—has been prepared by the moon and what I have described as the spiritual is already the basis for what will live on into Jupiter existence. But you should not say that the present-day sun, that we see with our eyes outside in space, is attracting the human will. This physical sun is only a symbol for the sun-like towards which the human will flows. Equally the physical moon is just a physical symbol for the moon-like, which constantly pours out in thought streams into earth existence.

You have to follow these thoughts if you want to understand properly what it means when in the following I talk about cosmic relationships, which express as images what is happening spiritually through humanity on the earth. And I have to add something to what I have already said. When we take our whole solar system seen from the earth, we have the sun, we have Mars, Jupiter, Saturn and so on as outer planets—the others are not so important—and closer to the earth than to the sun, the moon, Venus, Mercury [see diagram].

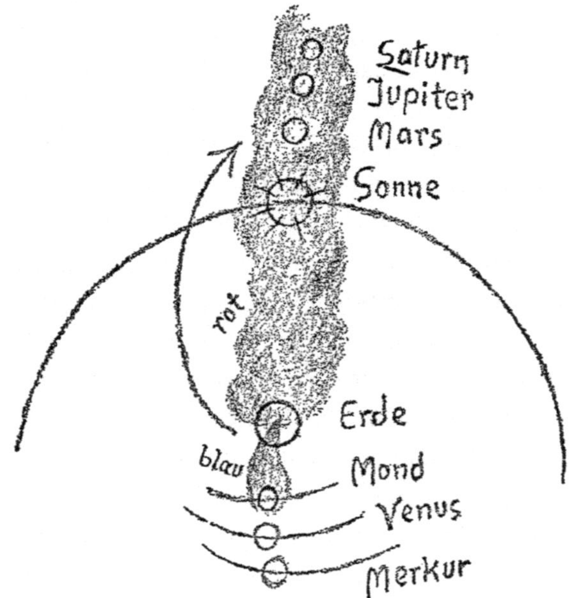

Merkur = Mercury, Venus = Venus, Mond = moon, Erde = earth, Sonne = sun, Mars = Mars, Jupiter = Jupiter, Saturn = Saturn, rot = red, blau = blue

Now stay with what I have said about the will of humanity flowing from the earth out into the cosmos towards the sun and also that when the body disintegrates, then the soul [red] also moves out into the cosmos along this will element. Thus, our will-like element arrives first at the sun existence, at the sphere of the sun.

Now you know that what I am presenting here as a fact had been discovered by the ancient initiates. They committed their questions to the stream of will, sending them towards the sun and then in turn they received the answers from the moon in the form of thoughts [blue], so that what I have here described to you can be taken as an established fact. And again, we have to connect to the old mysteries if we want to go further in our explorations.

Look at this fact once more: the initiates of the old mysteries send out their riddle-questions. They commit them to the stream flowing towards the sun's rays; they wait and after a while they receive the answers from the moon. In this respect they are speaking with the cosmos.

Now through this process the old seers only received certain answers, those which were related to the structure of the cosmos itself. Thus, what was contained in the old, more primitive wisdom, which despite being dreamlike was of course an exalted wisdom, that was accomplished by sending out the questions in the opposite direction to the sun's rays and then receiving the answers. These were the answers to questions concerning the structure of the universe, the forces at work in the universe and so on. In short, they received everything related to physical considerations, astronomical consider-ations, the music of the spheres and so on, all that was known in the ancient sciences about these aspects.

However, these old initiates sent out other questions into the cos-mos. For example, they knew the art of sending out questions as far as Mars, the Mars sphere [see diagram]. In the period when Mars was visible in the heavens, they sent out their questions counter to the rays from Mars. Now when they sent questions out to Mars, they did not await the answers from the moon, they awaited the answers when Venus was visible at such an angle that she seemed to be looking at Mars. The important point here is that they awaited the answers to the questions they had sent out to Mars from Venus. And furthermore, they awaited the answers to questions sent out to Jupiter from Mercury. They awaited the answers to the questions they sent out to Saturn, in a sense into the vastness of space, from the fixed stars, or from what in ancient times represented the fixed stars: the zodiac itself.

But what was in these questions that the old initiates sent out in this way into the cosmos and whose answers they then awaited? These were not the abstract, scientific truths concerning the structure of the universe, which I mentioned to you before; they were those questions the old initiates wanted to ask the divine spiritual beings directly.

To Mars they directed questions addressing the angel beings and awaited the answers from Venus. To Jupiter they directed questions to the archangel beings and awaited the answers from Mercury. And to Saturn they directed questions to the archai beings, the primordial forces, and awaited the answers from the zodiac.

Now while in a certain sense they spoke directly with the cosmos in a more abstract form, I would say an impersonal form, the way they spoke was such that they could retain consciousness: they spoke with real divine spiritual beings and they received their individual statements. In this way they received the declarations of will of the choir of the angels, the choir of the archangels, the choir of the archai. What was resolved as discourse between the sun, the moon and the initiates was related to the *externa* of the cosmos. What was communicated through the other planets and the zodiac had to do with the spiritual inhabitants of the cosmos.

So we know for a fact that human beings are constantly interacting with the cosmos, not just with its external structure, but with the inhabitants of the cosmos. The old initiates knew that when for example they directed their powers out towards Mars, it would not be sufficient to send out mere riddle-questions. Such riddle-questions would only go as far as the sun and the answers would only come from the moon. If the old seers wanted to direct questions towards Mars, they could not do so by merely thinking; rather they had to create formulas in a certain way, recitatives, mantras, which they could speak out loud. These were then sent out and formed what set Mars in motion, so that the answers, which they could hear through a kind of inner listening, would come back from Venus. If they wanted to direct questions to Jupiter, then this last was also not enough; rather they had to fulfil certain sacrificial rites in a specific ceremonial form. And what then flowed out into the universe as let us say the cosmic thought form of this sacrificial rite, that came back from Venus as certain signs that the old initiates knew how to interpret. When they were inspired by Venus and had sent out questions to Jupiter, then they could interpret these signs; when they were inspired by Mercury, then they could interpret the corresponding signs. These signs were very diverse. Someone not inspired by Mercury would see nothing in them. If they were inspired by Mercury, they knew: when I encounter this or that event, then it is this or that answer to a question posed through a sacrificial rite.

This is how natural events and also historical events, which otherwise only appeared to people as natural processes or historic processes, gained a certain substance; they could in a way be read. What had been put to Saturn as a question was particularly difficult, since it could only be asked by people performing complicated rites. In the old mysteries this would usually be done by the teachers of the mysteries giving their students a certain mission, a mission in which the student would dedicate their life to performing certain actions. The questions directed at Saturn consisted of these actions performed often over years by such a student. And the answers came back from the zodiac.

When the old initiates and their students practised these prayers, meditations and sacred rites of the ancient mysteries, it was really as if they were being woven into the fabric of the cosmos. There was nothing which would be completed in a short space of time; rather everything that went on over the years in such mysteries was continuous striving for knowledge or striving to create the right impulses for human actions.

By looking into these processes, we gain an impression of how those forces that we can describe as the forces of the sun, of Mars, of Jupiter, Saturn, the moon, Venus or Mercury affect human beings and of their significance for humanity. The meaning of the forces of the sun for human beings—you can see this from what I have said before—is that in a certain way they attract the human will towards the sun, and they draw up human beings themselves, when they have died, out towards the cosmos and through the cosmos into the spiritual world. The forces of the moon bring that organization into human beings which enables them to think, to reflect; but they are also those forces which carry human beings down from the spiritual world again and through the etheric sphere, when they must find their way into their earthly incarnation.

Similarly, we can give other forces the names of the celestial bodies which represent them and look at how they affect human beings. Let us take for example the forces of Mercury. These forces are not concentrated solely in the celestial body of Mercury. They fill out the whole of space accessible to us and the physical body of Mercury is just the concentrated, mineral embodiment of these Mercury forces. Imagine that we had filled up our whole solar system with the forces of Mercury [diagram below, yellow]. They permeate all the bodies of the solar system, including us humans, but where Mercury is to be found in the heavens they are just concentrated physically-minerally so that we can see them [yellow dot]. However, they are everywhere.

gelb = yellow

Now take the forces of Venus which are also everywhere [red]. But just at a certain point, where we can see Venus, they are physically/minerally concentrated [red dot].

gelb = yellow, rot = red

This is how it is with all these forces. In reality they permeate each other—Venus, Mars, Mercury and so on—but their mineral concentrations are to be found at specific locations.

If by learning to recognize Mercury we gradually develop an idea of how he gives answers for Jupiter, then we also learn to recognize the unconscious meaning of these Mercury forces for human beings. To take a simple example: when we want to walk we have to use certain forces so that the spirit can inform the bones and the muscles. We have to penetrate the physical; we have to get into the solid part of our bodies, into all the solid components of our bodies, with the soul-spiritual. That we are able to do this is due to the forces of Mercury.

So we can say the following.

Firstly, the Mercury forces allow human beings to take possession of the solid parts of their bodies. If there were no Mercury forces then we would always be outside the solid parts of our bodies.

Secondly, the Venus forces allow human beings to take possession of the fluid parts of their bodies. You already know that you consist of up to ninety per cent water. If there were no Venus forces in the world as a spirit you would only be able to continually circle around this column of water. You could not take possession of it.

Thirdly, the moon forces allow us to take possession of the aeriform content of the body.

We can realize these things by studying cosmology. Now we can go further in these studies, as did the ancient initiates, despite their having only a primitive knowledge, a kind of dreamy clairvoyance. Let us say for example that through their cosmological studies, they found out that the Venus forces allow human beings to take possession of the fluid element in their bodies. Then they experimented: they waited until they found a human being who had difficulty taking possession of their fluid element. This can lead to certain illnesses. For example, a certain illness develops when a person is not able to properly grasp just the one organ of their fluid being. So these old initiates asked themselves: What remedy is there for this? If a person was not properly attuned to the Venus forces, when taking possession of their fluid element was not functioning properly, then they saw that they had to use copper as the remedy. So by finding out that copper helped, that it helped the soul-spiritual take possession of the body, that it worked just like the Venus forces, they discovered that the same forces were at work in the metal copper as were at work in the Venus sphere. This is how they could connect the metal copper with Venus.

Furthermore, when it was a case of someone being ill because they could not properly grasp their solid components, then they found out that they had to use Mercury or quicksilver. Thus, they discovered the equivalence between the metals and the planets. Today all plausible accounts describe this equivalence, but no one asks themselves why Venus corresponds to copper and so on. This was all based on legitimate research.

Therefore, when someone speaks knowledgeably about copper as a medicine they have this knowledge from the study of the relationship between the human being and the cosmos. When for example someone is talking about whether a metal occurring in a certain plant is a medicine for some complaint or other, then they should look at the whole relationship of this plant to the cosmos. And from this relationship of the plant to the cosmos and in turn of the cosmos to the human being, they can gain insight into the workings of the plant as a remedy.

It is easy to understand why there is a certain reluctance nowadays to admit to these things. The modern approach, albeit open to question, is to learn all you need to know as a healer in five or six years. This is not possible; we have to go on learning continuously, but people want to be finished in five or six years and do not want to admit that they could learn much more, so that they develop resistance to what seems to have no end. However, despite our usual thinking, the world has no end, neither extensively nor intensively.

With the Mars forces it is a case not of helping us take possession of the etheric warmth forces, but that they protect us from the warmth element in the cosmos.

Fourthly, the Mars forces keep us from dissolving into the warmth element. If the Mars forces did not exist in the necessary way, then human beings would dissolve into the warmth element. The forces of Mars hold us together in the face of the warmth element. This is actually the most important force in human beings, as we have more warmth in us than is in our environment, so that we are constantly in danger of flowing out into the warmth element. That is most important. Therefore, the Mars forces in human beings must be concentrated and this happens because of the iron in the blood. Iron contains forces corresponding to those of Mars, which hold us together against dissolving into the warmth.

Human beings do not have the other forces, those of Jupiter and Saturn, within themselves in the same way. They are also in us, but in another form, not directly traceable. However, some of the recent research, including that of natural science, should get people thinking about these things. I will speak about this tomorrow.

Fifthly, the Jupiter forces protect human beings from dissolving into the element of light, in the light ether. Human beings would become clouds of light flowing ever outwards if there were no corresponding Jupiter forces.

Sixthly, the forces of Saturn protect human beings from flowing out into the chemical ether. These Saturn forces working on human beings are really forces related in a sense to innermost human nature. Usually, we speak figuratively when we say someone is sweet or someone is sour. But this is not just figurative, rather when someone seems sour in a moral or physical way, this is partly connected to their chemical configuration. And the Saturn forces are part of this chemical configuration. How a person lives from out of their organism depends on how Saturn affects them. So in fact someone is melancholic because of the way they are settled into their chemical constitution, in what is cooked up in the liver, in the gallbladder and in the stomach; melancholia is based on a certain settling in to the chemical configuration. And this is based in turn on the forces of Saturn being particularly strongly developed in such a person.

So we can say that human beings appear to be concentrated within their skin, but that in reality this is only illusion; in reality human beings are part of the whole cosmos and we can show in detail how the cosmos has its part in their shaping.

You can see that the planets close to the sun are connected more to the physical in human beings: the solid, the fluid, the air. The planets further away from the sun are more connected to the etheric elements in the human being. The sun itself divides the one from the other. The forces of Mercury, Venus, and the moon bring us to the solid, to the fluid, to the aeriform. Those of Mars, Jupiter and Saturn protect us from flowing out into the warmth, the light and the chemical. As you can see these are polar effects. And between them, so that they do not cause chaos, is the element of the sun. The forces of Mars would work unrestrainedly and they would affect for example the moon forces if the sun was not between them as a kind of partition which prevents them from coming together. Without this the Mars forces would help humans to be independent of the warmth element, but what had become independent would have to take possession of the air and would become an air wraith. In order that both processes can take place separately, so that human beings can grasp their aeriform, organic gestalt on the one hand and on the other can live independently in the warmth element, the two forces must be separated. The sun is between them.

This also the old initiates knew well. When for example a person developed a certain sickness because of the Mars forces working too strongly in them, so that in a sense they broke through the sun element and the person was living too strongly in the air element because they could grasp it more strongly, then the two elements had to be separated. To achieve this, they used aurum. In order to prevent the forces of Mars and those of the moon from flowing into each other, the sun forces had to be strengthened. This led to using aurum, which re-harmonized the organism, so that what was not supposed to flow together was separated.

From all this you will be able to see that knowledge of the world is not possible without knowledge of the human being and knowledge of the human being is not possible without knowledge of the world, particularly not when we are concerned with the scientific practice of healing.

Fourth Lecture

Dornach, 1 July 1922

Wʜᴀᴛ I presented you with yesterday was in a sense the outer aspect of what I want to talk about today. Yesterday I attempted to show how together with the universe human beings form a greater whole and specifically how what exists in humans is connected in various ways to processes and beings in the cosmos. So if today's discussion is not to appear to you as wholly lacking in any basis, then you should relate it to what was said here yesterday and also last Sunday.

We can view human beings in a way from the outside, either just by looking at them or by studying anatomy and physiology, which are also ways of observing them from the outside. But we can also look at them from the inside; then they reveal to us their soul attributes, their spiritual powers. When we look at the whole formed by human beings together with the cosmos, then we can also see it from two aspects, only these aspects behave in the opposite way to those concerning the individual human being. With the individual human being we speak of outside and inside. When speaking of the universe and of humans as just a part of this universe, then we should feel that we have to reverse this word usage. By first considering the mere existence of the world in space, our standpoint is in a sense from within this world existence towards the outside. So that when we first speak of the universe from the human point of view, then we are speaking from inside the universe. Our standpoint is somewhere within it. Seen from there, the universe offers us its sensual aspect.

Human beings show us their sensual aspect when we regard them from the outside; they show us their soul-spiritual aspect when we look at them from the inside. The universe shows us its soul-spiritual aspect when we regard it from the outside. The concepts we have to utilize here are very difficult, since they are almost totally unused in present-day language. We cannot find our way directly into the spiritual world with our present-day use of language. We first have to form the words in the relevant way. It is absurd to want to study the soul-spiritual by using words in their ordinary sense.

Now if we want to imagine schematically what I have just tried to describe, then we have to say something like this: if we take a human being then we speak of their exterior as being what we perceive with our senses. If we look at them from the inside then we speak of the soul-spiritual. With the universe, with the cosmos we have to think of it the other way around: we are at some point on the inside and so can see the sensual aspect. If we could view the world from the outside, we would be able to see its soul-spiritual aspect. Now of course the question arises: Can we view the universe from the outside?

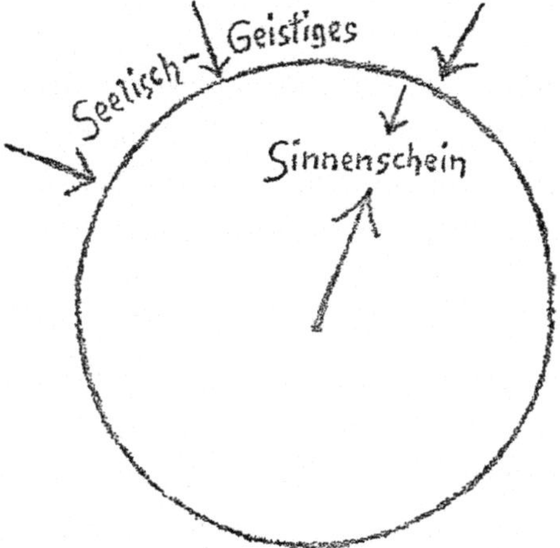

Seelisch-Geistiges = soul-spiritual, Sinnenschein = sense appearance

Now as we know human beings alternate between two states: that experienced between birth and death and that between death and a new birth. In the state between death and a new birth they can actually become aware of the universe, the cosmos from the outside. If you read what I wrote in my *Theosophy*[11] about the conditions that people experience between death and a new birth, then you will find descriptions in which I have described sufficiently how we have to find a new usage of language.

Now the world in which we find ourselves between birth and death is diverse enough. But it becomes much more diverse, much richer when we look at it in life between death and a new birth. Of course in talking about something like this I can only ever single out specific aspects to describe and I have always endeavoured to elaborate on those aspects which I had depicted at first in more simple terms. Today I would like to speak of the soul-spiritual aspect of what I described yesterday from the sensual-physical standpoint, the view of the cosmos from the inside. Now I want to describe it from the outside as it reveals itself when we look at it from the soul-spiritual aspect that we experience on our path between death and a new birth.

Now from all the various discussions that have taken place here, you know how necessary such an observation is and that an ordinary logical discussion of these things could not possibly correspond to reality. We have to offer the view which opens up when we use those methods depicted in the anthroposophical literature.

Now human beings only gradually find their way to a clear viewpoint outside the sensual-physical cosmos. When they have found such a viewpoint, which can only be some time after their death, then those questions are resolved which cannot be resolved through the intellectuality that we use when embodied. In philosophical discourse, questions such as whether space is finite or infinite have played a large part. But we can discuss as much as we like—in this respect Kant's *Critique of Pure Reason* was right—such questions as to the spatial or temporal end of the world will never be resolved through a discussion conducted in the physical body. There we can prove both the finiteness and the infiniteness of the world. These questions resolve themselves when the standpoint can effectively be moved, when we can in a sense look at the world from the other side, not from a point within it, but from the outside looking in. At least in the middle stages between death and a new birth we are truly beyond the limits of the sensual-physical cosmos. We can only say that the limits of the sensual-physical cosmos lie in the middle of what we see from our earthly standpoint and what we see in the life between death and a new birth.

It is a part of wisdom to know which questions can be asked within earthly existence, but not answered within it, because there we can only think on the basis of our physical bodies. Such questions can only be answered when human beings can move their standpoint to outside physical existence, either through initiation or through death.

Now if we can actually change our standpoint then we have experiences which we at first did not expect. When we stand here on some point of earthly existence and look at the cosmos, then it is one sole cosmos. It appears to us as one sole cosmos. We speak of our solar system as a unified, cosmic world. I will limit my observations for now to our solar system. When we change our standpoint, then it is not a question of finding another point outside; points finish here completely, not for the inner life of the soul, but for external space. The point becomes more and more a circle. When we are outside, then it stops being meaningful to speak of one world, for example of one unique solar system. In that instance when we turn life around so that in the disembodied state between death and a new birth we are able to look back at life in the world we are now, that means looking at our soul-spiritual from outside, in that moment, it ceases to have meaning, to speak of *one* solar system. There are innumerable solar systems, as many solar systems as there are human beings on the earth. Here I am describing external experience, what can be experienced. So this is also completely turned around. Here we have the clear feeling we are standing in a physical-sensual world. At that moment when we look at this physical-sensual world from a soul-spiritual viewpoint, it becomes meaningless to speak of a unity, because there are as many such worlds, including suns, as there are human souls connected to the earth. And there is also another surprising experience. When we look back at the earth from outside, then human nature also appears, the human being appears. Even in public lectures I have ventured to say that when we are looking from earth out to the cosmos we are really looking inwards from outside, but when we humans are between death and a new birth then what we are seeing is really the inside of the human being. Thus when we are moving towards earthly life, then our outer world is really the organic interior, not the soul interior, but the organic interior of the human being. This is what we always see when we look back from outside at the cosmos in which we exist between birth and death. We are looking back at human nature. We never really lose human nature. When we die, we still have the view of human nature, just that now we do not experience it from inside; we are not inside it as we are between birth and death, but experience it from outside, we look at it from the outside. But the strange thing is that the diversity of human beings disappears when we come outside. And while we see many cosmic formations, as many as there are human beings connected to the earth, in looking back to the earth temporally and spatially, we see but one human being. Between death and a new birth there are many worlds and just one human being.

You see, we can only hint at this in human language and we have to consider it meditatively and thoroughly—it is of momentous importance—otherwise we cannot fully understand the radical difference in our view of the world through our experience between birth and death and through our experience between death and a new birth. Between birth and death we experience one world and many people; between death and a new birth we experience many worlds, which constitute our present world entity, and only one human being. When in our life between death and a new birth we look back at earthly life, then there are not multiple human beings, but rather all humans are included in just one human being. So it is all completely transposed and we have to make ourselves aware of this radical transposition. For it is absolutely necessary that we are completely clear about how impossible it is to gain adequate insight into the spiritual world without completely transforming our concepts. It is just not possible to gain real insight into the spiritual world using those comfortable methods that are usually employed in the attempt. We have to be prepared to metamorphose our ideas even as far as completely transposing them. This is not what many people want and this leads to enmity against a real science of the spirit.

Now yesterday I showed what kind of relationship human beings have on the one hand to the sun-like, on the other to the moon-like and also to the individual planetary beings. I spoke about all this from the point of view of the development of the earth. I explained the relationship between humans and the Venus being, the Mercury being and so on, and I said that through modern spiritual science we can arrive quite independently at insights which were cultivated in the ancient mysteries in an old, dreamlike inspired way. All that I described to you yesterday is just a depiction from one point of view. As long as we only try to gain knowledge in the manner that the old initiates of the early mysteries did and as we do today, in life between birth and death, we will only get insights into our planetary cosmos such as I described to you yesterday. But when we go beyond this, when we are in a way standing outside this cosmos in which we live between birth and death, and are looking at the soul-spiritual from outside, then those things we described yesterday reveal themselves to us in their other aspect, their transposition.

Yesterday we said that when we look at the Mercury-like in the world—be it the substance, be it the planet—then we have the force that flows through the universe so that people are able to grasp with their soul-spiritual aspect the solid parts of their organism. The Venus-like enables human beings to grasp the fluid parts of the organism with their soul-spiritual and so on. At that moment when we transpose our whole point of view, all these characteristics present themselves differently. If we leave out Neptune and Uranus for the moment, then Saturn is at the edge of our planetary system and when we now look at the Saturn beings from the other side of existence so to speak, we have the possibility of looking not at what we said yesterday about Saturn helping people to maintain their soul-spiritual in the face of chemism—this is the aspect seen from the earth—but looking from the other side and with all the faculties that we have between death and a new birth, we get to know the real instinctual life of human beings. With those faculties we have on earth we cannot comprehend human instinctual life flooding up from the unconscious depths; we have to comprehend it either between death and a new birth or through higher, supersensible perception, through the science of initiation.

So we can say that if we look at the Saturn being from the earth with our spiritual eye, then we get an idea of the forces which enable people to assert themselves as independent soul-spiritual beings in the face of the forces of chemism at work in their organism. If we look from outside at the Saturn being in its soul-spiritual aspect, then it represents those forces in the cosmos that put the instincts into human nature.

And the Jupiter being [see diagram below], represents all which in humans is more of a soul-like nature than are the instincts, what exists in people as inclinations, sympathies and so on; the instincts are definitely more animal, whereas the inclinations are more animal-psychic.

The Mars being represents what is not directly a moral precept that we impose upon ourselves, but more the impulses emerging from our characterological constitution. Whether someone is courageous in their ethical behaviour, or more nonchalant, that is located in the forces that we get to know when we look at the Mars organization from the other side. These are not the fully conscious moral impulses I described in my *Philosophy of Freedom*[12] as being rooted in pure thinking, but impulses still very much tainted with a strongly unconscious element.

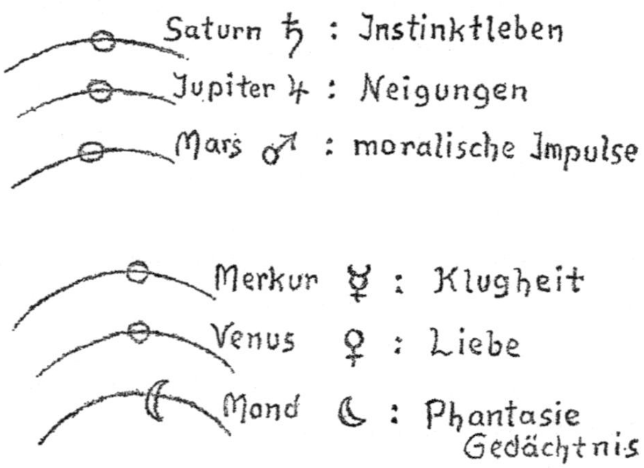

Saturn ♄ : Instinktleben

Jupiter ♃ : Neigungen

Mars ♂ : moralische Impulse

Merkur ☿ : Klugheit

Venus ♀ : Liebe

Mond ☽ : Phantasie
            Gedächtnis

Saturn = instinctual life, Neigungen = inclinations, moralische Impulse = moral impulses, Merkur = Mercury, Klugheit = cleverness, Liebe = love, Phantasie = fantasy, Gedächtnis = memory

So when we look at the relationship of human beings to these external planets, we have something connected more to those human virtues bound up in a sense with the human organism. What is born with us stems from the cosmos, stems from the universe. What is more instinctive and floods up so to speak out of the organism is Saturn-like. What flows up as inclinations, as affects, is Jupiter-like. What bubbles up as directly active, initiative forces, but is bound to the organism, that is Mars-like.

Now we come to the more internalized human characteristics. They also belong here in as far as they stem from forces which are also in the cosmos. For example, if we leave out the sun, then we first have Mercury. Normally people do not want to believe that human cleverness is something stemming from the whole cosmos. But it is. And if you only look completely impartially at world phenomena, then you will say to yourself: What my reason can see as active in itself, that is fulfilled in the phenomena of the world. Reason is there, within world phenomena. Now the forces representing this reason in the cosmos, which is born with us as our cleverness, as our faculty of reason, that is the Mercury-like in the cosmos.

Traditionally Venus has been well described: it is represented in everything to do with love. The moon-like represents all activities having to do with fantasy, including memory, not what is connected to the organic function behind memory, but rather the shaping of the images. The images of memory are actually identical to the images of fantasy, just that the first are formed true to real experiences. So we can say that fantasy and memory, the more internal virtues and faculties, are connected to those forces that appear as the moon being, the Venus being, the Jupiter being and so on. So we could also say that if we look at the sensual-physical aspect of Jupiter, meaning we are looking from the standpoint of the interior of the universe, then in the sense that I was talking about yesterday, it represents the concentration of those forces that enable human beings not to flow out into the light, to be able to maintain themselves as soul-spiritual beings in the light. If we imagine the soul-spiritual being of the forces of Jupiter—meaning Jupiter from the outside, whereas for the soul-spiritual in humans we would have to say from the inside—then it represents all those forces that humans have within themselves as inclinations, as affects and so on. Hence, we could say that the faculty of independent soul life in the face of light is the outside of Jupiter. The development, the forming, the creation of inclinations and affects is the inside, the soul-spiritual of Jupiter. When human beings go through the stages after death or in initiation, then as I have described in my book *Theosophy*,[13] at a certain point for example they no longer see the stars—whether planets or fixed stars—as we do from the earth with our sense organs. It is understandable that they cease to see them, but they do not cease to know about the stars. They know about them. Initially they know what I described yesterday. And from a certain time onwards they learn to recognize the moral aspect of the star beings. Thus they are looking back at the cosmos. However, they no longer see the cosmos as a physical being, but as a moral being and after going through an interim state, where they see what I described yesterday, then they see from the outside, particularly in the middle between death and a new birth, not what we could call Saturn in an earthly sense, but the seething life of instincts that they then take possession of as human beings on their way down to a body and into physical earthly existence. They see the weaving life of inclinations and so on. Obviously materialistic thinking can deny all this, but that would be just as clever as denying the soul-spiritual aspect of human beings in the face of their physical body.

To behold what I would like to call the moral cosmos, to behold the moral world of the planets, this is something that fulfils human beings in the time between death and a new birth. However, their view is dependent on the way in which they go through the gates of death. They see the life of instincts, inclinations, the life of moral impulses and so on in a way corresponding to the unconscious insight they have developed during their earthly existence.

For example, take a person who has known many other people in their life, who deviates in a way from the norm by not seeing other people as philistines, but by approaching them with a certain kindness, a certain understanding, who values rather than disparages them. This person has developed a depth of conscious understanding, but also a wealth of unconscious impulses; we benefit enormously when we value other people, when we try to understand them and not to disparage them. Equipped with these impulses we are able to observe the secrets of Saturn from the other side of existence, from that side of life that exists between death and a new birth. In this way the various secrets of planetary life reveal themselves. According to our ability to perceive them, we can connect them together to a whole and integrate them into our own human being when we descend again to the earth.

And now you can already sense that a certain experience develops in accordance with our perception, just as on earth an experience develops in accordance with what we perceive. On earth we get to know one person after another. This is how we develop our knowledge of human nature. And we gain experience according to what we perceive from the other side of life. Only the experiences that we gain in that way become creative in the second half of life between death and a new birth and we bring them with us into the organization that we receive through heredity. You will sense that this has something to do with the configuration of karma, that here something takes place that we could call the technique of the creation of karma. By having such perceptions from the other side of life as I have described here, human beings gain the experiences that they need, so that between death and a new birth they can shape their karma.

Today I have to describe things a little more subtly, because we are dealing with subtleties and because I have to point out that we must transform our concepts when we want to understand the universe. This is because in all that we see on earth, both sensual-physical and then through spiritually deepening our understanding, in all this we have only the one side of existence. Even when we look out at the cosmos, we see only the one side of existence. The other side of existence only reveals itself when we can observe the cosmos from outside the body in a purely soul-spiritual way. Then the cosmos is revealed as a soul-spiritual being, a moral being.

In very old times when human beings came down to their physical earthly existence, they brought with them what I would call 'cosmic memory'. In comparison to today, the outward appearance of these people of ancient times was certainly more animal-like, even if the crude theory of evolution is not true. However, even within their earthly lives they still knew something of the other side of existence. They brought it with them into their still imperfectly developed human body. And the evolution of human beings on the earth consists of them losing more and more the memory of the other side of existence, where we live between death and a new birth. And by losing this memory, they become solely dependent on the experiences they go through within their earthly life. Only through this process can human beings absorb as a force what cannot be learned anywhere else in the cosmos. Freedom of action can only be acquired here during earthly life; human beings acquire it here and then we have it for all our earthly and cosmic future existence.

Since people are naturally shocked when they first hear about these things, in public lectures today we have to speak in abstract terms about the fact that when human beings dwell in soul-spiritual existence, the world reveals itself in inverted, in transposed form. But as you see, we can describe the relationship of human beings to the whole of the cosmos in the actual, concrete facts of planetary existence—and we could go even further out into the world of the stars. Only in the light of this knowledge is it possible to say that the cosmos, as seen from the earth, is firstly the physical cosmos, including the earth, and then the etheric cosmos. You know what is meant by these terms. Only the physical cosmos and the etheric cosmos exist in our ordinary physical space. At that moment when a person passes through the gates of death or goes through initiation and experiences themselves in a purely spiritual way, thus looking at the universe from the other side, these ideas about space cease to have meaning for them.

As long as we have to speak in human words, we can say that we look at our spatial universe from the outside and it seems to us as if what we are looking at is spatial too. However, it is no longer spatial, since we have to say that when we look from a point here, then we have to imagine the point being spread out. The point is no longer a point, it is spread out. In a sense we enclose space within us and are looking at the non-spatial. Just as we look at space from a certain point, when we move outside the body we see the point, we look back at the point from space. And this is linked to what we experience: we see as many worlds as there are human souls connected to the earth, but we see just the one human being. When we look at ourselves from the outside, we are all just the one single person. This is why in the science of initiation we talk of the secret of the number, because the number itself only has meaning depending on the point of view. What is a unity here on earth, the cosmos, is a multiplicity seen from the outside. What is a multiplicity here on earth, human beings, is a unity seen from the outside. Even seeing something as a unity or a multiplicity is an illusion, Maya. Seen from a different aspect, a unity reveals itself as a multiplicity, or a multiplicity as a unity. This is something that took place here on earth in the development of the science of mathematics. I have already pointed this out. Nowadays we count by linking one unit to another. We say one, then two by joining it with another unit, then three and so on. In ancient times people did not count like this, they did so as follows: the unity one, in the unity two, in the unity three. They did not join the one to the other, rather unity always encompassed all numbers. All numbers were in the unity. For us the unity is in all numbers; in old mathematics all numbers were in the unity. This comes from the different way people thought back then, which was connected to the memories of an extra-cosmic science existing in those primeval times of humanity.

Fifth Lecture

DORNACH, 2 JULY 1922

In these last days I have described for you the relationship of humanity to the environment as seen when we turn our gaze away from the earth and out towards the world of the stars, the planetary world. Today I would like to enlarge on this, at least aphoristically, with some observations and experiences which show the relationship of human beings to their immediate earthly environment. We tend to look at what surrounds us in a kind of homogeneous way and arrive thus at a quite unreal concept of existence. I would like to remind you of what I have often mentioned here to clarify this point. When for example we look at a quartz, from our earthly point of view we can say that this is an object grounded in itself. In the self-containedness that the quartz presents to us we can only ever see in a certain way just this self-containedness.

However, this is not the case when we pick a rose, for example, and put it in our room. Within earthly existence this rose with its stem is inconceivable; we can only conceive of it growing on the branch of the rosebush with its stalks and roots. Hence when we mean to speak realistically, we should not call a rose an object in the same sense that we do a quartz. Speaking realistically means we have to include only those objects which can exist comparatively in and of themselves. Of course looked at another way the quartz cannot be seen as something existing in and of itself, but that would be from another aspect. The standpoint of a simple observation of earthly existence offers us a very different concept of existence for the quartz than for the rose. Unfortunately such things receive very little consideration. This is why human thought is so unreal and it is so very difficult for human beings to link what must be said from the point of view of spiritual observation to explicit concepts. They would be able to arrive at explicit concepts if they would observe the simplest things more as I have just described.

Now if we look at the earth, the immediate environment of human beings, we find at first on the surface various kinds of soil. Here if you look around you in this part of the world you will find chalky soil. If you move southwards, you will find shale. For now I want to stay with these two main soil types, the chalky, limestone formation, which you can observe here in the region as Jura limestone, and the shale formation, where the stone is not so densely packed as is the chalk formation, where it is more slatey. Just think of slate or even gneiss or mica slate and so on, which can all be found in the central Alps. In earthly existence these are very significant antithetical states: the shale formation and the chalk formation. Looking at these rock deposits, as they are also known, contemporary science attempts to explain them from a solely mineral-physical point of view. No thought is given to the fact that the earth is a whole. Let us look at what the science of geology consists of today.

Look at the various soils. Look at the various ores, metals, and minerals in general embedded in these soils. By looking at the earth in this way, a geological way, we regard it as if there were no plants or people living on it. This kind of observation of the earth that geology makes is really just the same as if we looked at a human skeleton on its own. If you look at a human skeleton in isolation you really have to say that actually this is not a being in and of itself. Nowhere in the world could such a skeleton develop just for itself. It can be the leftover rest of a total human being, but it could never have developed without the corresponding muscles, nerves, blood vessels and so on. So we should not regard a human skeleton as a self-contained existence or try to explain it out of itself.

For someone who thinks not just abstractly but realistically it is impossible to understand the earth with its various rock formations without taking into consideration that the plant kingdom, the animal kingdom and the realm of human beings belong as much to the earth as do the muscles, the blood and so on to the human skeleton. So we have to be clear that to look at the earth 'geologically' means that from the outset we relinquish any search for reality. We would not arrive at anything real. We would arrive at what in reality can only exist within a planetary being when this planetary being also contains the worlds of plants, animals and human beings.

When we first look at the shale formation, which I would like to call part of the skeleton of the earth, then we see that to all appearances it is considerably different from the chalk formation, which is in itself very compact. And if we use those methods I have used in the case of the greater contours of earthly development in my *Occult Science—An Outline*,[14] then in fact we have to trace back the difference in the shale formation and the chalk formation to their respective relationships to the existence of plants, of animals and of human beings. We have to look at how the soul-spiritual of the earth influences the rock formations.

You cannot understand a human skeleton when you leave out the will nature of human beings and you cannot understand the shale formation or the chalk formation if you neglect the tasks these formations have in relation to the soul-spiritual of the earth's existence. And there you will find an intimate relationship between the shale formation and the realm of plants, between the chalk formation and the realm of animals.

Of course as the earth is now, the rock we find in shale is also to be found in plants. We can find stone or minerals in the animal kingdom, in various forms according to their origins. However, this is not as important here as is the question of how for spiritual observation, for spiritual experience, the plant being, all the plant beings of the earth, reveal their relationship to the shale formation in their own particular way.

To illustrate this I would have to sketch it as follows: the earth [white], then the shale formation [purple] as a layer on it, schematically, and then the plants which grow out of the earth towards the skies [red]. Spatially the plants do not necessarily correspond to the shale formation, just as for example the thought, which has its basis in the instrument of the brain, does not need to correspond spatially to the big toe when it is moved. It is not a question of corresponding spatially, of being in the same place, but of trying to understand the shale formation not only by examining it chemically and physically, but with the help of spiritual research as I present it in *How to Know Higher Worlds*[15] or *Occult Science*. Then we can see that if the forces contained in shale were solely at work on earth, then they would have to be connected to something living that develops exactly as does the plant world. The plant world develops only the physical body and the etheric body; these are both in the plant itself. When we come to the astral aspect of the plant world, then we have to think of this astral aspect as an astral atmosphere surrounding the earth [orange]. Plants do not have an astral body. But the earth is surrounded by this astral atmosphere. And in the process of blossoming and of bearing fruit, for example, this astrality plays a part. The whole plant world of the earth has a coherent astral body, which never descends into the plant itself—at most just a little when the flower transitions to the fruit— but essentially floats above the vegetation like a cloud and stimulates the development of the blossom and the fruit.

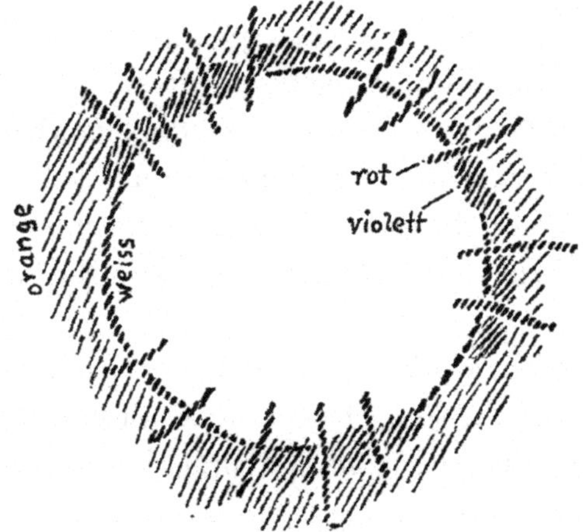

weiss = white, rot = red, violet = purple, orange = orange

What is developing in these processes would collapse into itself if not for the radiating forces from the shale rock formations. So that in the shale formation we have the quest to make the whole of the earth an organism. In fact in relation to the earth we have to view the plants as similar to our hair in relation to the whole human being, as homogeneous. And holding the whole organization of the earth together are the radiating forces coming from the rocks of the shale formation.

At some point these things will be confirmed by natural science. For example it will be said that human beings have their physical body and their etheric body. The foundation of their whole organism is the plant. In fact we can view humans as plant beings onto which the animal and human are superimposed. If we treat human beings in healthy or sick states with minerals from the shale formation, then even externally, we will be able to determine their effects—what I am saying here can be validated by spiritual observation. And it will be particularly significant to identify which symptoms in human beings are based on an overgrowth of the plant element. An overgrowth of the plant element in humans can always be treated with minerals from the shale formation. This is because all that belongs to the shale formation maintains the normal state—so to speak—of the plant element in humans, just as it normalizes the plant life of the earth. The plant realm would grow uninhibitedly out into the cosmos if it were not held together by the corresponding mineral forces of the shale formation. In future we will be able to study a living geography and geology of the earth from this standpoint, when people have recognized that for geology we should not just look at what is in a sense the skeleton of the earth, but at its connection with the whole of the earth being, with the organic and with the soul-spiritual of the earth.

Now all the plant world is intimately connected to the sun-like, to the influence of the sun. The sun does not just produce warmth and light through its etheric and physical elements, but within this warmth and light is also the soul-spiritual. This soul-spiritual is connected to what is incorporated in the shale formation. The fact that shale is in a sense distributed over the earth is connected to how the plant beings are spread out over the earth. The localisation is not the most important aspect. We should not imagine that, for example, the shale formation must be present for the plants to grow out of it. The shale formation streams out; the rays are carried over the earth by various magnetic currents and the plants live from this flow of radiation from the shale formation. Quite the contrary, plants cannot thrive where the shale formation has developed most strongly, since the plant's own forces would be drawn too strongly into the earth itself and would not be able to unfold. In this case the forces that bind the plant to the earth are so predominant, that the development of the plant, which also needs cosmic forces, becomes impossible. We can only really get a picture of the shale element in the earth when we go back to when the earth itself was in its sun existence in the sense described in *Occult Science*. Then the shale-like was being prepared within the earth, not fully formed as it is today, but in the making. At the time the earth was in its sun stage the physical aspect of the earth had only developed as far as a sprawling plant life. And really, we should say, that when we look back from its present form to the earlier moon and sun stages of the earth—these are the earlier planetary stages—then in the sun stage neither plants nor animals could develop. Plants as they are today did not exist in the sun stage, but the earth itself had a kind of plant existence and on the one side the plant realm developed from this plant existence of the earth and on the other side, through the hardening of the creative forces of the plant, the shale formation. So the shale formation is what has been retrieved from the plant existence of the earth as earth intellect.

When we look at the chalk formation however, supersensible perception reveals its intimate connection to what endows all animal existence on earth with independence. The plant cleaves to the ground; it is bound to the earth as is our hair to our scalps. The animal moves about. However, the chalk formation is connected less to this moving about, which is a local movement, and more to the independent configuration of the animal.

When you look at a plant you can see that it grows with the root down into the earth; it sinks down into the earth, strives in a way towards the centre of the earth and then develops outwards. In the plant's gestalt we can recognize how it is completely regulated by its relationship to the earth. Of course with more complicated plants we have to provide a more complicated description, but it is essentially the same. The plant is not independent. Where it is rooted in the earth it constricts itself and connects itself to the life of the earth; where it projects out over the soil it expands and spreads out in all directions towards the light. We best understand the form of the plant when we see it as intimately connected to the earth.

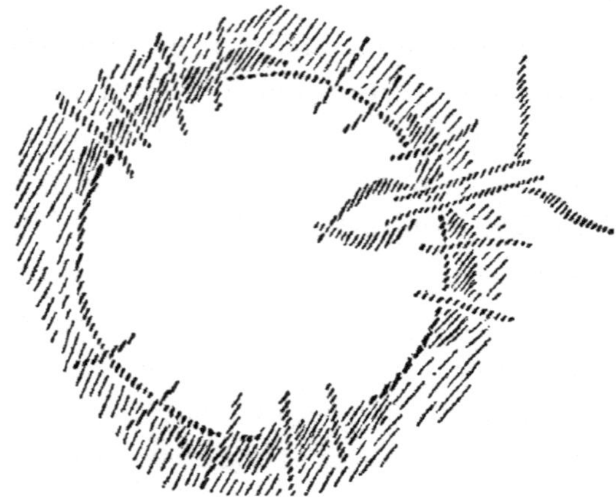

In the basic outline of the animal form, for example in the horizontal position of the spine or the downward tendency of the limbs, we can of course also find aspects adapted to earthly existence. However, the animal form is also independent of the earth. In each animal form we can see that it is not adapted solely to the earth as is the plant, but that it has something independent, something autonomous. The animal has broken away from the earth, as has its form.

Supersensible perception shows us that all that I have talked about these last few days in the sense of what shines down from the moon, the reflected light from the sun that streams down to the earth through the moon, the configurations that then flow into and form our thinking life, all this also brings the forms of the various animals. In essence what is in the animal as indeterminate and formless will can be found within the range of direct sunlight. What gives the animal its independent gestalt, not adapted to earthly existence, all this drifts in—and we have to express it thus—on the light of the moon.

All these particular configurations come down to the earth from the moon. The fact that the various animals are differently formed is because the moon traverses the zodiac. The moon exerts its formative influence differently on the various animals according to whether it is in Aries, Taurus or Gemini. This results in an interesting relationship between the zodiac and the animal forms themselves, of which the old dreamlike wisdom had a premonition. It is the forces flowing out of the chalk formations that draw down these forms, which would otherwise be lost as mists in the surroundings of the earth. The minerals of the earth send out not only radium rays, but much else besides. So on the one hand we have to look at the shale formation for maintaining plant life on earth and on the other at the chalk formation for drawing down from the moon all that lives in the specific animal forms. Thus through spiritual observation we can appreciate how the shale formation of the earth is connected to the forms of the plant world and the chalk formation to the forms of the animal world.

We have to be clear that what we find in the chalk formation is also to be found in every detail of organic life. If we have the proper means, we can observe quite clearly that for example some people have a strong tendency to skeleton development. With this I do not mean that they have a strong skeleton, but that they have calcification also in the rest of the organism. There are, so to speak, chalk-rich people and chalk-poor people. Of course you should not think that this is as coarse as it sounds; you have to imagine a more homeopathic dose, but it is still significant. The more chalk-rich people are generally cleverer and capable of holding together and then differentiating very fine concepts. Now you must not think that here I am describing the human being materialistically; that would never occur to me. Whether a person has more or less calcification in their organism depends on their karma. Both backwards and forwards everything depends on the spiritual. However, a real, incisive knowledge of the world consists not of talking about the spiritual and the material in generalities, but of knowing how the spiritual is creatively active in forming matter from out of itself. So a person who through their earlier lives is destined for an incarnation as a particularly clever human being, for example as an extremely good mathematician, develops between death and a new birth soul-spiritual forces that then lead to calcification. We need the calcium deposits in our organism in order to be clever. In contrast we need silica deposits, which are to be found in shale or slate, in order to develop our will.

We can only understand matter when we always consider it in relation to the spiritual. So we can say that the chalk formation contains those rays and currents which lend themselves to developing not only the animal forms on earth, but also what exists in us as the material basis for our ability to form thoughts in ourselves. Outside in space there are the various animals. Inside in our intellect there are the thought forms. They are the animal forms transposed into the spiritual. The whole animal kingdom is at the same time our intelligence. The whole animal kingdom projected into the inside of the human being, so that it appears as our moving thought forms, that is our intelligence. And just as the animal kingdom outside needs the chalk formation for its configuration, so we need, in a sense, the fine, inner calcium deposits, also a chalk formation, in order to be clever. Of course this should not be excessive. If a human being secreted excessive amounts of calcium, then their cleverness would separate out of them; it would not remain with them. This would lead to the development of an objective cleverness which would, however, not stick with this person. Everything depends on proportionality. And if we look deeper into this then we will find it interesting how minerals have a certain significance in the lives of human beings, animals and plants. Now as we have just said, if we look at all the effects the chalk-like forces have on us, then we arrive at what needs structuring, at what helps us to become stable human beings. And if we look at what in us is related to the effects of silica, of the shale-like, then we see that this develops us into human beings who struggle against, who resist this solidness and dissolve it, liquify it and turn it into something plant-like. The human being is always a kind of collaboration between the chalk-like and the shale-like, meaning of course the inner forces found in the chalk-like and in the shale-like.

Now let us take a closer look at the shale-like. In much of the shale-like we find siliceous rock, particularly in rock crystal or quartz. The forces found in rock crystal or quartz also flow and radiate within the human being. And if the human being had only these forces, which they absorb with the harder shale-like into themselves, if to a certain extent they had only this quartz-like in them, they would be in constant danger of trying with their soul-spiritual to get back to what they were between death and a new birth before they set foot on the earth. The quartz-like forever wants to bring people out of themselves, to bring them back to their not yet embodied being. There has to be another force working against the one trying to bring humans back to their unembodied being and this is the force of carbon. Human beings have carbon in them in various forms. Of course carbon is seen by modern science only externally, only through the methods of physics or chemistry. In truth, however, carbon is what helps us to always stay with ourselves. Really it is our house. It is what we live in, whereas silica forever wants to lead us out of the house and bring us back in time to before we were here, before we moved into our house of carbon.

Thus the carbon and the silica in us are continually in conflict. But this struggle is where we live. If we only consisted of carbon—for example the plant kingdom is based on carbon—then we would be bound only to the earth. We would not be able to have an idea about our existence beyond the earth. That we can know this is due to the silica element within us. When we comprehend this then we can see what healing powers silica or quartz has. If a person is ill because they have a strong tendency towards the carbon, which is the case with all diseases related to deposits of metabolites in the body, then they need silica as a remedy. This is especially true when the metabolite deposits are in the periphery or in the brain; then silica is a strong remedy.

So you see, when we understand these things, when we see them from the point of view of a holistic knowledge both natural and spiritual, which looks for the spiritual in all things material and finds the material in the spiritual, which is seen as the creative instance, only then do we find what really explains human existence and also what we have to do when this human existence is malfunctioning.

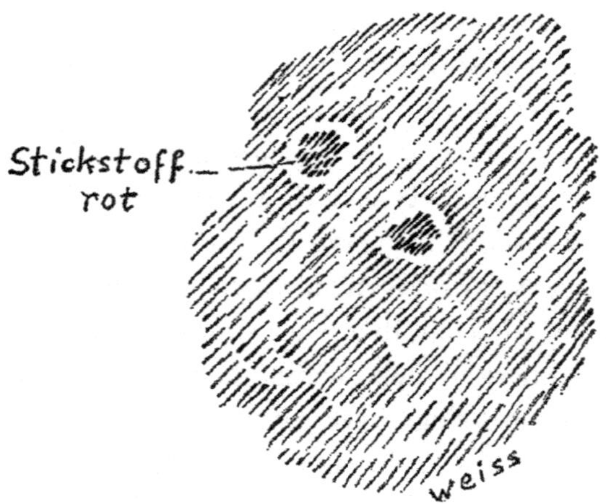

Stickstoff = nitrogen, rot = red, weiss = white

It is particularly important to pay attention to what exists in human beings as nitrogen-like: nitrogen itself and its various compounds. The fact that human beings have nitrogen in them enables them to remain open in a way to the universe. I can only sketch this roughly. Let us assume that this is the human organism [white]. By having nitrogen in their bodies human beings have gaps in which the laws of the body are suspended; along the lines of nitrogen contained in it, the body ceases to enforce its own laws. Through this, cosmic laws can come in along these lines [red]. The cosmic asserts itself along the lines of nitrogen in the body. You can say that to the extent that nitrogen is at work in me, the whole cosmos up to the most distant star works in me. What exist in me as the forces of nitrogen bring into me the forces of the cosmos. If I were not an organism containing nitrogen, then I would seal myself off from all the forces coming from the cosmos. And when I need to develop these forces particularly strongly, as for example after conception, when the human embryo, which is a recreation of the cosmos, is growing in the body of the mother, this is only possible because the nitrogenous substances open up the human being for the effects of the larger world, the effects of the cosmos. However, everything in the universe and in the human being is arranged so that no extremes develop. Everything working on its own would produce an extreme. If nitrogen were to unfold its whole power within the human being, then humans would fall out of themselves not only through the silica-like, where they fall into their spiritual past, but also through nitrogen, which continually strives to spread out spiritually; through nitrogen humans would continually be passing out, becoming unconscious. They would not be able to maintain themselves in themselves. They have to be held in themselves.

Now it is always of interest how when we observe something in nature or in human beings, significant factors play a double role. What is on the one hand in humans the physical imprint of cleverness, the chalk-like—is on the other hand the antagonist of the effects of nitrogen. Hence, we can say that in human beings, silica and carbon form a polarity on the one hand and nitrogen and chalk a polarity on the other.

The chalk-like in human beings enables them to repeatedly substitute their own organization for the cosmic that is attempting to work in them through nitrogen. The cosmic is trying to get in through nitrogen [red] and what is in opposition to it from the human organism oscillates against it [blue] through the chalk effect. Thus the cosmos is working in the body at various points and also being thrown out. And this is always an oscillation backwards and forwards: nitrogen effects, chalk effects, nitrogen effects, chalk effects. So you see we can not only relate human beings to the world of stars but also to their immediate environment.

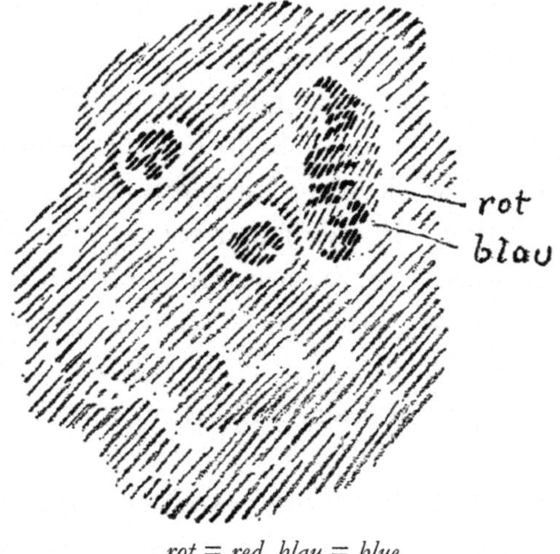

rot = red, blau = blue

In the last edition of *The Goetheanum* I emphasized in an aphorism[16] that materialism as a world view does not really come from an understanding of matter, but from a lack of understanding of matter. What do they know of carbon? They know that it appears in nature as coal, as graphite and as diamonds. Then they describe the physical properties of these forms. But they do not know that carbon is what holds us in ourselves, so that we are a cohesive human organism, or that silica is constantly working against this, trying to take us out of ourselves.

We can only truly know matter when we also recognize its spiritual aspect. For wherever there is matter, spirit permeates it. Of course we will not get anywhere if we get stuck in such a vague and woolly pantheism, saying where there is matter there is spirit. Just as in life itself, where we only progress by looking at things from every possible vantage point, so we need to know more than just that chalk, silica, carbon, nitrogen contain spirit. That is obvious, but obviously not enough. We need also to know how the various substances are, in a sense, embodiments, materializations of spiritual forces. We have to be able to see how the chalk-like organizes human beings in themselves and how nitrogen is always trying to permeate them with the cosmic.

Plants, which always have to be connected to the cosmic, since they grow out of the earth towards the cosmos, need nitrogen for growth; and when we grasp this connection then we are able to study the growth of plants in the right way.

These things have first their cognitive aspect: we only get to know the world when we understand them. But they also have a practical side. And we get stuck in the most primitive world view if we neglect to look at things in their larger context. We also need to go into details and look at how the necessary nitrogen compounds are incorporated into plant growth. Now you know that this is a very significant area of study, but agriculture can only really be studied properly through spiritual science. Spiritual science is the true science of reality.

You see, all that I am describing to you today has to be rediscovered by spiritual science through the methods now used and those to be developed in the future. Older sciences only know these things through a kind of dreamlike clairvoyance. We have to achieve a fully conscious clairvoyance. I have often spoken about this. We cannot today just accept these things that humanity knew on the basis of their very different human organization. It is obviously just nonsense when people only want to study the old sciences, because they cannot help us to understand things. Just the opposite: we understand even the older phenomena only when we can illuminate them spiritually in the right way. Still it is wonderful how basically, through a kind of instinct, modern science is tending towards what was discovered through dreamlike clairvoyance.

Let us take a specific case. The ancients supposed that everywhere in earthly etheric existence there was lead. They attributed what was working in the human gestalt from top to bottom to lead radiation. They saw in lead, which is to be found all over the earth, something linked to the inner configuration of human beings, particularly to human self-awareness. Now of course the modern materialistic thinker will say that lead plays no part in the human organism. The old initiate would have responded: We were not thinking of such a coarse form of lead as you were, but of a really fine lead, existing only as a force. This form of lead is to be found everywhere. This is what the old initiate would have said.

What would the modern scientific researcher say? They would say that minerals exist which give off radiation. Included in these are those that give off radioactive radiation. We all know about uranium radiation, that there are certain rays—known as alpha rays—which radiate out so that at first there is the radiation and then as radiation continues, there are certain changes: what is radiating develops a different atomic weight (relative atomic mass), as they say in chemistry, so that in short a transformation occurs within the radiating matter. Today some people even speak of the revival of the alchemistic metamorphosis of matter. Now people who have studied this say that within this radiation something then develops as a product which is no longer radioactive: radium G [pb-206] and this has the properties of lead. So you can find out solely from modern natural science that there are radioactive substances and within these radioactive substances is a force which is in the process of forming something. And behind all this is lead.

So you see the research of modern natural science is coming astoundingly close to the old science of initiation. And just as today with the instruments of physics they are discovering the properties of lead, so they will discover those of other metals. And then in time they will begin to realize what it means to say that we always find lead in the Saturn-like. You see that only through the vision of spiritual science can we understand what even natural science is discovering today, but which this latter is not able to put into the right context of what is already known.

Now another important aspect in this field is as follows. You know that the air which belongs to our immediate surroundings consists of oxygen and nitrogen. We do not really need nitrogen for our physical existence. We breathe in oxygen. This then transforms itself within us, carbon dioxide develops, which we then breathe out. So we could ask the question: What is the significance of nitrogen, which is not chemically bonded to the oxygen, but exists more in a kind of mixture with the oxygen in the air. We cannot live in nitrogen. We need oxygen in order to live. However, without nitrogen our I and our astral body would have no possibility to go on existing when they are outside the body in sleep. Between falling asleep and waking up we would perish, if we could not immerse ourselves in nitrogen. Our physical body and our ether body need oxygen from the air. Our I and our astral body need nitrogen.

Nitrogen is generally what brings us into connection with the spiritual world. In the state our souls are in during sleep it is the bridge to the spiritual world. Now take what I have said previously and what I have said here about nitrogen. Nitrogen draws the cosmic out of our surroundings. When it is inside us it makes us ready for the cosmic. When outside us it allows what is not of this earth to live in it soul-spiritually. So we have to say that the air is not mixed with a great deal of nitrogen to no purpose; it is mixed in because it is what deadens the physical and enlivens the spiritual during earthly existence. And when, from falling asleep to waking up, we escape from the deadening of the physical to another level of soul existence, then we immerse ourselves in the nitrogen element that forms a bridge between our soul-spiritual and the soul-spiritual of the cosmos. With our earthly, personal existence we are rooted in carbon, with our soul-spiritual existence in nitrogen. In earthly existence carbon and nitrogen have this connection to one another and to human beings that I have described here.

Now look at carbon. It is in common coal, in graphite and in diamonds. Those are the three different forms in which carbon can occur. What you see as carbon in black, sooty coal, in a diamond or in graphite, we carry within us in another form. Up to a certain point we are a diamond. This holds us in our earthly house. That is where our soul-spiritual lives when it inhabits the body.

Nitrogen which is to be found in the various nitrogen compounds, nitric acid and so on, in the saltpetre-like, this is what allows us to go out, what forms the bridge to the soul-spiritual of the cosmos. This too has to be found through the new spiritual science. It was once known on earth, but only in a dreamlike way. The ancient initiates could see it through the old clairvoyance.

As I have often said, we only have the appropriate respect for the old initiates when we rediscover things which we could not have recognized from the ancient lore. Only when we discover them ourselves can we appreciate them in the old traditions. Thus when we rediscover these things, we learn to revere the ancient wisdom of humanity.

Now next time[17] I will speak about how this rediscovery is connected to the Mystery of Golgotha. To do so we need a certain prior knowledge of spiritual science and of natural science, so I think that what we have talked about today should help to clarify some aspects of cosmic and human existence in this regard.

Sixth Lecture

DORNACH, 7 JULY 1922

Today I would like to introduce some of what I will be talking about in the next few days by linking it to the life and teachings of a personality about whom I have spoken in various lectures and about whom I have written more extensively in the third chapter of my book *Riddles of the Soul*.[18] I will be talking about this personality, *Franz Brentano*,[19] as one of the representative minds of the second half of the nineteenth century; the reasons for this will become clear when we continue our studies here. Some observations can also be found in the journal *The Goetheanum*.[20] I particularly want to begin today with his life and teachings as it is the occasion of the publishing of the first volume from Brentano's legacy, which contains one of the most important chapters of his world view, namely on the teachings of Jesus as Franz Brentano understands them.

Franz Brentano, the philosopher, died aged 79 in 1917 in Zurich. There came to an end a philosophical life which is undoubtedly one of the most interesting in history and above all in the second half of the nineteenth century. Not only was Franz Brentano a teacher of philosophy, in him lived a philosophical personality, a personality whose philosophical aspirations came from the breadth and the depths of his whole being.

The philosopher Brentano was a scion of the family to which the German romanticist *Clemens Brentano*,[21] who was his uncle, belonged. And Clemens Brentano was part of that family which was acquainted with *Goethe* through *Sophie La Roche* and through *Maximilian Brentano*. As a family they united two schools of thought, which were prevalent at the beginning of the nineteenth century and often linked to one another: on the one hand Catholicism—the Brentano family were good Catholics—and on the other the Romantics. Clemens Brentano created the most beautiful German romantic poetry and, reflective of the romantic atmosphere of German intellectual life, he was an eminent teller of fairy tales. We could say that German fairy tales as told by the German Romanticists were transformed, so that a real light shone from the spiritual world onto those who listened to them. And as a small child our philosopher, Franz Brentano, listened to these tales told by his uncle Clemens Brentano.

Now for us two things are important here. The one is that Franz Brentano grew up in this spiritual atmosphere. He was born in 1838. In 1842 Clemens Brentano died. The other thing that is important for us is that Franz Brentano, coming from this Catholic romanticism, grows into the strictest ideas of natural science, which dominated the intellectual life of the new civilization in the second half of the nineteenth century. Franz Brentano grew up in such a way that piety filled his soul. For him the religious element is something completely natural in the soul. Catholicism is not something absorbed from outside, but rather an integral part of the soul. The boy, Franz Brentano, fervently embraces and grows up in Catholic piety. Nurtured through Romanticism, he has awakened in himself a great appreciation of the spiritual. For a romantic genius such as Clemens Brentano the spiritual lives more in the form of fantasy, tending not to abide by the rules of logic, but to reach the spiritual world and to dwell there through flights of fantasy. Whereas with Franz Brentano this highly developed sense of spiritual life transforms itself into a special talent for developing stringent concepts.

To add to this it was just a matter of course for Franz Brentano as a Catholic to immerse himself in philosophical and theological studies. His subtle intellectuality led him to immerse himself early on in the thoughts of *Aristotle* and then in the strict schooling of the mediaeval scholastics. As I have already explained in more detail, Aristotelianism lives on in mediaeval scholasticism. And we could say that while Franz Brentano retained his highly developed sense of the spiritual, he was not able to disregard the logical faculties of the human soul as did Clemens Brentano, but developed the most stringent logic through which he was then able to form his ideas. However, as significant as his skill at logical thinking was, the genuinely Catholic piety of his early youth was more important for his theological and philosophical development.

There is something quite unique about a modern scholastic education such as Franz Brentano underwent as a result of his Catholicism. We have to emphasize that a really strict logic, not that fleeting, superficial logic taught in schools today and prevalent in natural science, but a really stringent logic connected with the whole person and not just with the human head, this developed out of scholasticism. Scholasticism is to the highest degree the art of the logical development of ideas. However, this scholasticism was used in the Middle Ages and in Catholicism until today to support the Catholic doctrine of revelation, as I have discussed in my lectures on Thomism.[22]

In the case of Franz Brentano there developed a specific intellectuality from his Catholic piety and from his strict schooling in scholasticism. He developed the faculty of seeing the existence of a spiritual world as completely self-evident. Being on intimate terms with both Catholicism and scholastic theology he lived in spirituality and was unable not to do so. And he understood spirituality by means of the strictest logic. He was actually a true Catholic. He was such a true Catholic in the strictest sense, that despite the fact that he had developed the strictest logic, he would never have allowed himself to criticize the Catholic doctrine of revelation—at least up until a certain point in his life.

Now I ask you to imagine a person in all their human profundity, someone who lives in the most stringent logic and who has heard the most derogatory criticisms of the Catholic doctrine of revelation from many a modern thinker. This would cause him the most terrible doubts, all of which he has thrust down into the unconscious, none of which he allows to become conscious; as soon as they surface into consciousness, he represses them. He says to himself: The Catholic doctrine of revelation is a closed system and shows clearly that it has come down to earth from the spiritual worlds through human beings, even if in many a roundabout way. It reveals its own truth and when there are doubts, we must always assume that as a single person, we can always be mistaken in the face of an all-encompassing system of such venerable greatness as Catholicism. Since this is one of the doctrines of Catholicism and only the synods can ever speak about the dogmas, when those doubts about the doctrine of revelation emerged from his unconscious, Franz Brentano would never have allowed himself to take them seriously. He repressed them all and told himself that it is impossible to accept such doubts. But those terrible doubts churned about in his feelings, in his sensations, in the unconscious regions of his soul. He did not do as did the thinkers of the Enlightenment of the eighteenth and nineteenth centuries and accept these doubts, but rather he repressed them again and again as being forbidden.

Then something happened that caused a great turnaround in his soul. Brentano was born in 1838. In the 1860s he was ordained as a Catholic priest, the state of his soul as I have described above, and became professor of philosophy at the university in Wuerzburg. There he was confronted with the movement for the dogma of infallibility, which developed towards the end of the 1860s. This dogma was meant to be declared in 1870. As an excellent theologian and a pious Catholic—at the time he was relatively young—Franz Brentano was given the task of saying what there was to be said on this subject from the point of view of Catholic theology by the famous *Bishop Ketteler.*[23]

Now I will just describe the external sequence of events. Ketteler was one of those German bishops who firmly rejected the adoption of the dogma of infallibility. He commissioned a memorandum from Franz Brentano, which the bishop would then read out in the assembly of bishops in Fulda so as to stipulate that the German bishops would not support the doctrine of infallibility. Ketteler did read out the full text of Brentano's memorandum against the doctrine of infallibility at the assembly of bishops in Fulda. This is what happened externally and we have to add that the German bishops later retracted their decision when they were assembled in Rome and the doctrine of infallibility was about to be declared; they backed down and voted for the doctrine of infallibility. So Franz Brentano had criticized this dogma for Bishop Ketteler as being not Catholic. And then the doctrine of infallibility was declared.

Where did this leave Franz Brentano as a distinguished theologian and as a devout Catholic? He would never have allowed himself to criticize a dogma that he had inherited. However, when Bishop Ketteler called upon him to criticize the doctrine of infallibility it was not yet dogma, but on its way to becoming one. In this case he took the liberty of attacking the dogma intellectually. This was exactly what Bishop Ketteler, who was also at first against the dogma of infallibility, had wanted. From his own perspective at that time, the end of the 1860s, Franz Brentano would never have challenged an established dogma. But infallibility was not yet a dogma and so he criticized it with all his usual brilliance. And Ketteler presented Brentano's memorandum at the conference of bishops in Fulda.

Now infallibility had become legitimate Catholic dogma. You see, the crucial turning point for Franz Brentano was not only rational considerations, but rather this course of events connected to one of the most important decisions in modern Catholicism. Perhaps it would never have happened from a mere intellectual aspect, but his turning away from the Church took place as a result of these events. He was the most important critic of the dogma of infallibility and so he had to ask himself whether as the devout Christian, Franz Brentano, who had criticized the dogma of infallibility from the depths of his Catholic conscience before the year 1870, was still a Catholic after infallibility had formally become dogma. So you see here that events have played a larger part in a person's life than any worthless intellectual decision usually can. And so it came about that a person with such an upright and spirited conscience as Franz Brentano had no choice but to leave the Church. We only have to look at this whole course of events to see how deeply Franz Brentano was connected to a particular aspect of the intellectual life of the second half of the nineteenth century.

Now Franz Brentano was a philosopher who had abandoned a Catholic career. He also had a completely different education from that of the other philosophers of the nineteenth century; among non-ecclesiastical philosophers his education did not count for much. However, he had now joined the ranks of these non-ecclesiastical philosophers. At the same time the scientific way of thinking of the nineteenth century had made a great impression on him. Since the beginning of the nineteenth century this scientific way of thinking had set the tone for the whole of scientific life. And Franz Brentano had qualified as a professor in Wuerzburg with a thesis entitled *The true method of philosophy is none other than that of the natural sciences.*[24] The methods of natural science had made such an impression on him that he could only say that if it is to be a real science, philosophy has to use the same methods as does natural science.

It really is not easy to unravel the soul knot into which Franz Brentano had become entangled in the 1860s. Let us look quite objectively at what the situation was. A human being, who was perhaps the most knowledgeable expert of his times on Thomism and Aristotelianism, on the one hand an incredibly keen thinker and conceptualizer, but all from the point of view of Catholicism and on the other hand someone greatly impressed by the methods of natural science. How is this possible? But it is possible if you look at it as follows. First take mediaeval scholasticism—it is an intellectual science based on scholastic concepts, a science which, however, confined itself to knowledge of the external world of the senses and to some findings gained through insights from the sense world, whereas the supersensible was to be left to revelations, into which field intellectual knowledge should not stray.

Thus mediaeval scholasticism strictly differentiates between the field of sensual knowledge with some implications, as for example the existence of God or other such inferences; they belong to human knowledge. Then in contrast the actual mysteries, the contents of the spiritual world, which can only be attained through revelation, meaning what the Church has preserved of the revelations of supersensible worlds, which at various times have been revealed to humanity in a way that the Church finds acceptable.

This was already the preparation for the modern scientific view. This modern science wants only the knowledge of the senses and at most some inferences arising from this sensual knowledge. Modern science has no idea that it is the continuation of scholasticism, with the exception of a few radical spirits, who have done things slightly differently than the scholastics. Let us epitomize it with a diagram.

The scholastics say to themselves: With the intellect and with ordinary science we can gain knowledge of the ordinary world of the senses and also of some inferences we can draw from this [yellow]; then there is a border beyond which lies the supersensible world, into which we cannot enter [red].

rot = red, gelb = yellow

Modern natural science does the same! They say: We can penetrate the sense world with our human knowledge and we can infer various things resulting from it. The scholastics said: Above this there lies the supersensible world, which we can only know through revelation. Radical thinkers of the modern world said: We can only perceive the sense world; we leave out the supersensible one, either it does not exist or at least we are not able to perceive it. This is how they became agnostics. What was common practice among the scholastics in relation to knowledge of the sense world and some inferences resulting from it then resumes in the modern scientific attitude, so that a mind which has absorbed a scholastic education for the whole of their youth does not need to see in modern scientific methodology anything other than the continuation of the scholastic outlook. And because he was a devout Catholic, for Franz Brentano the existence of the spiritual world was self-evident. So he was actually more consistent than hundreds upon hundreds of others, both Catholics and non-Catholics.

Thus Brentano turned to scientific methodology. The methodology of natural science, however, has either to become aware of its limits, or to declare itself either agnostic or that the spiritual world does not exist. However, if the existence of the supersensible world is for you self-evident, but you can no longer accept the truth of revelation—because you no longer accept the Church's truths—as was the case with Franz Brentano, then you are in a special position.

A superficial mind would easily cope with this. Either they would deny the supersensible world or they would just ignore it. This was not possible for Franz Brentano. But because of his scholastic training he could utter the following thesis: *The true method of philosophy is none other than that of the natural sciences.*

Now as you all know, someone who despite accepting the methods of natural science still wants to reach the spiritual world through cognitive means, must advance from ordinary scientific methodology to what I call exact clairvoyance or exact vision, which we attain by developing supersensible faculties according to the methods I have described in my books. However, Franz Brentano shied away from developing this vision, from developing any kind of cognitive methodology which went beyond that of natural science. The same disposition was at work in him here as in his attitude as a Catholic towards revelation. Science had no place in this revelation. Thus he could understand a scientific method that confined itself to the world of the senses; however, it is precisely when we take this seriously that we should also develop supersensible faculties. He shied away from this.

So in this mood Franz Brentano became a philosopher, no longer a theologizing one, just a simple philosopher. We could say that such a personality, one who experiences deeply all the storms and struggles to be found in the intellectual life of those times and who was not victorious in their own soul, such a personality is often much more significant and much more interesting than others, who cope with all possible difficulties more easily and with more superficial ideas.

Now in this soul mood Franz Brentano was summoned to Vienna, to that Austria about which I have spoken here recently.[25] And I have described his special intellectuality, so that if you keep that in mind, you will be able to understand how such a philosopher could make such a great impression in Vienna. Brentano did this. Even in his outward appearance he was an extremely interesting person. He had a highly intellectual head, his eyes sparkled with intelligence, which probably reflected something of the eyes of the romanticist Clemens Brentano. Franz Brentano was a striking personality, so that when people saw him walking towards the podium, the lectern, he always gave the impression of not having completely descended into his physical body. Almost every movement, walking, the gestures of the arms, the facial expressions, the forming of words, there was something unnatural about it all. You always had the feeling something is moving this physical body about as you would move a piece of clothing. And still he made the most congenial and intelligent impression. You could not resist the feeling that for this personality with the serious tone of voice, the constant striving to form the most stringent of ideas, who gave the impression of not inhabiting his head with his thinking, but of floating slightly above it, that for this person it was quite natural to wear the physical body like a suit of clothes that fits badly, that is too large or too small, perhaps too large. And some gestures that in another person would seem provocative were in Franz Brentano interesting.

Franz Brentano was at pains to emphasize the methods of natural science. When he dealt with intellectual problems, he did so with a mentality learnt from natural science. However, I have to say the theologian still existed in his way of speaking. It was an enormous difference to hear scientific methodology spoken about by an ordinary researcher or by this philosopher who came from theology.

For those who have an idea of Franz Brentano it seems quite natural that when he came to Vienna in 1874, he became the darling of Viennese society, meaning a society which particularly loved a figure such as Franz Brentano was at the time. Especially the women—in the 1870s the men of this society were less interested in culture—had a taste for Franz Brentano; he always had something witty to say. He was intellectually superior but at the same time not; you sometimes felt superior to him. When he arrived, he took off his coat in a clumsy manner. People would help him and so feel superior to him in certain respects, where he needed help, for example when someone supported him to prevent him tripping over the doorstep and so on. Or he failed to find his spoon, or he sawed at his meat from one side to the other so that it ceased to be a piece and became what in some areas of Germany is called a *slop*. So you could feel superior to him at the same time as the light of the spiritual world shone through him.

Then *Adolf Wilbrandt*, a writer, who was sometimes very ingenious, but not particularly sensitive to the depths of the human soul, tried to lampoon him in his *Guest of the Evening Star*.[26] In Vienna this novella was seen as ridiculing Franz Brentano, but in reality it does so only in the sense that I have described above.

When Franz Brentano gave a lecture in Vienna in this soul mood, he attracted what were for the time large audiences. You have to remember that then philosophy was not a very prestigious field. Franz Brentano had already had large audiences when he was an associate professor in Wuerzburg; this was in the same lecture theatre where students had hung a sign on the door reading *den of brimstone* after the first lecture of his predecessor—they boycotted the rest of his course. In this same lecture theatre Franz Brentano lectured on philosophy and attracted more and more listeners. It was the same in Vienna; whenever he gave a lecture there, the hall was full.

Now one of his first writings was his *Psychology*. His intent was to write a psychology with scientific methods. He reckoned with four or five volumes. In the spring of 1874 the first volume was published. He promised a second for the autumn and it was supposed to continue in this manner. He approached the subject with the most stringent scientific methods and—just as we can examine how a metal heats up or cools down or whether the heat from one metal is transferred to another metal—he wanted to examine how one idea follows from another, how the one idea correlates with another, in short, all the smaller conditions of the life of the soul. He got no further than that. But he said in the first volume: We must have a science for the study of the mind, for psychology. However, if we have to trade off this scientific approach for the fact that a modern study of the mind has nothing to say about what happens to the higher entity of the human being when the body is consigned to the earth elements, then we would have sacrificed something too valuable.

For Brentano—who lived so naturally in the mind that he could not of course verify with scientific methods—this mind was not something he was prepared to ignore as a subject for cognitive inquiry. He certainly wanted to access the spiritual world cognitively, but he also wanted to remain within the confines of natural science.

Therefore the first volume of Brentano's *Psychology* was also the last. He was too conscientious and true to science to be able to continue writing as a formality. Obviously, he could easily have done that and produced a psychology just like all the others. But if Brentano was to continue writing a psychology, then every page would have to be true, as was the case with the first volume within the limits of those truths a human being can attain. However, Franz Brentano wanted to remain scientific. This did not allow for extending into the field of the mind/soul. But just to deny it, as did those psychologists who wrote a study of the soul without the soul,[27] this he could not do. He could only keep silent. And so he never wrote a second volume, nor any further ones.

Followers of Brentano have resented the fact that I put forward this argument in the third chapter of my book *Riddles of the Soul*;[28] this is because they tend to explain all this much more superficially. However, even if we did decide to say that Brentano's followers knew better either from his legacy or because they were close to him, the first volume of his writings to appear after his death,[29] which was published in excellent form by Brentano's student *Alfred Kastil*, who also wrote the Introduction, shows Brentano in the same soul mood which prevented him from writing a second volume of psychology to follow the first. The first chapter of this first posthumous volume contains '*The moral teaching of Jesus according to the gospels*', which was written after he left the Church, long after he left the Church. He would accept nothing that was not in accordance with the strictest ethos of natural science. The second chapter is '*The teaching of Jesus on God and the world and his own person and mission according to the gospels*'. The third chapter is particularly detailed and is a critique of Pascal's *Apology for the Christian religion*. After a short passage on *Nietzsche* as an imitator of Jesus, there follows in the Appendix '*A brief description of the Christian doctrine*'.

After all that has been written in the nineteenth century about Jesus and his teachings from all possible points of view, orthodox, semi-orthodox, free-church, free spirit, even completely atheistic, with reference to all manner of mythology, such as that of *David Friedrich Strauss*,[30] it is very moving to have before you this book about the teachings of Jesus by Franz Brentano. It is moving to see how this distinguished philosopher, who had left the Church, characterizes the moral teachings of Jesus and their enduring significance, followed by the teachings of Jesus on God, the world and Jesus' own mission, then the whole significance of the doctrines of the Church and the administration of the Church, the significance of the Church as described by Pascal in his *Apology;* all this based exclusively upon the teachings of the Gospels themselves. It is moving to see how clearly Franz Brentano here shows himself as an astute opponent of Pascal and how he speaks out against Catholicism. It is moving because here is the young Brentano in all his devoutness and all his great ability to immerse himself in the spiritual, but still a man of the strictest scientific mentality, devoted to the methodology of natural science, someone whose thinking was profound and thus unimpressed by so-called modernism,[31] which is shallow even in its Catholic version. So even though he had left the Church, he had never spoken approvingly of modernism.

In the nineteenth century the question, in the truest sense of the word, arose for those who believed their thinking was firmly based on the principles of natural science, such as David Friedrich Strauss, as to whether they were still Christians.[32] Do we still believe in God? David Friedrich Strauss and many others put these two questions to themselves and answered in the negative. They just did not have the depth of education that Brentano had. Their intellectual life was therefore less tragic. They did not have to struggle with the methods of natural science since out of a certain shallowness they were able to accept it more easily than could Franz Brentano, who had the greatest difficulties because of his profundity. Still he saw scientific methodology as a necessity of the times.

I am telling you all this because I think that when we look at the facts of his life, both internal and external, through the example of this personality you will get a better idea of the way civilization was moving in the second half of the nineteenth century than if I just describe it in the abstract. Franz Brentano's soul mood is such that when we look at him first as a psychologist, we have to say that all his talents tend towards the development of supersensible perception so as to be able to study the soul. If Brentano had wanted to write another volume of his *Psychology,* then he would have had to develop imaginative cognition, then inspirative cognition and so on. But he did not want this. As a consequence of not wanting this, he conscientiously refrained from writing a second and third volume. So in a certain sense he was a casualty of scientific methodology, an honest and conscientious casualty. And just as only supersensible perception in the sense that I have described in my book *How to Know Higher Worlds*[33] can reach into the actual being of the soul, so only such a supersensible perception of natural science can penetrate into the all-powerful workings of the spiritual world.

A purely scientific astronomy only recognizes the heavenly bodies as they float about in space. At most with the help of spectral analysis they analyse the nature of the light of these heavenly bodies. But to them these are all just globes floating in space. This is all without spirit. And the subject matter of zoology, of biology, of botany, of mineral lore, all without spirit. By virtue of its methodology, natural science has to take account only of the spiritless and to discount the spirit. Spiritual science in the sense of anthroposophy must lead us to the spirit again. Supersensible perception leads to the spiritual not only in psychology but also in the world at large.

So just as with his strictly scientific approach Brentano was not able to reach the soul being in his *Psychology,* so, even after leaving Catholic dogma behind him, he was not really able to reach the Mystery of Golgotha. How can we reach the Mystery of Golgotha? Only when we are able to realize that the world is permeated by the supersensible spiritual. In this supersensible spiritual, as I have often described, there is a being, the Christ, who lived as the Christ being in the body of Jesus of Nazareth when the Mystery of Golgotha took place. Without spiritual science we would never be able to understand anything further than the personality of Jesus. Only anthroposophical spiritual science can show us how the divine Christ lived in Jesus. But Franz Brentano did not want this.

He still retained enough of his Catholic thinking, however, to know the central significance of Jesus for the whole of earthly evolution. This was clear to him. Just as the immortality of the soul was clear to him, even if he could not grasp it cognitively, so was the fact that Jesus is the pivotal point in the development of the earth. But he could not find the transition from Jesus to the Christ. So we see that from the feeling aspect and from the will aspect he was deeply touched by the significance of the personality of Jesus and by the teachings of Jesus. Take this sentence for example: 'The teachings of Jesus have not been superseded in history' as David Friedrich Strauss thought:

> on the contrary they have yet to be realized in their fullest sense. Because of human weakness, it will be a hard struggle for us to carry the decisive victory, but because of our inner strength it will be impossible for us to ever perish. Our conscience will forever bear witness to the truth and to the sacred beauty contained within it, as it has done in pre-Christian times with the Jews, with pagans, in the Asian orient and in the European occident, so that the moral teachings of Jesus do not signify a great advancement by proclaiming new commandments, but rather by the incomparable example that Jesus gave in his life and in his death, an example which revealed the possibility of such sublime virtue and thus inspired courageous imitation. This example will shine on forever and no prophecy is more reliable than when we say: Jesus forever.[34]

This from the philosopher who had left the Church, the distinguished theologian Franz Brentano, who could not advance from Jesus to Christ because of his scientific ethos!

Compare these wonderful words about Jesus as the midpoint of the earth's development with much of what theologians who have remained in the Church have written and see what conclusions you arrive at. Also see what you think about what it means, when a personality with such a constitution as the man I described here, says the following about Jesus' world view: 'Jesus' world view was not merely geocentric'—meaning not centred only on the earth—'but christocentric in such a way that around this one human individual, Jesus, not only the whole history of the earth, but also that of the spirits, good as well as evil, are organized and that only through their relationship to him do they find their purpose. We can call the world a monarchy not just because of the omnipresent God, but also because of the one who was created in his image.'

This is how Franz Brentano approaches the personality of Jesus. But despite the fact that he says of Jesus that his world view is not just geocentric but christocentric, that not only the people on the earth, but also higher spirits, both good and evil ones, organize themselves around him, despite all this he does not move on from the personality Jesus to the Christ being.

So he is in great inner conflict. He asks himself: What about Jesus, the human being, around whom all human history revolves? But Franz Brentano has no ideas which could lead him to the reality of the existence of the Christ in Jesus. Only someone who realizes the reality of the existence of Christ in Jesus can think of making this the pivotal moment of history.

Here too, even though he had managed to reach some conclusion in his writings, published not by him but by his students, even here he has not reached the end of his quest, despite standing so to speak at the gates, which he only need open to be able to see the immortality of the soul and the Mystery of Golgotha. This is why this slim volume of his, *The Teaching of Jesus and its Enduring Significance* is so very interesting, because Franz Brentano had a real vision of this enduring significance. And after having described the teaching of Jesus and its enduring significance in the second chapter, he again asks: Are we still Christians? He writes that the answer will depend on the spirit in which the question is asked. And then, after he has blamed modern education for the fact that no real idea of the Christ is possible, he says once again: 'Perhaps one could say that the hopes I express here are in vain, because the enormous influence that the teaching and example of Jesus has had on humanity, is essentially a result of the fact that people see in him a divine being and thus embrace a faith to which according to my understanding the most progressive of human beings today no longer adhere.' Here he starts to become rather obtuse.

> However these people overlook the fact that his influence did not set in with belief in the godhead of Jesus, but on the contrary in his example, available to us through the reports of the Gospels, which is one of the most powerful motives leading to the belief in the divinity of his person. There has been nothing like it, nothing we could put beside it in all these centuries and millennia that have passed since then, so that what he gave us remains unique as a beacon for how we live our own lives.

So you can feel how near Franz Brentano came to the gates of the supersensible world and how he was held back by the most powerful authority of modern civilization: the methodology of natural science, the ethos of natural science.

So after this publication from Brentano's estate, we have to say the same that is to be said about those writings published during his lifetime: Franz Brentano is a thinker of the second half of the nineteenth century, who was driven in each phase of his soul life to realize the supersensible world, but who could not allow himself this realization of the supersensible world in the face of natural science, just as earlier on he had not allowed himself to criticize dogma because of the dogma itself. Thus exactly through what he was unable to achieve, Franz Brentano stands before us as a shining personality, one of the most significant personalities of the second half of the nineteenth century, and teaches us as do few others to recognize the intellectual legacy of the nineteenth century, which has come over into the twentieth century, and how it affects human evolution.

SEVENTH LECTURE

DORNACH, 8 JULY 1922

I SPOKE at length about *Franz Brentano* because of the fact that the first work to be published posthumously by his students is one about the life of Jesus, the teachings of Jesus. This was the external connection. However, by describing the life of this philosopher I also wanted to go deeper. Through the example of a person who was a genuine seeker after truth, not just with his intellect, not just with his scientific methods, but as a whole person, I wanted to show how such a personality had to position himself in the intellectual life of the second half of the nineteenth century.

Franz Brentano was born in 1838, so that he was a student at exactly the time when the ethos of natural science was on the rise in modern civilization. As a student Franz Brentano was a devout Catholic, as you have seen, and as a devout Catholic he held fast to the spiritual world, but only as far as that is possible within Catholic religious practice and Catholic theology. At the same time this person, who had grown up with a certain understanding of the spiritual world, the immortality of the soul, the existence of God and so on, is a scientist and an extremely conscientious one at that, in a time when scientific thinking was everything. So that with Franz Brentano more than with any other personality of the time we have the feeling that he is a person of deep spirituality, who in the face of the ethos of natural science in the nineteenth century, was not able to get through to an actual realization of spiritual life. I know of no other personality of recent times who so characteristically demonstrates the necessity for the anthroposophical world view. With Franz Brentano you constantly want to say: he just needs to take one or two steps forward and he will be in anthroposophy. He did not do this because he wanted to stay within the parameters of natural science. It was precisely through what I described yesterday as characteristic for his personality, through the dignity of his behaviour and the gravity that shone through everything he said, that Franz Brentano gave the impression of someone who could have been a kind of leader personality in the second half of the nineteenth century.

Now you will rightly ask how it came about that this personality remained generally unknown? Franz Brentano is really only known within the small circle of his students. All these students are people who have received from him the most profound inspiration. You can see this in the impact the students of his students—those who are left—are still having. Franz Brentano made a significant impression on a small circle of people. And certainly, from this small circle of students, most of them would regard him as being one of the most inspiring and important human beings in centuries.

Now it is precisely the fact that Brentano has remained largely unknown to the general population that is characteristic for the whole development of civilization in the nineteenth century. We could cite several personalities who in one way or another are representatives of intellectual life in the nineteenth century. But however diligently we search, we will not find such a significant, such a representative personality as Franz Brentano. This is why I want to say that it is through Franz Brentano that we can see that in the form it had taken in the nineteenth century natural science may become a great authority, but despite being such a great authority it is not able to take the spiritual lead in culture as a whole. To do so natural science must first develop into spiritual science, then together with spiritual science it will contain all that is needed to guide the spiritual life of humanity.

To appreciate this we have to take the larger perspective. If we look back at the most ancient times of humanity then we know that everywhere as a general faculty of human beings there was a kind of dreamlike clairvoyance and the initiates of the mysteries added to this dreamlike clairvoyance their higher, supersensible knowledge as well as knowledge of the world of the senses.

If we went back to ancient times in humanity's development, we would find no difference in how they treated the supersensible and the physical. All spiritual life emanated from the mystery schools, which were both churches and centres of art. In those old times, this spiritual life influenced all human life, including the life of the State and of the economy, in the most profound sense. Those who worked for the State took advice from the priests of the mysteries, as did those who wished to give impulses in economic life; there was no separation between the religious and the scientific element in those ancient times. The leaders of religious life were also the leaders of spiritual life as a whole and of the sciences. However, the development of humanity became more and more organized so that the currents of human life which were once united, began to separate. Religion separated from science and from art.

This happened slowly and gradually. If we look back at ancient Greece, we find that there was no science in the sense we know it today and then next to it philosophy; rather Greek philosophy spoke about science and there was no separate natural science. But in acting as an independent entity, philosophy in ancient Greece had already detached itself from the actual religious element. They still took the most profound truths from the mysteries, but in the later stages of ancient Greece they criticized what the mysteries revealed from a philosophical standpoint. However, the revelations of religion continued to be transmitted and when the Mystery of Golgotha took place it was essentially religion which was prepared to understand this mystery. Today people have no idea of what existed in the earliest years of European civilization as an intelligent theology; they call it disparagingly 'Gnosis' and such like. However, there was a deep spiritual understanding in this 'Gnosis' and they were aware that we have to understand spiritual matters just as today we understand gravity or light phenomena or anything else in physics. They did not have the attitude that there was a science separate from religious life. In the Christian faith too it was the same with the Fathers of the Church, the first great teachers of Christianity; they treated knowledge as a unity. Of course the Greek separation of religious life was already taking place, but they still included both religious considerations and also rational observations of the physical as belonging to spiritual/intellectual matters. This only changed in mediaeval times. Scholasticism developed in the

Middle Ages and differentiated strictly between human science and what is really knowledge of the spiritual. This last could not be achieved by applying independent human powers of cognition, but only through revelation, through acceptance of what was revealed. And increasingly people said that human beings cannot attain the highest truths through their own cognitive power, but must accept them as they are given by the Church as revelations. Human science can only extend to what the senses give us as truths and to various conclusions that can be drawn from what the senses give us, just as I said yesterday.

Thus there was a strict separation between science, which covered the world of the senses, and what was contained in revelations. Now in many respects, the last three to five hundred years have been of great importance for the development of modern humanity. If you had told a person of those times, when religion and science were one, that religion is not based on knowledge of human beings, this would have been nonsense to them; for all religions developed originally from knowledge of the human being. However, they said that if a human being is limited to everyday consciousness, then they will not attain to the higher truths, for to do so we have first to raise our consciousness to a higher level. The ancients said from their point of view just as we have to say today, according for instance to what I have described in my books *Knowledge of the Higher Worlds—How is it Achieved?* and the second half of *Occult Science—An Outline*:[35] human beings have to develop their soul faculties to a point where they can achieve higher knowledge. This is also what they said in ancient times. They were aware that with normal consciousness human beings can only recognize what is spread out around them, but we can develop this consciousness further and become able to recognize supersensible truths. Also in those old times they would not have said that a revelation had appeared to someone without their having done anything for it. That would have been nonsense to them. All the dogmas contained in the various teachings of the Church originate from the old truths of initiation. Today we say in a facile way that all dogmas such as the Trinity or the Incarnation must be revelations, since human understanding would not be able to reach them. However, they originally developed out of human powers of cognition.

In mediaeval times human beings began to use their intellect more intensively. It is a characteristic of scholasticism to use the intellect in such an impressive manner, but only in relation to the world of the senses; at this stage in humanity's development people no longer felt capable of developing higher cognitive faculties, at least not in those circles in which the old dogmas were taught as revelations. There they rejected the idea that a human being could reach the supersensible world by developing higher cognitive faculties. So they just adopted as tradition, as historical transmission, what in earlier days had been won through actual human cognition and they said we should not try to examine it with our human science.

This was what gradually became the accepted viewpoint. People became used to designating as faith, what had before been knowledge which, however, no one dared aspire to any longer; and as knowledge they designated what they could discover through human cognitive ability in the world of the senses. This teaching developed particularly strongly within the Catholic Church. But, as I said yesterday, basically the whole of this modern attitude of natural science can be traced back to scholasticism. Just that people got stuck there, saying that the human intellect could only gather knowledge about nature, so they did not need to concern themselves with supersensible cognition. They said we were not able to attain this through our own faculties. Then they left it up to faith to accept the old wisdom as dogma or not.

The eighteenth century had already led the way in proclaiming only the knowledge of the senses and of what we can conclude from it and in the nineteenth century there was a growing tendency to allow only what we can gain through these human faculties from the sense world as valid science. In this regard the nineteenth century achieved a great deal; indeed even today there is great work being done in research through the methods of natural science.

I would say that the last public attempt to reach the spiritual worlds took place at the turn of the eighteenth to the nineteenth century with that movement we call German idealism. The philosopher Kant,[36] who was a forerunner of German idealism, wanted to express this separation of knowledge and faith philosophically. Then those forceful thinkers Fichte, Schelling and Hegel appeared; they stand at the end of the eighteenth, beginning of the nineteenth century as the last great figures who wanted to advance human cognition beyond mere knowledge of the world and what we can conclude from it.

Fichte, Schelling and Hegel are very different from each other. Fichte based his thinking on the human I, developed an enormous vigour in the understanding of it and attempted to conquer the world cognitively through the human I. Schelling developed a kind of imaginative configuration of a world view. Indeed, this foray into imaginative thought configuration actually brought him close to an understanding of the mysteries. Hegel believed in the thought itself and that the eternal actually existed in thoughts that a human being can grasp. It is a lovely idea that Hegel gives us[37] when he says that he wants to know and grasp the spirit through thought. However, only someone who grasps his main thrust, his quest for spirit, can really relish Hegel. For when we read Hegel—most people soon stop reading—we see that for all his faith in the spirit of thought, when he expresses his own thoughts, he is an extremely abstract thinker. And it is sadly true, that despite the fact that his impulse towards the spiritual was very strong, Hegel has left to humanity only an inventory of abstract concepts.

Why was this? It is a great tragedy that these robust and powerful thinkers, Fichte, Schelling, Hegel, could not penetrate through to the spiritual.

This is due to the fact that civilization in general humanity was not mature enough at that time to really open the gates to the spiritual world. Fichte, Schelling and Hegel only came as far as the idea. But what is the idea, the thought, that lives in ordinary human consciousness?

Remember what I said a little while ago. If we follow the life of a person from birth until death, then we see that person as a living being, the physical being warmed and illuminated by the soul and the spirit. When the person has died for the physical world, then we have the corpse in the physical world. We bury or cremate this corpse. Just imagine what an enormous difference there is for an unbiased human observer between a fully alive human being and a corpse. If you grasp this deeply with your heart, then you can understand what the spiritual scientist has to say in relation to another phase of life, when we look at human beings between death and a new birth, how they exist as soul-spiritual beings in a soul-spiritual world, how they develop there, how in contrast to earthly existence where they grow ever older, in the spiritual world they become younger and younger up to the moment where they find their way down to a physical embodiment. With our higher spiritual faculties we can grasp what lives in human beings in that world, just as we can grasp what lives in a physical person. And then we can ask ourselves: When a human being is born, what is left of what we could see of them in the spiritual world, before the soul-spiritual descended? What is left is what lives discernibly in the human being as their thoughts, their ideas. But these thoughts which the person then carries here on earth through their physical bodies, they are the corpses of those thoughts accorded them when they live in the soul-spiritual world between death and a new birth. The abstract thoughts we have here are for all intents and purposes a corpse in comparison to the living thoughts we have between death and a new birth, similar to the corpse of the physical body in comparison to the living human being before they die in the physical world.

Someone who does not want to vitalize their abstract thoughts allows the corpse of what they were before they descended to the earth to live on in their ordinary thinking. So it was just this corpse of thinking that lived in Fichte, Schelling and Hegel, however great these thoughts were. We could say that in ancient times, when religion, science and art were one, some of the vitality characteristic of human thinking in the spiritual world lived on in earthly thinking. Even with *Plato* we can see in the power of his thoughts how something transcendental lived on in him. This has gradually diminished. Humanity preserves the knowledge of the supernatural as revelations. However, human beings could not have become free otherwise; they could not have developed freedom. The thinking of human beings is increasingly becoming just a corpse of their inner life before birth. And just as with some people for a few days after their death the corpse can have an enormous freshness, so it was with the corpse-thinking of Fichte, Schelling and Hegel: their ideas were fresh but a real spiritual science has to see them as being still the corpses of the supersensible.

So now I ask you: Do you think that we could ever encounter a human corpse in this world if there had never been a living person? Whoever encounters a human corpse knows that this corpse was once alive. Similarly someone who looks impartially at our abstract, our dead thinking will realize that this had once lived, namely before the person descended into the physical body.

However, humanity had already lost even this knowledge, so that people were only able to experience dead thinking and if they attached any importance at all to what came from living thinking, they venerated it as revelation. This position was substantiated by the great discoveries of natural science, which took place at the time when, as I have already mentioned, Franz Brentano was young.

I have to add two special features of Franz Brentano to those we have already looked at. Yesterday I wanted to characterize more his personality, today I want to point out more his development through time. Therefore today's observations will be more abstract.

Next to all those qualities that I described to you yesterday of this Franz Brentano, who had outgrown Catholicism and had become a more universal philosopher, there was the fact that he had a great antipathy towards Fichte, Schelling and Hegel.[38] He did not rail against them as did *Schopenhauer*, who sometimes spoke in the most obnoxious way about Fichte, Schelling and Hegel, probably because Brentano was more well brought up, but he did speak out harshly, if in a more refined manner, against them. Now we have to appreciate that someone who has grown out of Catholicism and into a new world view, cannot basically assume any other position towards Fichte, Schelling and Hegel than that which Franz Brentano took. Thinking was for Hegel the highest cognitive faculty in human beings, but for someone who has been through scholasticism, it should only be applied to the world of the senses as an expedient.

Just think about it. We approach the sense world through this corpse of thinking, we grasp at first only lifeless nature. We cannot grasp living nature with this thinking. For inanimate nature this corpse-thinking is exactly right. But Hegel wanted to understand the whole world with all its secrets through this corpse-thinking. Thus in Hegel you will not find anything about immortality or God; what you will find will appear quite strange.

Hegel divides his system into three parts:

<table>
<tr><td>Logic. Philosophy of nature. Philosophy of the spirit.</td><td>{</td><td>Art
Religion
Science</td></tr>
</table>

Logic is an inventory of all concepts which human beings can develop, but only those which are abstract. This logic begins with *being*, moves on to *nothingness* and to *becoming*. I well know that if I quoted the whole list to you, you would hit the roof, because in all these things there is nothing of what you are really looking for. Yet Hegel says that what appears in us when we develop *being, nothing, becoming, existence* as abstract concepts, this is God before the creation of the world.[39]

Take Hegel's logic, it is really nothing but abstract concepts from start to finish, as the last concept is that of purpose. There is not much you can do with this. There is nothing about the immortality of the soul or of the existence of God that you would recognize as valid, but only an inventory of abstract ideas. Now think of these abstract concepts as existing before there was nature, before there were human beings. This is God before the creation of the world, says Hegel. Logic is God before the creation of the world. And this logic created nature and in nature became conscious of itself.

So first there is logic, which according to Hegel, is God before the creation of the world. Then it segues into otherness and becomes conscious of itself, self-aware; here it becomes human spirit. And the whole system finishes with the highest aspects: art, religion, science. These are the three highest forms of spirit. So on the earth God lives on in religion, art and science. Hegel only takes note of what lives on in ordinary life on the earth. He only proclaims the spirit which has died, not the living spirit.

People who have been educated in natural science and who are looking for science in the modern sense have to reject this. They have to reject it because when we approach nature we cannot stick with abstractions, with these dead concepts. Even if you have been taught botany badly, so that you convert all the beautiful flowers into a number of stamens, descriptions of seeds, of carpels and so on, even if you have such abstract concepts in your heads and then you go out with the botanist's container and bring back only abstract ideas, at least the withered flowers are left over and they are more tangible than the most abstract concept. And if you are a chemist in the lab, you can fantasize about all sorts of atomic processes and such like, but you still have to see what is happening in the test tube, to describe what substance you have put in it and the flame you have used to melt it or evaporate it or whatever. You still have to describe an object. And finally when in optical science the physicists record how light rays break and whatever else they think light rays do, when they are making their nice diagrams of how the light rays pass through a prism and are refracted in various directions, they are still reminded of the existence of the colours. Even if all colour has been drained from the way physics explains the colours, still they are constantly reminded of their existence. But if we try to understand the spiritual with these completely abstract ideas, then we end up with mere abstract logic.

Someone like Franz Brentano, or the other scholastics, could accept this as a real description of the spirit, as they have at least the tradition of revelation. Thus as a student in the middle of the nineteenth century, Brentano stood there with an irrepressible thirst for truth and knowledge and an inner scientific conscientiousness beyond compare and was unable to accept anything from the last philosophical greats of modern civilization. He could only accept what had been filtered through the strictest scientific methodology. In his heart he had what Catholic theology had given him. With all this he could not push through to a new understanding of the spiritual.

But it is very engaging how truly honest this person was. And now I come to the other theme I wanted to mention. If we look at a human being, how they are born into the physical world, how in their first clumsy movements we can see the development of what before the descent to the physical earth was immensely wise, then if we understand spiritual science in the right way we have to say that we can see how the child's head organism is born. In the head we have an image of the cosmos. Only at the base of the skull do the earthly forces push back. If the base of the skull were as rounded as the rest of the head, then the head would be a complete image of the cosmos. Human beings bring this with them. If we look at it as something physical, then the head is an image of the cosmos.

People have resented that I have publicly mentioned an important fact,[40] but we cannot understand cosmic interrelationships without mentioning such facts: I have described in public how in the human brain the grooves and furrows are arranged in a certain way, there are certain centres and so on. Down to the last detail this human brain is an image of the starry heavens in that moment when the human being is born. In the head we see the image of the cosmos that we can see with our external senses, even if most people do not see the spiritual side of it. In the chest organism, in what is the main basis for the rhythmic system, we can see how up to a point the roundness of the cosmos is already overcome, but if we follow the chest organism with the specific form of the spine and the ribs and see how this chest organism is connected in the breathing to the cosmos, then we can still see, if already somewhat modified, an image of the cosmos. However, in the metabolic-limb system this is no longer the case. Here it is not possible to see anything emulating the cosmos. Now the head structure is connected to thinking, the rhythmic organism to feeling and the metabolic-limb system to the will.

Now why is the metabolic-limb system, the earthliest part of the human being, the medium for the will? The connection is as follows. In the human head we have a true image of the cosmos. The soul-spiritual has flowed out into the head, has flowed into the formative life forces. We could say that before they descended to earth, the human being has learnt from the cosmic forces and has formed the head accordingly. In this way they also form their chest organism up to a point, but not any part of the metabolic-limb system.

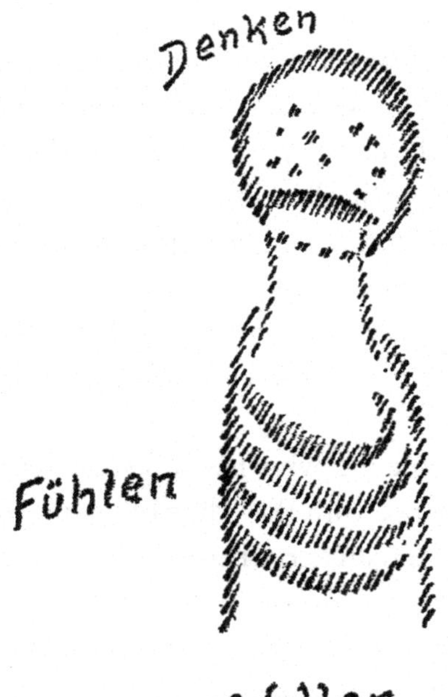

Denken = thinking, Fühlen = feeling, Wollen = will

This is where the will is. Hence when we look at the external human organism thinking has to be assigned to the head, feeling to the centre of the person and the will to the metabolic-limb system. The spiritual can maintain itself best in what is the basest, the metabolism and the limbs, and in our thinking we only have a corpse of what we were before we descended to the earth. And in our feeling, we have a little more, but feeling remains dreamlike, as you know, and we are completely unable to grasp the will with our ordinary consciousness. The will remains entirely in our unconscious; it is also the most alive of what we were before we came down to the earth. When we develop as children, the will contains the most of our immortal soul.

Most people, however, just go ahead and say: Human beings have three soul forces: thinking, feeling and willing. You know how people just number these three soul forces as if they were visible for ordinary consciousness, whereas we know that anthroposophy has had to make people aware of them. Really we are only completely awake in our thinking. Feeling is like a human dream and we know absolutely nothing of our will. I have to emphasize over and over again that when we want to raise an arm, then the thought 'I raise my arm' flows into the organism and becomes will, so that then the arm raising takes place; however, we know absolutely nothing of this; we sleep through it although we are awake, just as we sleep through everything from falling asleep until waking up. So instead of saying in our thinking we are awake, in our feeling we dream and in our willing we are asleep, people say we have thinking, feeling and willing, which they leave next to each other as if they were all of the same quality.

Now imagine someone who has a strong feeling for the truth and who, in accordance with the ethos of natural science, only uses thinking. A modern researcher, whether using a microscope or a telescope to look at the cosmos, or studying astrophysics using a spectroscopic instrument, only ever applies conscious thinking. This is why for Franz Brentano it was axiomatic to reject the unconscious. He wanted to restrict himself to ordinary conscious thinking and so refused to develop higher cognitive faculties. What could we then expect from such a person when they speak of the soul, when they try to speak as a psychologist? We could only expect that when they stick to just the conscious they cannot speak about the will in psychology. We could expect that they would completely obliterate the will, that they are doubtful about feeling and that they can only really deal with thinking.

This did not even occur to other more superficial minds. Franz Brentano divided the faculties of the soul not into thinking, feeling and willing, but into conceptualizing, judging and into the phenomena of love and hate, meaning the phenomena of sympathy and antipathy or feeling. Willing is completely missing in his concept. Proper active willing is missing in Brentano's psychology because he was a thoroughly honest seeker after truth and had to say to himself: I am not able to find the will.

It is poignant to see how thoroughly sincere and honest this personality actually is. Will is missing in Brentano's psychology, since he differentiates between judging and conceptualizing so that he can have three components of soul life, whereas judging and conceptualizing are really one, so that he actually only has two components.

Now think of the consequences of what Brentano presents us with. What is really missing in his idea of the human being? Through being a modern scientist and refusing to count anything but what was available to conscious thinking through scientific methods, he disconnects the will from the human soul. And what is he disconnecting? Precisely the most alive of what we bring with us of what we were before we descended into a physical body.

Brentano was confronted with a science which disconnected the eternal from the soul. Other psychologists did not sense this. He sensed it and so faced an enormous gulf between what he had previously absorbed as the teaching of revelation, which spoke of the eternal in the human soul, and what he found based on scientific method alone, which erased the will and with it the eternal from the human soul.

Thus Brentano is a personality who is typical for all that the nineteenth century could not give humanity. The gates of the spiritual world were meant to be opened. And this is the reason why I have spoken to you about Franz Brentano, who died in 1917 in Zurich. In him I see the most characteristic of all those philosophers of the nineteenth century, who strove earnestly for the truth but who were constrained by the shackles of the ethos of natural science, who rejected a spiritual understanding of the world, but constantly demonstrated that the time for this spiritual understanding had come. Now where is the difference between what spiritual science in the sense of anthroposophy strives for and the tragic quest of a person like Franz Brentano? It is that with great brilliance Franz Brentano gathered together all the ideas that we can develop in our ordinary consciousness and then he said: Here we have to stop. However, this insight is not complete; to seek real knowledge in this way is to seek in vain. He was never satisfied; he always tried to find a way. But his scientific ethos would not let him. And so it was until he died. We could say that spiritual science begins where Brentano finished; it has to venture beyond ordinary consciousness to a higher consciousness. This is why he is so very interesting, the most interesting philosopher of the second half of the nineteenth century, because his quest for truth was really something personal. It must be said that if you want to study the symptoms of what a person experienced through the development of natural science, through the intellectual development of modern times, then this nephew of Clemens Brentano, the philosopher Franz Brentano is a good example. His case is typical for all that people are searching for, but because of prevailing scientific methods cannot find. His is such a typical case because we have to go beyond what he sought with such integrity. The more we study him, including his classification of mental phenomena, the more we realize this. He is a prime example of those thinkers through whom we can see that humanity needs a spiritual life which embraces all aspects of reality. Natural science cannot offer us this. But natural science is the destiny of modern times, just as it was Brentano's destiny. Brentano was a real contemporary Faust of the nineteenth century, living first in Wuerzburg, then in Vienna, then in Florence, then in Zurich, and all the time struggling with the great problems of humanity. He does not allow that 'we can know nothing', but he should have, if he had been fully aware of his own methodology.

Really, he should have said: Natural science is what prevents me from finding the way into the spiritual world.

However, natural science presents itself as the great authority. And so it is in public life today. But natural science cannot offer people what they need for their souls. The greatest achievements of the nineteenth and twentieth centuries could not give people spiritual guidance. On the contrary this ethos of natural science is a great obstacle precisely because of its great authority; everywhere anthroposophy appears, science opposes it and despite the fact that science itself cannot give people what they need, they still ask whether anthroposophy is compatible with natural science. This is because even those people who know little of science still have the feeling that the authoritative voice of science is right and if it says anthroposophy is absurd then this must be true. People need not even know much about science to do this—what for example do the advocates of monism know about science? Usually they have some vague idea about science in general as it was three decades ago! But they act as if they were speaking with the voice of modern science. Thus many people accept them as an authority.

We can see in the inner fate of Brentano the external fate of the anthroposophic world view.

Eighth Lecture

DORNACH, 9 JULY 1922

T HIS time I want to use a personal example to show how what we now call anthroposophy had to grow out of intellectual life as a whole. It is a valid argument to say that when we discuss such things we are only speaking to a small circle of people. We look at individual human beings, who are interested in scientific, philosophic or other pursuits and are unknown to most people, and so we position ourselves outside what is important for the great mass of humanity. However, you just need to take a more impartial look and you will see that this view is not tenable. You only have to consider that what lives in most people as soul content, as the impulse to act or not to act, stems from the influence of leading personalities, even though they may have no knowledge of what people, such as the ones we have considered, have experienced in their inner lives.

But we must bear in mind that it is in exactly such a personality that the age with its ideas and sensibilities pulsates, so that at least a large number of those people who pursue a higher education learn about what such persons experience and carry it with them into those places where the leaders of humanity, who influence the greater masses of humankind, are educated. Thus what we can observe as the intimate experiences of such a personality, can become an impulse which then permeates into the lives of the greater mass of people. It is just that the channels through which these intellectual impulses flow into the greater mass of people remain invisible. So we can only look at what really and truly lives in the culture of the times in the way we have done in the last few days and we are justified in saying that out of the deepest, spiritual experience of the nineteenth century something like anthroposophy had to develop, because the culture of the times had crushed the human soul, as we have seen in the example of *Franz Brentano.*

To achieve what I set out to do with these observations, to make them more universal, I would now like to broaden the discussion.

We find Franz Brentano as a devout Catholic, a teacher of philosophy in Wuerzburg. After what I explained in the last two days, we have an idea of the content of the lectures Franz Brentano gave at his lectern in Wuerzburg. He tried to substantiate his arguments through reasoning, but behind this there was all he had absorbed as a believer in Catholic theology. Some extremely important ideas appeared here. For example, Franz Brentano knew about the latest scientific theory of evolution, which was based on the notion that the human brain is similar to the brains of the higher apes. The purely naturalistic theory of evolution drew from this observation the conclusion that human beings were related to the higher mammals. Franz Brentano accepted this proposition, just as he always accepted the claims of natural science. He said that now science can show that the human brain is not very different from that of an anthropoid. However, if we look at the soul life of a human being and the soul life of an anthropoid, then we find a huge difference. The main difference is that even the highest of the ape species are unable to develop abstract concepts. Human beings can develop abstract concepts. If the human brain is similar to the brain of the ape, then according to Franz Brentano, we have to say that the thoughts that humans are capable of developing cannot originate in the brain, because otherwise they would also originate in the brain of the ape. Hence we have to conclude that humans have something like a special soul substance, where thoughts which an anthropoid cannot develop originate.

So from scientific knowledge Franz Brentano could deduct the existence of an independent soul substance. This was in the years 1866 to 1870 when he was teaching philosophy in Wuerzburg, because in the background of what he was developing philosophically there was still the whole Catholic theological world view. However, Franz Brentano later left Catholic theology behind and immersed himself in his own individual point of view, which first had had to be informed by Catholic theology; he came increasingly to a purely scientific understanding of soul phenomena and lost sight of this soul substance, could no longer stand by this soul substance. Quite simply, his cognitive faculty weakened when he tried to reach up to a level beyond the mere association and separation of ideas about the internal life of the soul itself.

Now as I have already mentioned, this scientific way of thinking is just a direct continuation of scholastic thinking, despite the fact that some of its proponents object to this view. Scholastic thinking said that revelation deals with the supersensible world so that only the world of the senses, together with conclusions drawn from it through sense observation, can be the object of human cognition. And what was so important to the scholastics, on the one hand what was only accessible to sense perception as scientific knowledge and on the other what existed as knowledge of the supersensible world through revelation, this developed in the course of the sixteenth, seventeenth and eighteenth centuries into the stance that natural phenomena would be studied according to the principles developed by the scholastics and that for science the teaching of revelations would be abandoned. Therefore we can see modern science as a legitimate child of mediaeval scholasticism in the sense I have described here and so it should be no surprise for us to see that people hold on to revelation, as did Franz Brentano in his youth and as Catholic scholars still do today, who accept a science limited to the world of the senses and hold that we should not attempt to gain knowledge of the supersensible, which remains accessible only through revelation. So we can imagine that scientists and Catholic theologians can work together in one institution without any dispute arising about the area of influence of the Catholic theologist and that of the scientist. Here I would like to offer you an example.

Let us look at how Franz Brentano taught logic, metaphysics, ethics and the history of philosophy in Wuerzburg from 1867 to 1870. So as to make this as vivid as possible I will stay in one place, in Wuerzburg, and ask you to envision Brentano's auditorium around the year 1869, where he lectured on subjects as described above, where he spoke about the similarities in the brains of humans and the higher apes and how there must be a soul substance which brings forth thinking in human beings.

Now let us take another chapter, which he also lectured on at that time: on the existence of God, on the proofs of the existence of God. There in his usual astute manner, he offered all that human reason can bring forth to prove the existence of God and of course he pointed out that with human cognition we can only approach the existence of God, but the final truth of the matter has to be given through revelation. Now let us imagine how in front of a large audience Franz Brentano lectured on his metaphysics, his philosophy in a Catholic sense, but with great regard for science, how he approached the deepest problems of humanity in this fashion. Now let us go from Brentano's auditorium in the university in Wuerzburg to that of the physiologist *Adolf Fick*.[41] At the same time as Franz Brentano was lecturing in metaphysics and philosophy in Wuerzburg, Adolf Fick was lecturing there on physiology.

Now I would like you to imagine what a listener in Adolf Fick's auditorium would have heard, a listener who perhaps had listened to Franz Brentano's philosophy as I have described to you. I only need to mention it, as what I want to show you is all preserved in the lectures that Adolf Fick held at the University of Wuerzburg at that time. What he said can be summarized in the following sentences. We look for example at the warmth that we notice at first through sensation. When we touch a body, it will seem warm or cold; we have sensations of warmth.

What these sensations of warmth correspond to in the outside world is the movement of the smallest parts of the body, the movement that takes place in atoms and molecules, or by atoms and molecules in space. If for example we look at a gas, then this gas has to be in an enclosed space; in there we find the atoms and molecules of the specific gas. However, they are not in a resting state; they are swimming here and there, bouncing against each other, bouncing off the walls. In there it is all movement and uproar [see diagram]. And if we touch this, which inside is all movement, with the surface of our skin then we have the sensation of warmth.

This was the general view in science at the time, the view that developed particularly out of the teachings of *Julius Robert Meyer*[42] and from what *Helmholtz*,[43] *Clausius*[44] and other scientific thinkers of the times had achieved. *Joule*,[45] the English brewer, who was also a scientific researcher, had discovered that through a movement, for example that of a paddle wheel moving in water, the water can become warm. We could then measure how much work the paddle wheel does and how much warmth develops and we could then assert that through movement, through mechanical work done, warmth develops. This is nothing less than the conversion of what the paddle wheel moving in water produces in visible movement; it converts into movements that are invisible, but can be perceived as warmth. Hence warmth was considered to be a form of movement.

Now at the time they had also discovered that not only warmth is converted into movement, but that other forces of nature can be converted into movement as well. So a physiologist such as Adolf Fick could proclaim that all forces of nature, magnetism, electricity, chemical forces can be converted, that one can be converted into the other and that basically the only difference between them consists of the fact that we perceive the various forms of movement in different ways with our senses. So if we disregard what we have in us as warmth sensations, light sensations and so on, and look just at what is outside us in space, then there is only movement everywhere. The physiologist continues his observations by saying that when we look at our body, the most highly developed organism—and Adolf Fick now comes into his own field of physiology—we cannot assume there is a special life force, which makes the molecules of this organism move about in this way, but rather what moves around outside when we feel warmth, some kind of tension force, electricity or magnetism, this is also at work in the human body. Now he discusses how in the human body, through the absorption of oxygen, carbon is metabolized to carbon dioxide, hydrogen to water, and thus by absorbing oxygen combustion processes take place within the human body. He then explains that we can determine how a certain amount of oxygen is absorbed and how a person then gives off warmth. Back then there had already been trials with the calorimeter, measuring how much warmth is emitted by one animal or another, and some tests were also made on humans, which showed that this whole thing was wrong. However, it was said that mistakes had been made in the experiments, but that despite that they had found data which showed that what corresponded to the absorption of a certain amount of oxygen was then emitted as warmth. They assumed that part of what was processed internally went into the movement of the muscles, so that effectively the warmth that developed in the human being through the burning of carbon to carbon dioxide or of hydrogen to water produced these movements. The human being breathes in oxygen. Hydrogen burns down to water, carbon to carbon dioxide. What makes a person warm inside, what they then emit is only the movement of their smallest parts. Only after the conversion of these forces, do those parts convert to what forms the basis for the movement of the muscles, when the person does not only give off heat, but also works with their muscles or even just moves their limbs. Therefore we can say that the human being is in the main a complicated physical-chemical organization, which through breathing in oxygen emits heat and performs work.

Adolf Fick went on in this vein, saying that when, however, humans continually breathe in oxygen and use it up through combustion, then in the historical development of the earth, we should have noticed that there is now less oxygen. However, this is not the case. We could explain this by the fact that oxygen is continually being produced. The sun shines on the plants and when they absorb sunshine, they give off oxygen. Thus oxygen becomes available.

Humans can breathe it in again. The oxygen that humans and animals need is produced by the plant world.

In his lectures Adolf Fick continues: by continually emitting light and heat, the sun at least must be getting colder. He then shows how we can calculate how much cooler the sun should become. Julius Robert Meyer had done this before him and had shown that the sun should really have cooled down completely and that according to the amount it gives off, it really should not be able to emit heat any more at all. Therefore Julius Robert Meyer assumed, and Fick submitted this in his lectures, that comet masses, which according to Kepler must be more numerous in space than there are fish in the sea, are continually plunging into the sun. When something plunges into a body new warmth is created. Through this continual plunging in of comets, the warmth of the sun and with it the sunlight is constantly created anew. There was only a bit of a dilemma, as Adolf Fick assured his listeners, because we would have to assume that these comet masses were always there. Therefore we would have to assume that the masses which fly into the sun are then thrown out again, so that they can fly back in again. Here too he found a way out by showing that according to the second principle of the mechanical theory of heat it is not necessary for the heat of the sun to exist continuously, since it is a law of development that we can prove with the strictest logic—at the time Clausius had published the second principle of the mechanical theory of heat—that through conversion forces are continually converted into heat, but that heat cannot convert itself back into forces, so that heat is always left over; this means that in the end all events in the world must be transformed into heat states which level themselves out. Then nothing will be left of all that has happened in the world but the so-called heat death. In the end everything will culminate in this so-called heat death.

Thus Adolf Fick put forward how the earth, with all that takes place upon it including human life is moving towards this heat death, how all will find its end eventually in this heat death. A strictly physical view of the world!

We can imagine how Adolf Fick, the physiologist, was presenting this teaching as the world view of physics, while Brentano in his own lecture hall across the way presented what I described to you earlier. Now I would like to tell you about how these two finished their lectures. Let us assume that Brentano closed his lecture as follows: when we look at the scientific view of the evolution of the world, then we have to postulate an initial state which natural science can recognize. We arrive at a final state, which today even science characterizes as heat death. However, all this is illuminated and ensouled by divine-spiritual processes. We are guided to a beginning where a creative act of God brings to life all that science can study today. Then we arrive at the heat death, out of which only a creative act of God can further guide our evolution. Franz Brentano could have said something like this at the end of one of his lectures—and he did say it.

Let us assume that the two lectures were held one after the other, not simultaneously, so that after listening to Franz Brentano, a student could have gone across to Adolf Fick and listened to the last lecture about physiology. What would they have heard there?

Now I am quoting;[46] I am only saying what Adolf Fick said himself at that time, about 1869, at the same university where Brentano taught. After he had made the remarks I have described above in several previous lectures, he said: We will arrive at that point where all events both around us and in us will go into the heat death, meaning the end of the world. When, however, according to all the rules of science we can assume such an end to the world, when we have forgotten nothing, when we have to postulate such an end according to the strictest science, then we cannot suppose otherwise than that there was a beginning to the world. For it is inconceivable that a world with all its scientific processes that has existed since eternity has not long suffered the heat death. Since this heat death will only develop after some time, the world must have begun at some point, so that according to Adolf Fick, it must have begun through a creative act of God.

So you could hear in the one auditorium Catholic theological philosophy from Franz Brentano with the conclusion I have just described to you and then go across to the physiologist—not however to someone like Vogt[47] and others, who could not think things through consequently, but a physiologist who could—and he said the same on the basis of natural science.

This is an extremely interesting fact. It means that when scientists only went as far as pointing out a creative act of God, then they were in line with what could be heard in the next lecture hall on the basis of Catholic theology.

What could a listener do, who had heard about the physical constitution of the world and that it could even be proved that its beginning was a creative act of God? Adolf Fick would have said to him: If you want to know something about this act of God, then go over to the auditorium where Catholic theology is taught! At least this is what students must have thought.

And now imagine the soul of Franz Brentano. At that time it was still possible for him with his scientific ethos to come to such a conclusion, because what seemed to him proven about the supersensible worlds came from Catholic theology. Ten years later this was no longer possible. As I described already, ten years later he could not fully accept the Catholic teachings of revelation as a basis for the supersensible world. In other words this means that when the student of science then went across to hear the continuance, which science itself demanded, the lecturer, who could no longer hold on to the old tradition of revelation, had nothing to say to them. This was basically already the case when Franz Brentano was lecturing in Vienna. At the time he had just left the Church. In 1874 he came to Vienna; he had only left the Church completely in 1873, even though he had fallen out with the Church since the dogma of infallibility. He was so attached to the Catholic Church that it took him years to consider the matter carefully.

Now we are no longer able to imagine that from the lecture hall of Adolf Fick in Wuerzburg, or of *Bruecke*[48] in Vienna or of some other physiologist—they would of course all say the same—a student could go across to Franz Brentano and as was possible in the 1860s find the appropriate continuance. In Franz Brentano's lectures they could hear stimulating and interesting ideas about ethics and about psychological problems, but nowhere was Brentano able to move from direct perception to the supersensible. This example shows clearly how, if you refused to return to the old faith in revelations, the possibility of reaching the spiritual on the basis of established intellectual culture was disappearing. This is the most important spiritual fact of our modern age. For it is the atmosphere, which grew out of this, that has brought forth our leading thinkers. And through their influence we have landed in the great cultural chaos of our times.

Now I would like to show you the problem from another point of view. One of the students present when Franz Brentano was lecturing so brilliantly was *Richard Wahle*.[49] Richard Wahle wrote a book in 1894, which was much more significant than is usually assumed among philosophers: *The Whole of Philosophy and its End—its Legacy for Theology, Physiology, Aesthetics and Public Education*. If we want to look impartially at the development of intellectual life, then we have to point out the importance of this book. I just want to characterize how Richard Wahle viewed the world. For this view had developed out of what was undoubtedly the enormous inspiration Richard Wahle had received from Franz Brentano and also out of what was otherwise available in the intellectual culture of the time.

Richard Wahle said: Our experience of the world, what is it exactly? Now our experience of the world is that 'events' appear before us. Here I stand; in front of my eyes there appear walls, brightness, lamps, people. I have to make these events into my own personal experiences by means of my own ideas. Everywhere are events that become my own through ideas. All I have within myself are concepts of events. The world is a sum of events represented to me by my ideas. But let us take an impartial look at what we have here. Do we ever really have a table before us? We have an event, an occurrence, that is represented to us through the concept of the table. Do we have a human being before us? Again we have an event represented by the concept of a human being. All we have are representations of events. It is ingenious when someone so under the influence of Franz Brentano could see how he cancelled the will and only accepted the life of concepts and at the most of feelings, as I said yesterday. This life of ideas only allows for subjective representations of events. And what are these events? They are anodyne, completely anodyne! For if I have an event—I will use a drastic example here—in which someone slaps someone else's face; this is an event or a series of events, but I do not know what is behind it all. Richard Wahle says quite rightly: We only have events represented by subjective ideas. We cannot reach the determinants behind it. He freely admits that hidden behind what we have as human beings are determining factors, but we are unable to reach them. Therefore we can only become agnostics. We have to confess that when one person hits another in the face, then my idea of the moving fist is feeble, without strength, and does not connect powerfully with the face of the other person. I only have the idea of it. This is how Wahle dissolves all that is accessible to us humans into subjective representations of events. Even what we perceive inside ourselves are events, just that they surface from inside instead of being occurrences outside ourselves. Again we know nothing of the determining factors inside ourselves. We have not even an idea of the determining factors behind the event when, because of my thinking which is powerless and unable to slap anyone around the face, my hand lifts up to do exactly that. What factors are at work here we do not know; what is at work in us we do not know. However, we cannot possibly concede that the mere thought hits the other person in the face; thoughts are powerless and even if we turn to the great heroes of history, they only exist as subjective ideas. Think for example of Bismarck: he only exists as a subjective representative of events. The content of his soul life, or that of the great heroes, has not done these great deeds. The deeds happened through the determining factors, which we humans are unable to reach.

With Brentano you see someone struggling to get away from a world view that still tries for reality, but is based on belief in revelation, and into a pure intellectualism in the life of ideas, where he gets stuck, so that he cannot even continue to write his *Psychology* beyond the first volume. And you see how Richard Wahle, coming from the same contemporary trend, felt obligated to stick to anodyne concepts, the content of the intellect. It all becomes feeble, powerless. The human being cultivates only intellectual ideas and finally sees how feeble they are.

It was an important experience, when after my first lecture in Vienna[50] Richard Wahle said to me: I do have my ideas about the determining factors, but basically in comparison with the ancient philosophers, we are just gravediggers. In Richard Wahle we find something quite harrowing: he was condemned to admitting, in the most brilliant manner, that what human beings can obtain for their souls from this new culture is but feeble and powerless. I briefly mentioned to him the names of people who were teaching in Vienna when Wahle was still a student, Zimmermann, Franz Brentano. He responded: Yes, they still dared to make arguments; we do not dare do even that any more.

And just look at the book that appeared in 1894: *The Whole of Philosophy and its End—its Legacy for Theology, Physiology, Aesthetics and Public Education.* Theology! Does this mean we should take up theology as it was taught before? Should we completely give up trying to reach the supersensible? Should we just go back to what Brentano had to abandon with such consequences? What kind of process is it that takes what philosophy could once offer us and gives it back as a legacy to theology again, at least in part? How should what philosophy once offered become a legacy to physiology?

Just think—physiology in the sense of Adolf Fick leads us to the act of creation by God at the beginning of time. This legacy would not be able to give us anything satisfactory. And according to the demands of science at the time, aesthetics would not be acceptable as a way of discovering truth. And public education? Now it is quite understandable that someone who is unable to establish a relationship to the spiritual world should turn to ideas conceived of by human beings within human society, so that what determines our actions should be incorporated into public education in the broadest sense. Thus whatever leads to action by a human being, whether child or adult, should be determined by the laws of the State, a certain orientation should be provided by the laws of the State. So we see that in his book *The Whole of Philosophy and its End* agnosticism blossoms most ingeniously, most vigorously and most conscientiously.

And how could it have been any different? I will express what I have to say here in an image. Philosophy is love of wisdom; we can only love what we know to be alive. As long as Sophia was seen as something living, we could speak of philosophia. Nowadays when Sophia is just an aggregate of all sorts of ideas about the lifeless, gathered together from all over the place, now Philo also has to wither away.

Essentially this revolutionary, Richard Wahle, took the argument on a philosophical level to its logical conclusion. He simply stated what had become of philosophy under the influence of the intellect alone. This we cannot love. It has to fall apart into indifferent fragments. This is how it must end. After the death of Sophia, there can be no love left for her, or at most in memoriam. Thus philosophy has become a dead subject. We could honour its memory. And of course we could still write a history of philosophy. We could also resurrect old systems. This is basically what the new philosophers have most often done. We have had neo-Kantians, neo-Fichtians, Haeckelians; whatever commemorates our adoration of a deceased lover. And if we look at the insipid, subjective representations of events, which are just intellectualistic notions, then we can understand the whole process. Then we also understand the fact that philosophical thinking has reached its end, that it had to reach its end.

This is why in my *Riddles of Philosophy*,[51] after I have depicted the whole course of philosophy from the ancient Greek philosophers up to the second half of the nineteenth century, I attempt to show that what was philosophy had to be transformed into anthroposophy. Hence the last chapter is a schematic description of anthroposophy.

That we have to proceed in this way, that we have to see anthroposophy as the last chapter of philosophy is not the result of subjective considerations, but of the objective course of historical development itself. And it is precisely by looking at those personalities who are most typical of modern times that we are compelled to see things this way. For, as humanity has arrived at these insipid ideas that no longer contain any reality, after humanity has forgotten that these concepts are just the corpses of what was once life before we descended from the spiritual worlds into earthly existence, now it is necessary that we revitalize these ideas through the methods found in my book *Knowledge of the Higher Worlds—How is it Achieved?* through meditation, through concentration. And we are faced with the task not of just stopping at the ideas of science like Franz Brentano, but of absorbing and revitalizing them through inner spiritual work consisting of meditation and concentration. Then the most modern scientific ideas will lead us directly to the supersensible world. Then they will lead to the development of that method which is the method of anthroposophy; then the method of anthroposophy develops out of natural science. This can then fill the wishy-washy representations of events with life again, with vitality, because for a humanity that has advanced as far as the intellect, this life, this vitality has to originate in the intellect itself.

And I want to say that in relation to the more intimate aspect of this problem, Franz Brentano seems to me again especially typical. As a quite young man he wrote a letter to an acquaintance about meditation,[52] for he was attached to the meditation he had been taught in Catholicism which, however, never led him to the independent development of an inner spiritual life. Franz Brentano wrote approximately this about the meditation he had learned: I do advise you not to stop meditation. Someone who lives only a life of action, with no contemplative, no meditative life, they are only living a quarter of life; we must live three quarters of life in meditative contemplation. All that brings us closer to God can only come from meditative contemplation. Then he closes with the characteristic sentence: I would rather die than give up meditation.

However, this was a meditation taught in the ancient life of the spirit. And here we can sense the tragedy of someone who loves meditation, but because they are bound by scientific bonds, they cannot develop further into a free meditation that leads them to a new understanding of the spiritual, the supersensible life. Perhaps it is this letter that shows us how Franz Brentano was led by inner necessity to the gates of anthroposophy, but could not open them, because he had to repudiate all that he believed must be rejected by the scientific ethos and way of thinking.

It is a simple fact that science has certain limitations. If science does not just say there is nothing more to achieve, but following Adolf Fick, Franz Brentano's university colleague, says there is a creative act of God, an act of creation, then we can also say that just as it is legitimate to consider the whole field of the physical, so we must consider this aspect too. The physical does not only set limitations, it also points to the fact that there is something which must also be considered positively. It is truly not an arbitrary subjectivity when we point these things out, when we point out how necessary anthroposophy is for universal human culture. On the contrary, whoever considers the history of intellectual life impartially will see from that the necessity for anthroposophy.

Let us assume anthroposophy was recognized as a scientific approach, then it would be easy for someone like Adolf Fick to teach the following: physical research goes only so far, for the rest it has nothing to say, but there is a continuation and that is anthroposophic research. However, what from the physical point of view is the end of the world, something like the heat death, will only be seen in its proper light when all of evolution is seen according to what I have described in my *Occult Science—An Outline,* where Saturn existence leads us back to the beginnings, where we have nature consisting only of warmth, and then at the end Vulcan existence consisting also of warmth. Not only at the beginning and at the end will we see the creative, spiritual act, but during the whole of evolution the physical will always be seen in connection with the spiritual powers and spiritual deeds of spiritual beings, who do not go through a physical incarnation. So that of course the anthroposophical and the physical are not just next to each other, but the one permeates the other. When we consider individual physical facts, we will hear much about how spiritual forces work in physical-sensual existence. Then nobody will speak of events and undetermined factors, rather they will speak of how in what occurs as events we can find those hitherto unknown factors at the end and at the beginning of evolution and throughout the whole unfolding of evolution as well.

I would like to make this clear using an image. Assume that you have a mirror and you see in it what I have described. We can stay with this symbolic image even if it is rather drastic. You see in the mirror what I described: someone slaps someone else's face. In the mirror image you have the whole process. There you have images and you can certainly not say that the one image is so powerful that it slaps the other in the face. However, this is just how the modern philosopher thinks about his ideas. They are as powerless as images in a mirror. The one mirror image cannot slap the other in the face. But the philosopher Richard Wahle, for example, goes on brilliantly. He says: We cannot get to the determining factors, even if right in front of me I have two people, where the one slaps the other's face, I still only have the idea of it and the idea of person A cannot slap person B in the face. And I cannot get to the determining factors that are really giving the slap.

This image is quite a good symbol: the mirror image of person A cannot give the mirror image of person B a slap. However, if you look carefully at the mirror images, you will see all sorts of movement patterns. But you will not believe that the slap has really hurt the mirror image of person B; you will not feel sorry for the mirror image for having been slapped like that. And if you look more closely, look at the face of the mirror image after they have been slapped, then you will find something in this face that would be inexplicable if it was just an insipid image.

In other words, philosophy had come to a standstill with Richard Wahle, when there was only talk of events, but no possibility of reading these events since all the atavistic clairvoyance, which alone would have made such reading possible, had been lost. You can read in the image of the person who was slapped, in the expression of the face, that all this points to determining factors. If you open a book then you can read in it, if you have learnt to do so, and you will not say: Here I cannot see the determining factors. This is because what you are reading leads you to a certain understanding of these factors. We have to learn again to read the phenomena, the manifestations. We can easily acknowledge that in the intellectual age there are only representations of events; but if we are able to go to work on these subjective representations with inner fortitude, then we will learn to read them. Then we will become not Kantians, but anthroposophists, who say: Of course from the ideas that we have, we can know nothing of the determining factors. But if we understand how to read the world then we will gradually learn how through reading the events we can attain knowledge of these factors.

This can only happen however, when we bring strength into our inner life. And we can only achieve this through those methods given for meditation, concentration and so on. Thus we can say that modern philosophy has dried out, squeezed out of itself all that is life-giving for intellectual life. This was due to human beings who could not find the way into the supersensible worlds and also due to the times in which they lived; so we must now learn how to strive for inner development, so that we can find again the way into the supersensible worlds.

This was what I wanted to put before you through this quite detailed historical description of the second half of the nineteenth century. I also wanted to lay the groundwork here for some of what I will speak about in the next few lectures.

Ninth Lecture

DORNACH, 14 JULY 1922

T HE lectures from last week were in a certain sense meant to show how in the history of the second half of the nineteenth century those personalities of a more profound disposition struggled and how the contemporary scientific mentality prevented exactly such deeper natures from finding their way into the spiritual world. When we look at the personal, as we did with *Franz Brentano*, at the inner struggles of the soul, at what went on spiritually within these people, then we can see much more intimately what the great struggles of the time consist of than we could if we just described them abstractly. I pointed out in the last edition of *The Goetheanum*[53] how Franz Brentano, who starting from Catholicism, immersed himself in the ethos of science and then, in a manner of speaking, got stuck in the physical, the earthly and was unable to find his way back to the spiritual, can be seen alongside another personality, who apart from a few variations, suffered the same fate. This is the figure of *Nietzsche.*[54]

With Brentano we can show how from his devout Catholicism, his truly Catholic piety, he was then gripped by the scientific view of the world, which never again let go of him, and how his whole path as a philosopher can be characterized through this. We can show something similar with Nietzsche. We can show that Nietzsche starting out not from Catholicism, but from another way of thinking, was also held back in the physical, sense world by science and just like Brentano was unable to rise up to the spiritual, so that his fate took a similar but different turn.

Brentano immersed himself in scientific thinking in the eighteen-sixties and we have seen how, like a great wave of destiny breaking against him, the dogma of infallibility alienated him from the Church completely. Nietzsche is a few years younger and went through a similar development in the seventies. However, he came not from Catholicism, but from an artistic view of the world, from the kind of view that a modern person can develop, who has in their youth immersed themselves in Hellenism; the way of looking at the world of the ancient Greeks. And we can say that Nietzsche was as fervent in his Hellenist way and in his artistic view of the world as was Brentano with his Catholicism. He believed to have found in *Richard Wagner* and his art the renewal of ancient Greek culture. And just as Brentano took part in all the rites of Catholicism and absorbed himself in all that the Catholic ritual can arouse in a human being, Nietzsche absorbed the art of Wagner, in which he believed to have found a renaissance of the way the Greeks had seen the world. So he produced his first writings and then in the seventies he experienced the influence of natural science on his soul life.

Before that he was filled with the idea that human beings have received the great ideals from the independent sphere of the spirit, that we humans can put before our souls these great moral and religious ideals and that through them we are able to rise above the physical human level. And with great enthusiam Nietzsche finds inspired words to describe how humanity was immersed in the reality of these ideals. Then, however, the scientific view washes over him. And he begins to believe that he has to immerse himself in the notion that the physical side of a human being in the broadest sense produces these ideals out of itself. It is shattering for him to have to give up his old belief that the ideals are independent, rooted in an independent spiritual world and accept that they are just the results of physical processes. With all these ideals existing in his mind, Nietzsche submerges himself in a way in the physiological aspect of human nature. What before seemed of divine-spiritual origin now seems to him only human, all too human. Before he saw how human beings devoted themselves to the world of ideals, how through this devotion they had risen above base nature. Now he thought he knew that the base nature of humans just strives to develop the instinct to become stronger and stronger and that providing them with ideals only serves as a means to strengthen the inner intensity of power in human beings. In short Nietzsche strove to declare all ideals in a sense as simulacra produced by physiological processes in the broadest sense. However, he did not think of these physiological processes in humans as narrowly as does modern science, but he did want to view ideals as the product of physiological, physical processes in the widest sense. Thus ideals became for him something that people, unable to see through them, bemuse themselves with, whereas those who do see through them understand that ideals, just like common instincts, emerge from the physiological background of human beings and are only meant to reinforce and accentuate their physical nature.

Of course this is a rather radical description, but it does express the essentials which so shattered Nietzsche, namely when he thought he had discovered that even conscience can be explained by physiological means.

But the natures of these two personalities were rather different: Brentano is a fine spirit, attuned to ideas and cognition; with the scientific method he constructs in a sense an instrument with which he then aims to analyse human soul life, just as science dissects physical life. However, this instrument becomes blunt at exactly that point at which he tries to access spiritual life. In contrast, when Nietzsche realizes that according to science the basis of everything is physiology, or at least the consequences thereof, he constructs as an instrument not a fine analytical gauge as does Brentano, but a hammer that is robust enough to bust out anything spiritual from the physiological body. With this instrument that is robust enough to transform morals, ideals into something physiological, he grinds down the spiritual. He gave one of his writings the title: *Twilight of the Idols or How to Philosophize with a Hammer.*[55]

In a way Brentano recoils from the spiritual. Nietzsche batters it down. Basically someone examining modern cultural history should be able to find a profound similarity between these two personalities, despite their differences. And yet in his latest publication, that I have already spoken to you about recently, Brentano has a short chapter on Nietzsche, wherein he thoroughly rejects him. He calls him a writer of trivial literature, a fickle flash in the pan. He compares him to Jesus and claims that Nietzsche is a caricature of Jesus. Really, we have to say how strange it is that such a remarkably fine human being as Franz Brentano has not developed an organ to enable him to empathize with what another spirit experiences, who is basically so similar to him and who suffered such a similar fate, as I have described it all to you.

However, this is a contemporary phenomenon and just shows in the examples offered how people are today. They do not live in one another; they live asunder. I have often pointed out how people pass each other by without any understanding and how this is a social phenomenon of our times. People just go past each other, even the most dedicated seeker after truth. Everyone does this, but in such distinguished personalities this general phenomenon of our times shows itself in meaningful symptoms. Why do people just pass each other by with no understanding? Today we are in such dire need of mutual understanding! We are in great need of someone developing the ability to enter into both Nietzsche and Brentano, or say, *Haeckel* or *David Friedrich Strauss* and so on, so as to show how these various personalities view the world from the most diverse points of view. However, only spiritual science with its real access to the spiritual is able to consider what fruit a world view develops in various personalities. And this is exactly the reason why people are not able to understand each other: they have no access to the spiritual. We have to look for the reason why Brentano was not able to build a bridge to another person, who basically suffered a fate so similar to his own, in the fact that he got stuck in the scientific approach. Only a spiritual scientific in-depth study can penetrate the various viewpoints. For this, however, we need profound observation, profound knowledge of human beings. What are such personalities as Brentano and Nietzsche faced with when they are deeply impressed with the scientific methods of the nineteenth century?

Soner or later they will be confronted with the fact that as honest seekers after truth they have on the one hand the physical world and excellent scientific methods with which to explore this world; on the other hand they have a spiritual world. To be as superficial as many people of today and refuse to view the spiritual world as the great contrast to the physical world was of course not a possibility for people like Nietzsche and Brentano. They see the physical world, they see the spiritual world, but it is impossible to build a bridge between them. They see what human beings want on the basis of their physical natures; they see the will behind the instincts and drives, they try to explain these drives and instincts based on physiology and how in a way they coalesce into the will. Then, however, they notice that the spiritual world raises up ideals to which they should aspire; they notice aspiration opposite will and between will and aspiration they can find no bridge. Someone like Brentano becomes a psychologist, a scientist of the soul. Physiology has been more or less finalized. Now he wants to study the phenomena of the soul and in so doing imitate the methods of science. He is not even sure whether he has any soul phenomena because science disputes this in a sense. Brentano is only certain that soul phenomena exist not from a scientific viewpoint, but because he was a devout Catholic for so long.

This terrible dichotomy exists in the souls of these people: the spiritual world, the physical world and no bridge between them. How to move from one to the other? The ethical ideals exist. But it is not possible to understand how the thrust of ethical ideals can take hold of human muscles, can move a person to action. Science only tells us how the muscles and the bones are moved through the laws of physics, but not how aspirations influence the movements of the muscles and bones.

The fact is that basically however perfect the scientific method, this century of science was helpless when it came to the human being. They were not able to study the human being. They could not realize that humans are threefold beings as I have described in my book *Riddles of the Soul*. They were not able to get as far as dividing human beings up into the nerve-sense being, which of course fills out the whole person but is located primarily in the head, the rhythmic being, which again fills out the whole person but is concentrated primarily in the organs of breathing and blood circulation, then the metabolic-limb being, which is all the rest of a person. This is such a significant fact that we have to link all our other knowledge of human beings to it. Of course we should not just say that the threefold human organism consists of head, chest and limbs. As I have already said humans are nerve-sense beings all over, just that this is most pronounced in the head. Now look at this head. Its structure demands our admiration, all the more when we look more deeply, when we examine closely the nerve structure of the human head. There is no reason in the world of physical phenomena for the human head, especially on the inside, to be formed as it is.

Now we have to realize what I have often spoken about here. The outer form of the human head, leaving out the base of the skull, is a replica of the cosmos. It is really a sphere [see diagram]. The form of the head is taken from the cosmos. All the cosmic forces are at work in the body of the mother so as to create the human head in its embryonic form. If we look at this from a spiritual point of view, then the human being, who exists as a soul-spiritual being in the soul-spiritual world before descending into physical earthly existence, first unites with cosmic forces and then embraces the forces of heredity. The actual soul-spiritual human being forms themselves first from the world ether and then goes into the physical substance that the body of the mother makes available. So really the head is made out of the cosmos and what then descends as a being from the soul-spiritual worlds onto the earth has incorporated this cosmic gestalt. Hence nobody can understand the physical construction of the human head, if they cannot explain it in this spiritual sense: the human head is a replica, a direct imprint of the spiritual. These wonderful cerebral convolutions, that we can discover in the physiology of the human head, all this is as crystallized spirit, spirit in the form of matter. As part of the physical body the human head is a direct replica of the spirit.

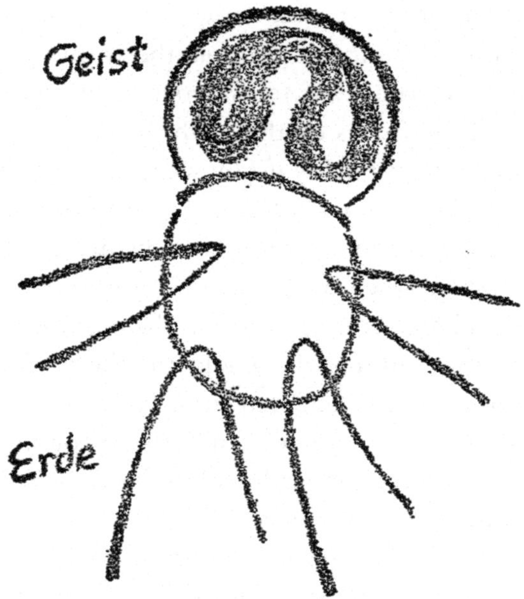

Geist = spirit, Erde = earth

If a sculptor wanted to depict the spirit as such, they would have
to study a spiritualized human head. Of course if they just work from
models, then they will not be able to capture it, but if they work
from the spiritual then they could create a wonderful image of the
innermost nature of cosmic spiritual forces. In the human head we
encounter the intuition, inspiration, imagination of the cosmic spiritual. It is as if the deity had wished to create an image of the spiritual
and had thus produced the human head. This is why it is basically
amusing when people seek an image of the spirit, while all the time
they have the best, the most sublime, the most powerful image in their
own human head; but of course just an image, not the spirit itself.

With the limb being it is just the opposite. If you compare this
to the above, then the limb being is only affiliated to the earth. It
only makes sense as belonging to the earth. Only the arms are a
little way above the earthly. In animals those limbs corresponding
to the arms in humans are also given over to gravity. Essentially
though the human limb being is organized in relation to earthly
forces. Just as the human head is a replica of cosmic spirituality,

the human limb organization shows us how the spirit is bound to earthly forces. Study for example the form of the human leg with the foot. If you want to understand its structure you have to understand the forces of the earth. Just as you have to understand the highest spirituality if you want to grasp the form of the human head, so to understand the form of the limbs you have to study what it is that binds human beings to the earth, what pushes us down to the earth, what causes us to be able to walk on the ground and maintain ourselves in the cosmos through gravity. You have to study all this, the whole way the earth affects a being connected to it as is the human being. Just as you have to study the spirit to understand the human head, so you have to study the physical aspect of the earth with all its forces so as to understand the human metabolic-limb being.

However, this has serious consequences. Only when we can look into the human being, when we are able to look at the human head and how in a way it is the crystallized world of the spirit which is active in the whole of the cosmos, and when we can see the origins of the structuring of the human limbs in the axis and swing lines through which the earth rotates, when we comprehend dynamically how the human being is formed and structured through the effects of these forces, then we can gain insight into how the soul-spiritual is at work in the human being. I would like to illustrate this with two examples.

Two things, which are in a sense opposed to each other, play a great part in human soul life. The one is what I would call doubts, the other belief or conviction. We could possibly find other more succinct expressions. However, you will all be able to sense that we have polar opposites in our soul lives, when on the one side we talk of doubts and on the other of convictions. Now imagine what happens when a person is caught between intensive doubts and intensive convictions. Try to imagine how suddenly something, even if it is only a specific event important to you, is thrown into doubt. It need not be a great universal truth or a cosmic riddle, just something in which you are extremely interested. Then you go to bed with these doubts. Imagine how you toss and turn, how restless you feel, how it leaves you no peace. Then try to imagine how a pleasant sense of conviction flows into you, quietens your soul, how a kind of soul warmth can pervade your whole being. In short when you actually look without bias at these two opposing natures, you will be able to see in your soul doubt on the one hand, conviction on the other.

Now what is the difference when we look at the whole human being? The human head is a replica, formed from the cosmic ether, of what we were in the spiritual world; the human head is a pure replica of the most human, namely the spiritual human. Notions of doubt approach the head, but find no place in it. The head does not take them up. They have to pass through the head and down into the limb being. In the limb being they unite with the grainy aspect of the human material being, with what permeates this being granulatively, that is what takes on an atomic aspect. Doubts go right through the head as if it was permeable. The blood then takes up these doubts and they are carried down to the rest of the organism, are first absorbed by the metabolism and then transferred to the nervous system; they live in all that is atomistic in human nature, what is granular or salty. They unite especially intimately with these last. The body receives these doubts and they go through the head. Only when we understand the specific nature of the human head and that the material of the head is not suited to doubts because the head is a replica of truth itself, from whence we come when we descend from the spiritual to the physical earth, only then do we understand that just as light passes through transparent glass, so these doubts pass through our heads and into the other parts of the nervous system and into our metabolism. The head only absorbs these notions of doubt in as far as it is also part of our metabolism. But it guides them through its specific nerve organization and only absorbs the convictions.

When they penetrate the human head, these convictions find related entities everywhere. They feel at home in the whole of the nervous system. They come to rest in the human head and flow into the rest of the body not through the blood but through the nervous system, which is itself in a kind of destructive process, so that in their spiritual aspect they flow directly into the rest of the human being. But primarily they settle in the head, they fill out the head. And in this head, they receive the gestalt appropriate for the whole person from the spirituality of the structure of the head, including the inner form, and then they are as if intimately related to the person, as if that person would live in them, as if they were that person. We could say that in these convictions the head of the human being forms something which is most suited to that person.

If you study the human embryo, then you will see that first the head is formed and then the rest of the organism; this is because those forces which form the rest emanate from the head. When the head absorbs convictions then this is what happens spiritually: at first, they are absorbed by the head and the head then sends them to the rest of the human being. Just as physically in the embryo the rest of the body follows after the formation of the head, so the spirit of the convictions and ideas is sent out to the rest of the human being and a human being is formed spiritually from these convictions [diagram on the left, red].

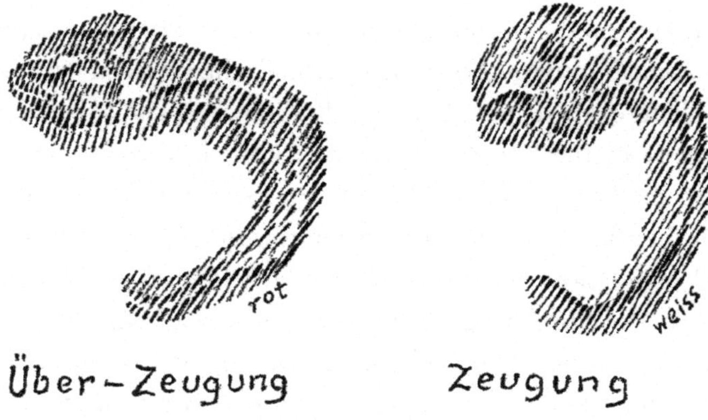

Überzeugung = convictions, *Zeugung* = procreation

An inner image of the human being radiates out into the specific human being. And the convictions unite with all the warmth that flows through a person. Just as the doubts unite with all the granular, the atomistic, so the convictions unite with the warmth that flows through the body, the first link of the etheric that permeates the whole person, and do not enter further into the physical.

Now try to imagine the presence of the doubtful and the convinced in human nature and whenever you experience the beneficial effects of a conviction and the tortuous effects of doubts, you will be able to understand the truth of the matter in real life.

I have often said that the spirit of language is one that works with reason/common sense. And if we attribute *Zeugung* [procreation—diagram on the right, white] to the embryo, then it is not surprising that to this structure on the left in red we attribute *Überzeugung* [conviction]. We should not see this as merely accidental. These are the deeds of the genius of language, which knows more than the individual human being. I am aware that modern linguistic science sees this as nonsense. But if they would really look deeply into the weaving of the reigning genius of language, then some aspects of modern philology and linguistics would appear as nonsense.

Now think of what this all means. You have now a picture of how two soul experiences, doubts and convictions, affect the physical human being. You have received an absolutely understandable bridge between the soul-spiritual and the physical. You can say to yourself: Here is the physical human being and what they experience in their soul shimmers and ripples through the physical granulates in the body: here is a sceptic, here is a doubter. You can see in the inner structure of matter how the disbeliever vibrates throughout the soul and then the body. You see the other person, whose warmth flows through their limbs and you can see in this quiet flow of warmth the physical expression of someone devoted to belief/conviction. You can see in the human being the direct physical expression of the spirit. Now you begin to understand the physical. When they analyse the human being the modern chemist and physicist would say that they contain calcium, phosphorus, oxygen, nitrogen and carbon. But in oxygen, nitrogen and carbon you will never find the spiritual. *Du Bois-Reymond*[56] is absolutely right when he says that oxygen, nitrogen and carbon atoms are completely indifferent to how they are arranged or how they are moving. If we only see matter in the body as carbon, oxygen and so on, then this is true. However, when we know that inside matter there is something which is receptive for the spirit in various ways and which in the head is a direct replica of spiritual being/quiddity, and in the rest of the human being is united with the earth, so that the earth holds on to what passes through the head as doubts, then it is no longer possible to think that in our brains there are a number of carbon atoms, nitrogen atoms and so on regardless of the nature of their arrangement or of their movements. We can see that matter is not indifferent to whether a stream of warmth flows through it, or whether there is a salt process, so that the body then tends to produce a grainy structure. These are two antithetical states which express themselves in the body but which originate in the spiritual. The fact is that we did not get materialism in the nineteenth century because humanity had never known the spirit. That most materialistic age knew the spirit in its most clarified form; all the earlier ages never knew the spirit in its purest form because in the images of the spirit that they developed there was always something material mixed in. Purely spiritual ideas were only first developed in the scientific age. However, what the scientific age had to disregard is precisely the actual knowledge of matter, of spirit in matter. Materialism has brought us to a lesser knowledge of material existence in the world, the loss of insight into the weaving of the spiritual in the material through ignorance of the way matter functions. By not knowing how the spirit works creatively people began to imagine the spirit more and more abstractly. Thus aspiration to ethical ideals became something you could not mention, because it could not even float around in space, having not a grain of materiality. It had just ceased to exist. Trying to catch a glimpse of it was like trying to breathe in an element which is not available. The human beings of the nineteenth century are like people trying to breathe by means of a bicycle pump! When they try to grasp ethical ideals—they are not there; they long for them, but they are not there, because people refused to develop an idea of how the soul-spiritual works in the physical body. This is why they developed all those curious theories about the interplay of the physical with the soul-spiritual; these were all just fabrications, whereas real knowledge can only be gained by following the facts exactly.

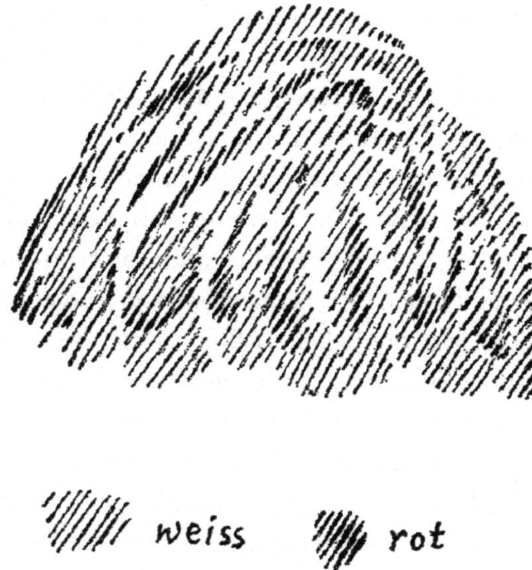

rot = red, weiss = white

When we realize how doubts and convictions flow through the body, then we are able to recognize in the world what we have already noticed in the human being. In the world we have the sphere of material functioning. We see for example how in the world outside matter has to take on a granular formation, how it crystallizes. Now if we have realized how in us doubts unite with the granular in our organism, then we can recognize doubts in the outside world. For example we look at the mountain [diagram, white], which is formed from granular rock, at the same time we can see how the same thing permeates the mountain that we know from ourselves as doubts [red] and we get to know the creative power of doubt. Doubts in us make us granular, because we are humans and not nature. Doubts outside in nature create the appropriate thing. When what works outside in nature permeates us then it creates something inappropriate. By walking on rocky ground you are walking on the physical formation of what God has sent out as doubts, so that the world can become granular. And in turn when you study your convictions or beliefs, steeped in warmth, then you find yourself in what is creatively coming into being. So that when you consider that basically in warmth we can find the source of cosmic creative forces, then you will find that what is working through warm matter is cosmic conviction, cosmic belief.

If you first truly learn to recognize these things in yourself, then you will be able to evaluate the active agents outside in the cosmos. When you can recognize all that crumbles away in the outside world, showing us the first signs of the decaying of our earth in the universe that lies ahead of us, as being the emanation of cosmic doubts, then you can understand much of cosmic existence. And conversely when you recognize conviction/belief in the cosmic then you can better understand the creative force. These are just examples through which I wanted to indicate how we first have to get to know the human being, so as to have a chance of understanding cosmic existence.

Now you see, Brentano studied scientific methods in the sixties, Nietzsche in the seventies; this research found that carbon, hydrogen, oxygen, nitrogen, phosphorus, some sulphur and so on were in the brain. There was no sign of the spirit. And when they used the methods which came up with these results on the spirit, of course they could only arrive at either spiritual helplessness as did Brentano, or at complete spiritual demoralization as did Nietzsche, who was more of a will person. But both suffered the fate of not being able to go from the physical to the spiritual, because they could not find the spiritual in the physical and so could not experience the spirit as powerful enough to create the physical out of itself.

Thus such minds were faced with a physical nature which really had no meaning, as it contained no spirit, and with a spiritual nature that had no power, no strength. This is the fate of two of the most significant minds of the second half of the nineteenth and the beginning of the twentieth century: they were faced with matter without meaning, spirit without potency.

Historians have spoken of ideas in history. This is also spirit without power. You cannot make of these ideas cultural instruments which influence civilization or through which historical events take place; abstract ideas are impotent, spirit without power. On the other hand we have nature, which they only studied as unspiritualized matter: matter without meaning.

We will never find the bridge when we have the one absurdity: matter without meaning. And the other absurdity: spirit without power. Only when we find power in the spirit, in conviction which causes strength and warmth to flow through the body, because this is the way human beings are organized; when we find strength in doubt to propel it through the head and downwards, because it has no affinity with the head, to soften up the rest of the human being so that it tends towards the granular; only then when we find power in the spirit to both dissolve the granular through warmth as well as to create it in the salt process, then we will find matter with meaning, because the spirit works so powerfully that what we perceive as matter becomes meaningful. Then we have matter with meaning and spirit with potency.

This is what such minds as Brentano and Nietzsche reveal to us in their tragic fates and their personalities.

TENTH LECTURE

DORNACH, 15 JULY 1922

WE have to bear in mind that the opponents of what we discussed at the anthroposophic congress in Vienna[57] called a meeting in which various people spoke in the materialistic tenor of our times and at the end of which a doctor with particularly materialistic views summarized the various speeches in a keyword, meant to become the motto of the opponents of anthroposophic oriented spiritual science: the fight against the spirit. It is a fact that nowadays there are people who see the fight against the spirit as a real rallying cry.[58]

When such words ring out, we are reminded of how many people there are today, good-natured, well-meaning human beings, who are trapped in a kind of sleep with regard to what is happening in the civilized world and who refuse to see the direction we are headed in. They mistake the most significant phenomena for unimportant contemporary events or for the opinion of someone or other, whereas in fact a strong tendency in the actual development of humanity is asserting itself today. And really all those who have an understanding of what is happening should be intensely involved, from their hearts, with assisting in this development.

I have tried to show by means of two personalities how people with more depth have experienced modern intellectual development. I compared these two personalities, *Franz Brentano* and *Friedrich Nietzsche,* so as to show you through them how people from very different fields, who were at first strongly oriented to the spiritual, then in a sense foundered on contemporary scientific thinking. When we look at actual people whose fate this was, then we can perhaps feel more moved than if we just consider these matters abstractly.

With Brentano I wanted to show how a personality who grew up and was educated in a completely Catholic environment had retained this disposition towards the spiritual world that Catholicism had planted in his soul for the whole of his life. It is exactly someone like Franz Brentano, born in 1838, so that he grew up in those times when the scientific way of thinking of the nineteenth century was flooding through all aspects of research and human intellectual ambition, who can show us what lingered on from the old ways of looking at the world.

When we look at the young Brentano, who studied at the Catholic theological seminary, then we see how his soul was filled with two things which at first guided him safely. The one is the Catholic teaching of revelation, which he accepted as did all theologians of the Catholic Church since the Middle Ages. The Catholic revelation on all things spiritual is traditionally accepted. They accepted that there was a kind of grace which revealed to humanity knowledge of the spiritual worlds. For Brentano this was linked to the second aspect, where he tried to understand what had been received through the Catholic teaching of revelation. This was Aristotelian philosophy, that philosophy which was developed in ancient Greece. And so until the middle of the eighteen-sixties, perhaps slightly longer, Brentano's soul life was such that in the sense of the mediaeval scholastics he would have said: We should receive what humanity knows about supersensible beings as the Church reveals it and we can use thinking to examine nature and life according to the teachings of that great teacher of this way of knowledge, the Greek philosopher Aristotle.

In their soul life mediaeval scholastics combined these two things, Aristotelianism and the Catholic doctrine of revelation and saw them as compatible. This lived on in Franz Brentano. However, he was deeply shaken in this view when he was faced with scientific methods, so shaken in fact that when he began his lectureship in Wuerzburg, he had to make the case that the methods of philosophy must be exactly those of natural science. And he wanted to establish a psychology, a study of the soul, in which soul life is examined in the same way as science examines natural phenomena.

Thus we can say that this person has experienced a radical turn-around. He wanted to combine knowledge through revelation with knowledge gained through reason and limited to earthly matters. Hence his assertion that only what has been found through scientific methods can be considered science. We should try to empathize with what this radical change meant for him.

I want to draw your attention firstly to the fact that until this turn-around the mediaeval scholastic outlook illuminated an exceptional personality. Even today this outlook continues to influence many contemporaries of an honest Catholic persuasion and even many an honest adherent of Protestantism, when in a slightly different form. I have brought Nietzsche into this because although Nietzsche did not have this continuance of mediaeval scholasticism, something else lived on in his soul, namely what emerged as a kind of reaction to scholasticism during the Renaissance. Nietzsche had a kind of Greek artistic wisdom, which formed the basis for his whole view of the world. He had this just as did the people of the Renaissance. However, the people of the Renaissance did not have this impulse or tendency to deny the reality of the spiritual. They still sensed, still felt the reality of the spiritual. Thus in Nietzsche too something from olden times had survived in his soul. And as I described to you yesterday, he too had to immerse himself in the scientific world view of the nineteenth century and he completely lost the connection of his soul to the spiritual.

In what I have mentioned here lie immensely significant riddles for the contemporary seeker after truth. Let us look at the two spiritual currents which flow into mediaeval scholasticism. Let us try to illuminate what is here the case. I would like to do it as follows. Within mediaeval scholasticism we have a number of let us say tenets about the supersensible world, for example about the trinitarian nature of the primordial spiritual being, about the Incarnation of the Christ in the body of Jesus of Nazareth, a whole series of tenets of which we have to say that they are not related to the sense-world but to the supersensible world and which were discovered long ago by human beings who were initiates. Of course we should not imagine that something like the tenet of the Trinity or of the Incarnation were simply invented by someone in order to dupe people. Rather these tenets are the results of experiences of erstwhile initiates. Only later did people start to see them as supernatural revelations. Such tenets were found through the experience of initiation. Only later they no longer recognized that a person could undergo such an initiation and so for example experience the vision of the Trinity for themselves.

Something like this only becomes dogma when the origins of knowledge have been lost. When someone is an initiate and has a vision of the Trinity, then for them it is not a dogma, but an experience. When, however, someone asserts that to see the Trinity is an impossibility, that it is a revelation and has to be believed, then that is a dogma. Of course it is not legitimate to disdain dogma as such, but rather what is questionable is a certain attitude that people have towards dogma. If we can trace back those dogmas with a deeper spiritual content to the form they had when an initiate first uttered them, then they cease to be dogmas. However, in the Middle Ages people no longer wanted to tread the path that they would have had to follow in order to be able to see such things. They had the old tenets that had once been the wisdom of initiation. They had become dogmas which had to be believed. They had to be accepted as knowledge through revelation. This was the one tendency: knowledge through revelation. The other was knowledge through reason, which the mediaeval scholastics learnt according to the teachings of Aristotle. They thought as follows: to a certain extent we can investigate nature through this knowledge of reason. We can also draw logical conclusions from its findings, for example the conclusion that God must exist. We are not able to find the Trinity, but we can come to the reasonable conclusion that there must be a God and that the world had a beginning. This was knowledge through reason.

Mediaeval scholastics also accepted certain conclusions of rational knowledge that came very close to the supersensible, but they did not concede the *vision* of the supersensible. However, they did accept rational conclusions through which they could approach such things as the existence of God or the beginning of the universe, although it was not possible to actually understand the knowledge of revelation. These truths, which can be found through reason, are called *praeambula fidei* or preambles of faith and they can form a basis for advancing into what can never be known through reason and should be the content of revelation.

Now that we have looked at these two spiritual currents side by side, let us examine the mind of someone who has them coexisting in their soul. I have spoken about this several times in the last few years. In the days when scholasticism was blossoming, what lived in the scholastic was not the evil that ignorant people have called it, rather at a certain time in mediaeval development it was simply what this development needed. At a certain point in time no other view was possible. Today of course such things are outdated. Today we must find other methods of cognition and of human soul activity than those that were fitting for scholasticism. Therefore we have to take care to investigate scholasticism with understanding. And we can only do this when we ask ourselves how knowledge through revelation and knowledge through reason, based on the study of natural phenomena and on conclusions drawn one-sidedly from these phenomena, could exist together in the soul of the honest scholastic? How did they co-exist?

What did such scholastics want—and with them all their faithful, all those honest Catholics—when they put themselves in the soul mood of the revelations and said: We should not try to see what dogmas give us, no vision is possible, we have to accept them as revelations. The scholastics tried to evoke a certain soul mood towards the supersensible world. They were completely convinced that this supersensible world exists and is intimately connected to what lives in the human being as their soul. However, they did not seek a path of knowledge in the human being, directly in their own personality, which could reach into this supersensible world so intimately connected to them.

Now try to imagine this mood. It was a mood related to what I would call a known unknown, or a familiar stranger, someone we should honour and revere, but towards whom we should also feel awe, so that we do not care to raise our eyes to theirs.

Next to this there was the knowledge of reason. Scholastic reason was extremely acute, at a level which has never been achieved since. We could wish, as I have said many times here, that those people who study science today would learn to think as astutely as the scholastics could. It was a knowledge through reason which denied itself access beyond a certain border: knowledge through revelation on the one side, knowledge through reason on the other. But if we compare consequently the knowledge through revelation and knowledge through reason of the scholastics with similar entities of today, then we will find a great disparity.

The scholastics said to themselves: With your knowledge you should not go into that realm where you should have only revelation. You should not for instance enter into a vision of the Trinity or of the Incarnation. However, in the revelations that they received from their Church there were ideas about the Trinity, ideas about the Incarnation. There were descriptions. They told themselves that cognition cannot approach these things, but still we can think them. As long as we have thoughts corresponding to what has been revealed. You cannot say that the mediaeval scholastics had a dark and mystic feeling about the supersensible. This is not true. It was a skilled way of thinking in structured concepts, which encompassed the contents of the revelations. They thought about the Trinity, they thought about the Incarnation. However, they did not think as we do when thoughts are something we arrive at ourselves, but as one thinks when thoughts are given by revelation.

You see, this too corresponds to a particular precedent of higher cognition. Nowadays there are people who still have certain atavistic clairvoyant visions, as we could call it, dreamlike imaginations. There are even people who in such atavistic, visionary imaginations can for example attain visions of old Atlantis. This is still possible today. And do not think, that in the clairvoyant imaginations such people have, no thoughts exist. Such clairvoyants often have thoughts more structured than those of our peculiar logicians, who have learnt to think in the modern school. Sometimes we could despair of the logic used by people who learnt to think in the modern school, whereas we need not despair of the logic revealed in this atavistic clairvoyance—it has often been developed in the most stringent manner.

We can still show proof today for the way that in what has been revealed through supersensible means for human understanding thinking also lives. This is also true of mediaeval scholasticism. It is only in recent times that people think that knowledge through revelation should be free of thinking, so that today faith should filter out of its content not only cognition but also thinking. Mediaeval scholastics did not do this. They filtered out cognition, but not thinking. If you study the dogmatic theology of mediaeval scholasticism, you will see it dominated by a strictly formed system of thinking.

This lived on in someone like Franz Brentano. This is why he could think. He could form thoughts. You can see this even in the rudiments of his *Psychology*, of which he only managed one volume. You can see that he has a certain inner structure in the formation of thoughts, despite the fact that he trips himself up again and again in the worst possible way and so cannot progress. As soon as he has a thought about some soul formation—and he has such thoughts—he forbids himself to think about it. Such prohibition is exceptional these days. I have already told you how a very ingenious man who wrote the book *The Whole of Philosophy and its End* said to me in Vienna not so long ago: I have my own thoughts about what is behind events as the primordial factors. But scientifically he does not allow himself these thoughts. We could even imagine that, hypothetically of course, a person schooled in scientific thinking suddenly, through a miracle, becomes clairvoyant and that they would struggle against this clairvoyance in the worst possible manner. Hypothetically we can imagine this quite easily because the tendency to cling to external authority is enormously strong.

So knowledge through revelation lived in the soul of a mediaeval scholastic in a completely concrete form. On the other hand there was knowledge through reason, which focused on nature, but was not exactly like our modern knowledge of nature. Just to corroborate this, open a book about natural history[59], for example one by *Albertus Magnus*;[60] there you will find natural objects as also described today, but here they are described differently; alongside this you will find all kinds of elementary and other spirits. Then the spirit still lived in nature and natural history and natural science were not just described in the most arid way as they appear to the external senses. These two things coexisted: what was given through revelation where cognition was forbidden but which was still thoughts, so that it could be reached through the thinking of the human spirit and what was found through reason, which, however, still had spirit, but was nevertheless something that had to be investigated in order to discover its true reality.

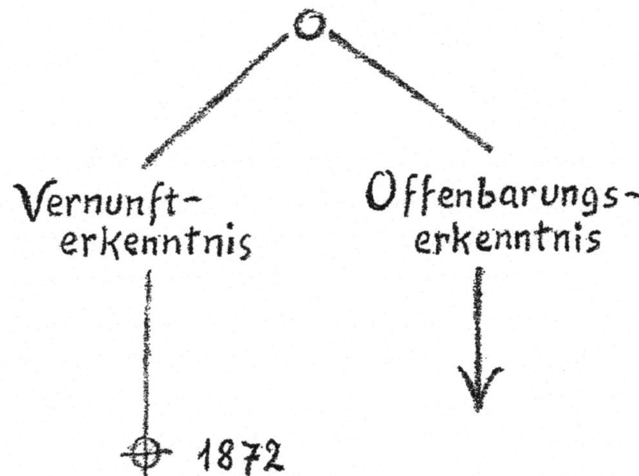

Vernunfterkenntnis = knowledge through reason, Offenbarungserkenntnis = knowledge through revelation

Knowledge of nature has developed out of the scholasticism of the Middle Ages. The one branch of scholasticism, knowledge through reason, has evolved further and become modern natural science. But what are the consequences? Try to imagine the scholastic view of nature as vividly as possible. There are still spiritual aspects in there. What did these spiritual aspects protect the mediaeval scholastic from?

Perhaps I should illustrate this with a diagram.

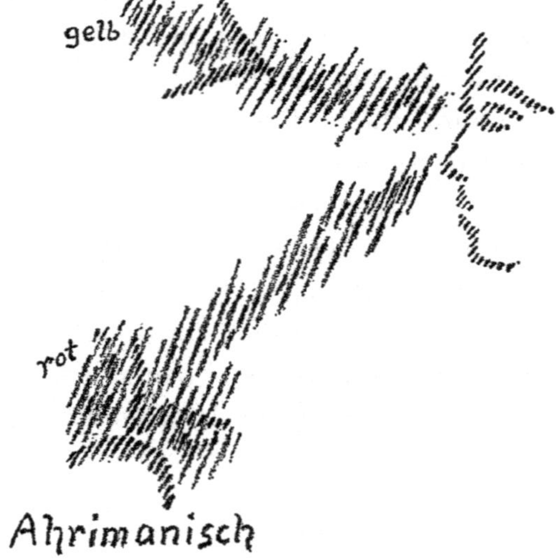

gelb = yellow, rot = red, Ahrimanisch = Ahrimanic

Let us assume that here is a mediaeval scholastic with their longing for revelatory knowledge going upwards and that for rational knowledge going downwards. However, in the rational knowledge there is also something spiritual, so I will put some red there too. And in the revelatory knowledge there is also thinking, so I will put some yellow in there. Now where does this rational knowledge want to go? It wants to go out to all the objects and phenomena which surround us. The thoughts we then make want to connect with the objects. You will not want to recognize a plant or get an idea of the plant without reckoning with the fact that the idea connects with the plant; it wants to connect with the plant. However, for the scholastic the spiritual aspects, which still permeate their rational knowledge, hinder their ability to connect fully down here. It does not completely connect; something is thrown back. So where does it not connect? When namely our modern, intellectual, rational cognition connects with external nature, when it completely connects, then it connects fully with the ahrimanic. So what does the spirituality of the mediaeval scholastic mean in relation to their rational cognition? Basically it means that with their rational cognition they want to reach something, which, however, burns a little. But they feel the burn and recoil from it again and again. Nature is sin! They are on guard against Ahriman! But in the nineteenth century further development then threw out all the spiritual from rational cognition and so rational cognition then connected fully with the ahrimanic.

And what does this rational cognition that is connected fully to the external ahrimanic say? It says that the world consists of atoms and the movement of atoms is the basis for all scientific knowledge. It explains warmth and light as the movement of atoms; it explains everything in the outside world as being the result of atom movements, since this satisfies our need for causal explanations.

In 1872 *Du Bois-Reymond* gave his famous lecture in Leipzig about the limits of our knowledge of nature. This is the lecture in which the rational cognition of the scholastics has advanced as far as throwing out all the spiritual; with the motto *ignoramus et ignorabimus* [we do not know and will not know] the human mind is meant to connect fully with the ahrimanic. And Du Bois-Reymond describes quite vividly how a human head, which now knows about all the atoms which swirl around in the universe, does not see green nor blue nor any colour at all, but only perceives all around it the movements of atoms. We do not feel warmth, rather everywhere there is warmth we feel the movements of which I spoke to you here eight days ago. With the power of suggestion he denies that all colours, warmth states, sounds and so on exist. He fills his head with an understanding of the world, in which it consists only of atoms. Just imagine: the whole world thinks of such a head as consisting only of atoms. He has in mind that already at that point in time where Caesar crossed the Rubicon there existed in the cosmos this particular constellation of atoms. Now he only needs to set up the differential equation and then by further calculation he can find the next constellation and the next and so on.

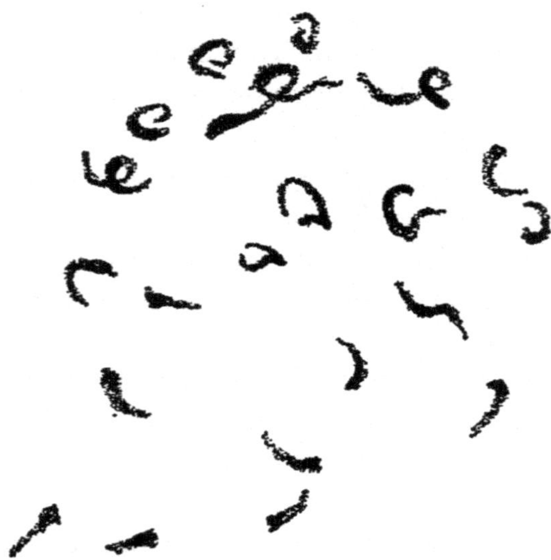

Now he can calculate the most distant future. As this was an idea of *Laplace*, Du Bois-Reymond called this the Laplace equation or the head of Laplace.[61] So in 1872 we had the description of an intellect which could grasp the whole wide universe, that everything is the movement of atoms and we need only know the differential equation and integrate it in order to have the cosmic formula.

But what have we really achieved here? What we have achieved is learning to think like Ahriman, like the ahrimanic ideal of thinking. We can only learn the real significance of what happens in time when we know what it really is. The lecture about *ignorabimus* will go down in the history of modern culture, but we will only recognize its value, its real significance, when we are in a position to show how the one branch of scholasticism connected fully with the ahrimanic. You see, the scholastics held their knowledge so to speak in abeyance. They could not completely reach what was in the outside world. They always recoiled cognitively from Ahriman. This is why they needed to develop such extremely ingenious concepts; these ingenious concepts still have to be developed through human creativity. In order to carry out experiments all you need from human creativity is the capacity to assemble the necessary apparatus and so on, but the ingenuity of scholastic thinking was not suited to this.

This means it was a watershed event as rational thinking connected completely with the ahrimanic. Because what you see around you outside as the sensual phenomena of the world, as your sensual environment, this only exists as long as the earth exists. When the earth perishes all this perishes with it. What lives on are the thoughts which connected with this external reality. When something is thought as Laplace thought or as what Du Bois-Reymond presented as an ideal of scientific thinking, this does not mean that it has merely been thought, but rather these are thought realities which connect to the external. And when all that we perceive with our senses on the earth has perished, these thoughts can live on, if they are not obliterated beforehand. Hence, when something like this becomes the general way of thinking, there is a real danger that our earth will be transformed into a planet which corresponds to the ideas of the materialists. Materialism is only a mere doctrine as long as it does not gain reality. But this is exactly what the ahrimanic powers are striving for, that materialistic thoughts become so strong and so prevalent, that all that will be left of the earth are the atoms.

When we say nowadays that we have to explain everything in terms of atoms, this is a fallacy. However, if all human beings start to think that everything has to be explained in terms of atoms, when all humanity embraces the Laplace formula, then the earth will actually turn into atoms. It is not correct that the earth has always consisted of atoms and their components, but human beings can actually cause this. This is the essential point. It is not just the tendency for human beings to have false ideas, but these false ideas create false realities; when false thoughts become prevalent, they create realities.

This ahrimanic danger is already present today. The mediaeval scholastics tried to avoid the other danger, inherent in cognition through revelation, by clothing these revelations in thoughts. The contents of the revelations became concrete thoughts. This thinking through of the dogmas, however, faded in time, so that many were gradually abandoned. And of course we should abandon what is not understandable; this is on the one hand completely legitimate and when people can no longer follow the dogmas as far as a real vision then it is self-evident that they should be dropped. However, what do they then develop into? Then they develop into the most abstract thoughts of a dependency on something vaguely eternal or infinite. Then the thoughts which carry revelations within themselves are no longer vividly formed, but there is just the dark, mystic feeling of a kind of dependency on something vaguely eternal. Then the thought content disappears all together. This is what has happened in recent times. It leads us to Lucifer. And just as the path of cognition through reason has led us to Ahriman, so the other path can lead us to Lucifer.

And now look at such a spirit as Franz Brentano in terms of what I have just described. Franz Brentano approaches nature with the feeling: do not touch Ahriman! And he approaches the supersensible world with the feeling: do not touch Lucifer! Thus do not become atomistic, do not become mystical. And with this feeling he turns to natural science, which is already such a powerful authority, so that he has to subjugate himself. He describes soul phenomena within the framework of the scientific method. If he had started out from a more superficial point of view, as do many contemporary psychologists, then he would have written an ahrimanic psychology, a 'study of the soul without the soul'. But he could not do this. This is why he let it be after the first volume and never wrote the following books—it was meant to be four— because there was something in him which would not allow him to think in such a way as to connect completely to Ahriman.

Now take Nietzsche. Nietzsche was just as taken with natural science. But how did he understand science? He paid little attention to specific methods, but studied scientific thinking in general. He said to himself that the soul is based on physiology and is human, all too human. What are supposed to be divine-spiritual ideals are in reality an expression, a manifestation of this 'human, all too human'. He rejected that form of knowledge which we find in Brentano: rational cognition. He cultivated the will in himself. And, as I said yesterday, Nietzsche hammered down the ideals, the spiritual. This is another phenomenon where a person comes in a sense into the ahrimanic, but collides with it. Instead of connecting with the ahrimanic, he collides with it. He wants to develop atomism, but instead he collides with it as with a wall.

And so we see how such minds of the nineteenth century develop their specific soul mood through coming so close to what we would call the ahrimanic powers. It is the fate of such spirits in the nineteenth century to come so unbelievably close to Ahriman. And then they either get into the position of Brentano and go no further, recoiling just at the border, or they start to struggle as did Nietzsche. But it is the forces of Ahriman which have surged up in this nineteenth century and then greatly influenced the twentieth century. We should be aware of this. And the original minds who experienced this partly disguised encounter with Ahriman in the nineteenth century suffered this tragic fate. And their students were then the recipients of their deliberations. These deliberations lived on in them. And ahrimanic forces had also worked on these deliberations. The first, original minds recoiled from Ahriman; their students received incomplete ahrimanic thoughts. They are now at work in them as 'the struggle against the spirit', against that spirit which refuses to abandon the earth to the ahrimanic powers, hate of the spirit, war against the spirit!

Today we have to see that as the actual situation. It lives on as a mood of the times, as a condition of the soul. We have to understand this so that we become really aware how necessary it is that we assert the reality of a spiritual world view in all the various cultural forms in which such a world view expresses itself.

Eleventh Lecture

DORNACH, 16 JULY 1922

IN my last talk I had to point out repeatedly how in European civilization at the height of the Middle Ages two currents of thought flowed through the best of souls, those two currents which I described yesterday as knowledge through revelation and knowledge through reason within scholasticism. Now we had to emphasize that knowledge through revelation as it appears in scholasticism is definitely not something mystical or an unclear abstraction, rather it is the expression of sharply defined, structured concepts. However, it was considered beyond the scope of human understanding and each person who sought this knowledge had to accept it as transmitted by the Church, which in its traditions and continuity has in a way the right to preserve it.

The second current, knowledge through reason, was free to be explored by human beings, but those who were firmly anchored in scholasticism had to recognize that with this knowledge through reason there is no possibility of attaining knowledge from the supersensible world.

Thus at the height of the Middle Ages it was acknowledged that what was no longer accessible to the people at the time had to be preserved historically. I have already indicated that this was not always the case. If we go further back through mediaeval times to the first Christian centuries, then we find that the special character of knowledge through revelation was not so keenly emphasized as was the case in the late Middle Ages. And if for example we had shown a Greek of the old Athenian school of philosophy the differentiation of cognition into a mere knowledge through reason and a knowledge through revelation—using revelation here as it was used in mediaeval times—then this Greek philosopher would not have understood it at all. He would not have been able to find a concept for the fact that when a power from beyond this world communicated knowledge of the supersensible to humanity that this should be static and could not be communicated anew. The Greeks understood that we cannot attain higher spiritual knowledge through ordinary cognition, but they also understood that through spiritual training, through the path of initiation, we can develop higher cognitive abilities. Then we can enter that world in which we have the possibility of seeing what is truth, what is knowledge in the supersensible.

And precisely in this respect the whole of Western culture underwent a great change from what existed in those centuries in which Greek philosophy blossomed in *Plato*, in *Aristotle*, to what then appeared at the end of the fourth century CE. I have often pointed out one aspect of this: the Mystery of Golgotha took place in a time in which there was still much of the old wisdom of initiation, of the old knowledge of initiation. And truly there were enough people able to use their initiate wisdom so as to understand the Mystery of Golgotha by means of supersensible cognition. Initiates strove to gather all the initiate wisdom they could so as to understand how the Christ being, who before the time of the Mystery of Golgotha had not been united with earthly evolution, had connected with an earthly body and was now united with human development. What kind of a being was this and how had they acted before descending to the earth?; these were questions for which they sought answers using the highest faculties of initiation at the time of the Mystery of Golgotha.

Then, however, we see that the old wisdom of initiation which existed in the Middle East, in North Africa, but also in Hellenic culture and even in Italy and farther into Europe, this wisdom of initiation was less and less understood from the fifth century CE onwards. Certain names are spoken as if the people they belong to are seen as rather contemptible within the Christian civilization of the Occident, or at least as personalities a proper Christian should have nothing to do with. At the same time efforts were made to obliterate all traces of the earlier knowledge that these people had.

It is curious that a man like *Franz Brentano*, steeped in the mediae-val tradition, inherited the hate people had towards what had existed in the soul of someone like *Plotinus*,[62] of whom we know very little, but who is seen as a philosopher with whom a true Christian believer should have nothing to do. Brentano even shared this hate of Ploti-nus.[63] He had allowed himself to inherit this hate. He wrote a treatise *What kind of philosopher sometimes makes the epoch?* and he meant Ploti-nus, the philosopher of the third century CE who was part of that current of thought, which then completely dried up in the fourth century CE and which later Christian development did not want to remember.

What is written in the customary history of philosophy about the outstanding figures of the first centuries CE is mostly not even just a minimum; it is impossible to gain a faintly coherent idea of these people from it. Needless to say it is very difficult in modern times to get an idea of the first three or four centuries of the Christian era. For example how what had lived in Plato and Aristotle continued and lived on in these personalities of the third or fourth centuries CE, even though it was already estranged from the deeper wisdom of the mysteries. In the usual histories of philosophy you will find hardly any real understanding of Plato. If you are interested in this, then look for example at the chapter on Plato in the history of Greek philosophy by *Paul Deussen*,[64] where Paul Deussen writes about what Plato thought about the idea of the good in relation to the other ideas. There you will find sentences such as the following: Plato did not assume the existence of a personal God, since otherwise the ideas that he taught could not have existed out of themselves; Plato could not recognize a God-being because ideas exist independently. However, Deussen goes on to say that Plato places the idea of the good above the other ideas. Only this does not mean that the idea of the good somehow stands above the other ideas as something intrin-sically independent; for what the idea of the good expresses, that is just a certain family resemblance that exists in all ideas.

Now we should pay attention and look more closely at Deussen's logic, the logic of one of the most outstanding contemporary philos-ophers. Plato has the ideas. They are independent. Now Plato has the idea of the good. This is not supposed to be something which leads the other ideas, rather the ideas have a common family resemblance. And this family likeness is expressed in the idea of the good. But where do these familial resemblances come from? If there is a family likeness, if you want to use such an expression, then it must at least come from some kind of parentage. The idea of the good points to a family likeness; hence we must be able to find an ancestor!

So this is what we find in pre-eminent contemporary writings on the history of philosophy. The writers of such things are the intellectual authorities of our times. People learn these things and fail to notice that it is complete nonsense. Obviously, we cannot trust someone who talks such nonsense about Greek philosophy to have much of importance to say about the wisdom of India. Still today, if you are looking for an authority on Indian wisdom, then you will be referred to Paul Deussen. This is how bad things have become.

I just wanted to point out that at present there is not much appreciation even of Platonic philosophy. Modern intellectualism is not even capable of this. This is why there is no understanding of what, however, is still part of traditional lore. This is that Plotinus, the neoplatonic philosopher—this is what he is always called—was a student of *Ammonius Saccas*,[65] who lived at the beginning of the third century CE, but wrote nothing, only teaching individual students. The outstanding spirits of this time wrote nothing, because they thought that wisdom must exist as something living, so that it cannot be transmitted from one person to another through writing, but only from human being to human being in direct personal contact. Now there is something else said of Ammonius Saccas, whose significance people are not clear about. They say that in the face of the awful quarrels between students of Aristotle and those of Plato, he tried to bring them to a consensus by showing how Plato and Aristotle actually harmonize with each other.

I just want to describe in a few words how Saccas could have spoken about Plato and Aristotle. On the one hand he says that Plato belongs to that era in which people could find their own soul path to the spiritual world, in other words when people still knew the principle of initiation. Perhaps Ammonius Saccas said that in older times logical, abstract thinking had not yet developed. Even now—here I mean at the beginning of the third century CE—there are only the first signs of it. Thoughts developed by human beings did not really exist in Plato's time. But whereas older initiates gave what they had to communicate to humanity in the form of images and imaginations, Plato was one of the first to transform imaginations into abstract ideas. When we envision the mighty contents of these images [red], which Plato wanted to guide people to see, then for older times the content of these images was expressed only in imaginations [orange], but for Plato they were already ideas [white].

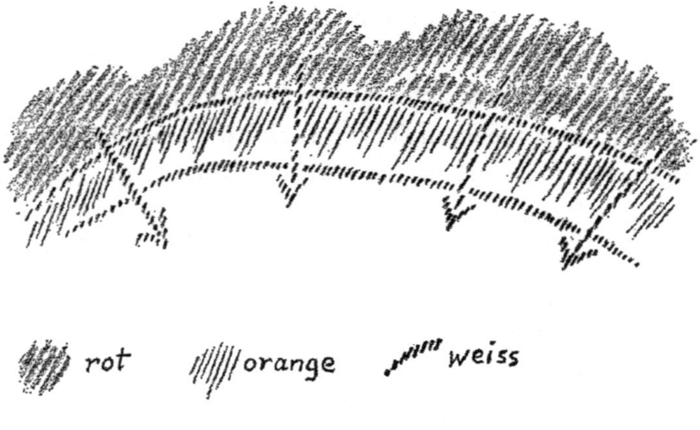

rot = red, orange = orange, weiss = white

But these flowed down in a way from the divine spiritual [arrows]. Plato said: The lowest manifestation, in a sense the most diluted manifestation of the divine spiritual, are these ideas. Aristotle no longer had the strong potential to rise up to this level of the spiritual. Thus he only had what was below the level of the images, he only had the content of the ideas. However, he could still understand these as revelations. There is no difference between Plato and Aristotle, said Saccas, just that Plato could see into higher levels of the spiritual world and Aristotle saw only lower levels.

Ammonius Saccas thought that with this he could sweep away the differences between the followers of Aristotle and of Plato. And even though at the time of Plato and Aristotle wisdom was already beginning to appear in intellectual form, there was still the possibility that some people could rise to quite high levels of spiritual vision. And so we have to remember that such people as Ammonius Saccas and his pupil Plotinus were still full of direct spiritual experiences and especially of such experiences where their vision of the spiritual world was quite specific. Of course we could not have spoken to such people about external nature as we do today. In their schools, they spoke of a spiritual world and of nature down below, which today is for most people the whole world, was only the lowest image of the spiritual worlds of which they were conscious. We can imagine how such people spoke if we look at one of Saccas successors, *Iamblichus*,[66] who still had deep insights and carried them on into the fourth century CE.

Let us imagine how Iamblichus saw the world. He spoke to his students as follows.

> If you want to understand the world then you should not look at space, for space consists of just the outer expression of the spiritual world. Also you should not look at time, for it is only the mirage of the real and true cosmos which appears in time. We have to look up to those powers in the spiritual world, which create time and the relationship between time and space. We must look out into the cosmos. Every year the same cyclical course of heavenly bodies takes place, exemplified outwardly by the sun. The sun moves through the zodiac, through the 12 signs. We should not just look at it passively, because 360 celestial powers are at work in all this and they are behind all the effects the sun produces for the whole of the world accessible to human beings; and they repeat this cycle every year. If they alone ruled then the year would have 360 days.

This is roughly what Iamblichus taught his students. However, there are five days left. These five days are ruled by 72 sub-celestial powers, the spirits of the planets. I will draw this pentagon in the circle because 1:5 is the same relation as 72:360. So the remaining five world days of the year, which 360 celestial powers would leave empty, are ruled by the 72 sub-celestial powers. Now as you know the year does not consist of just 365 days, a few hours are always left over; for these hours, according to Iamblichus, there are 42 earthly powers.

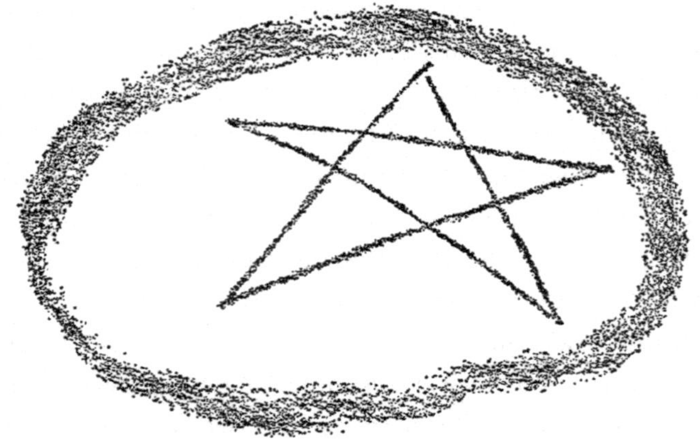

Iamblichus goes on: the 360 celestial powers are connected to the human head organization. The 72 sub-celestial powers are connected to the chest, breathing and heart organization, and the 42 earthly powers are connected to what in humans is the purely earthly organization of digestion, of metabolism.

So human beings were embedded in a spiritual system, in a cosmic spiritual system. Nowadays we begin the study of physiology by learning how much the human being ingests of carbon, nitrogen, sulphur, phosphorus, calcium and so on. We relate the human being to the lifeless in nature. In his schools Iamblichus would have described the human being as related to the 42 earthly, the 72 sub-celestial or planetary and the 360 celestial powers. Just as human beings are now described as consisting of earthly substances, so then they were described as something that flows down from the powers, the agencies of the spiritual universe. We have to say that an extremely exalted wisdom was represented in these schools. We can then understand that Plotinus, who only became a follower of Ammonius Saccas when he was 28 years old, felt that he was now in a different world, because he could absorb some of this knowledge. This wisdom was taught in many places in the first four centuries after the Mystery of Golgotha. And with this wisdom they attempted to understand how the Christ descended into Jesus of Nazareth. They tried to understand what was Christ's place in this whole mighty world of spiritual hierarchies, in this whole spiritual edifice.

Now I want to talk about another chapter of the wisdom of Iamblichus that he taught in his schools. He said: There are 360 celestial powers, 72 planetary powers and 42 earthly powers. Hence altogether there are 474 divine beings in diverse hierarchical order. Now look to the Far East, so said Iamblichus to his pupils, where you can see that there are peoples who all have names for their Gods. Then go to the Egyptians and they too will have names for their Gods; other peoples will also name their Gods. Then go to the Phoenicians, to the Hellenes or to the Romans and again you will find other names of the Gods. If you take all 474 names of the Gods then all the various Gods of the various peoples are included: Zeus, Apollo, also Baal, Amon, the Egyptian God, all the Gods are included in these 474. That the various peoples have different Gods is because the one people has taken 12 or 17 out of the 474, the second has taken 20 or 25, the third 3 or 4 and so on. And when we rightly understand the various Gods of the various peoples then we find 473. And the highest, the most noble of all, the one who at a certain point in time would descend to earth, that is the Christ.

It was this wisdom which tended to reconcile the various religions, not from some vague feeling, but rather because they wanted to recognize how, for someone who could distinguish the 474 Gods in the whole cosmic edifice, the various divinities of the various peoples are part of a great system and how this divine Olympus of all peoples of ancient times culminated in Christianity. And this whole edifice was meant to be crowned by the understanding of how the Christ in Jesus of Nazareth had descended into his earthly task.

When we look at the spiritual science of those times, which is, however, no longer valid today—now we have to study spiritual science differently—then we are full of admiration for what was taught about the supersensible worlds, the supersensible cosmos. However, this understanding of the universe was only transmitted on condition that it was handed down from the older initiates to their immediate students; this wisdom was only to be passed on to those who had been thoroughly schooled so that their cognitive faculties had reached a level where they were able to understand the nature of one or other of these various Gods.

We can say that everywhere in the relevant circles this was a prerequisite of spiritual culture, in Greece, in Egypt, in the Near East; but not in the Roman world. However, the Roman world did have some vestiges of the ancient wisdom. Plotinus himself taught for a long time in Italy, within the Roman Empire. But the spirit of abstraction had infiltrated the old Roman world, a spirit which could no longer understand in the old way the value of the human personality, or the value of beingness/quiddity itself. The spirit of abstract concepts had taken hold of Roman culture; not as extreme yet as in later times, but I think people clung to it all the more when it was in its rudimentary form.

And so we see that, as the fourth century CE begins, there is a kind of school in Italy which takes up the fight against the old principle of initiation, the fight against all preparation of individual human beings for initiation. We see a school developing which collects and carefully records all that has been transmitted from the old initiations. This school, which continues on from the third to the fourth centuries, is concerned with perpetuating Roman culture itself, of establishing historical tradition in place of the strivings of each actual, individual human being. And Christianity now starts to develop within this Roman principle. Standing at the beginning of that Christianity which originated in the fourth century CE, this school meant to obliterate all that could still be found in the old initiation about the Incarnation of the Christ in the person of Jesus.

In this Roman school they were convinced that what Ammonius Saccas taught, what Iamblichus taught should not be allowed to pass down to posterity. Just as they set about demolishing all the old temples, destroying the old altars, annihilating what was left of ancient paganism, so they tried to obliterate spiritually all the principles which made people able to find the higher worlds. And so, just to take one example: in place of what Iamblichus and Ammonias Saccas knew, that the individual human being is able to evolve up to a level where they can understand how Christus dwelt in the body of Jesus, they substituted the dogma of the one divine nature or the two natures in the Christ. This dogma was to be inviolable and insight or the mere possibility of insight was to be deeply buried. In ancient Rome this transformation of the old paths of wisdom into dogma took place. And they were at pains to destroy all the old information, everything that recalled the old ways, so that only the names of such people as Ammonias Saccas and Iamblichus remained. Not even the names of numerous other teachers of wisdom in the southern areas of Europe have survived. Just as all the altars were destroyed and all the temples burned to the ground, so the old wisdom was eradicated so that people today no longer have any idea of the wisdom that existed in the south of Europe in the first four centuries after the Mystery of Golgotha.

This knowledge at least found its way to people who were interested in such things and who could see how ancient Rome was swiftly heading for its downfall and how Christianity was spreading. However, after what would have enabled a glorious reception of the Mystery of Golgotha had been destroyed, it was only possible to see the uniting of the Christ with Jesus as a dogma, determined more or less by the synods of the Church in an abstract, Roman way. The living wisdom was extinguished and replaced by the abstraction, which was then regarded as knowledge through revelation.

The history of such processes has been more or less wiped out, but at the time, in those first Christian centuries, there were many people who said that initiates, such as Iamblichus once was, do exist. These are the people who talk about real Christianity. For them Christ is indeed the Christ. But what did the Romans increasingly do? The Romans made of Christianity what we should really call 'The Galileans'. For a while during the third and fourth centuries this expression was used to cover up a great misunderstanding. The less people understood about Christianity, the more they spoke of the Galileans; less and less was known about Christ and the human personality of the Galilean became more and more important.

Into this spiritual environment came the figure of Julian, the so-called Apostate, who had absorbed much of what the followers of Iamblichus had to say and who knew that there is a spiritual cosmos that reaches down into the various realms of nature. Julian the

Apostate had heard from students of Iamblichus how right down into the animal, into the plant, the forces of the 360 celestial powers, the 72 sub-celestial, planetary powers, the 42 earthly powers are at work. In those days people understood such things as are wonderfully expressed in the legend surrounding the personality of Plotinus, which has a profound meaning. This legend says that there were already many who refused to believe that someone could be inspired by a divine spirit and said that someone who claimed to know something of the divine-spiritual world was possessed by a demon. So Plotinus was dragged before the Egyptian temple of Isis, where it was to be decided which demon had possessed Plotinus. And as the Egyptian priests, who knew about these things, arrived and examined Plotinus in front of the altar of Isis with all the rituals possible at the time, then instead of the demon manifesting, it was the Goddess herself! So at that time there was at least the possibility of testing whether someone was possessed of a demon or of a benevolent God.

Julian the Apostate still heard about such things. But on the other hand he also heard about something like the text which in the first Christian centuries was doing the rounds within the Roman Empire and which was supposed to be a sermon of the Apostle Peter;[67] however, this was a forgery. This text said that we should look at the godless Hellenes and how they see the divine spiritual in all natural beings. That is profane and is forbidden! You should not look at nature, at animals, at plants and see the divine spiritual. You should not stoop to the belief that in the path of the sun, the path of the moon there is something divine. So Julian the Apostate heard these things from both sides. And he developed a deep love of Hellenism. He became that tragic figure who wanted to speak of Christianity in the sense of Iamblichus.

We cannot imagine what would have happened if not the Christianity of Rome but that of Julian the Apostate had won the day; if his impulse to rebuild the temples of initiation had won out, so that people could see for themselves how the Christ had dwelt in Jesus and how the Christ was connected to the other deities. Julian the Apostate did not wish to destroy the pagan temples. He even wanted to rebuild the temple in Jerusalem, the Jewish Temple. He wanted to rebuild the pagan temples and he also befriended the Christians. He wanted the truth. He was particularly against that school in Rome which aimed to and succeeded in destroying the old principles of initiation and replacing them with mere recorded traditions of initiation wisdom.

And they knew how to arrange it so that just at the right moment Julian was killed by a Persian lance. It was then that was said what has never been understood, not even by *Ibsen*,[68] but that now from the tradition of the times we can realize what it means: not Christ but the Galilean has won! For in his moment of death Julian the Apostate could see prophetically how the idea of the divine Christ would ebb away and the 'Galilean', the human being born of the tribe of Galileans, would gradually be venerated as a God. In his thirtieth year in a great prophetic vision Julian the Apostate saw the whole development of theology that continued into modern times, into the nineteenth century, and how it completely lost the Christ in Jesus. He was only apostate in relation to what was yet to come. In reality he was an apostle in relation to what was then a spiritual understanding of the Mystery of Golgotha that we must understand again.

Newer geological layers are deposited on the old and we always have to dig through them if we want to reach the older ones. It is difficult to believe how thick these historical layers in the development of humanity are. What has been laid down over the Mystery of Golgotha since the fourth century CE under the influence of Romanism is indeed extremely thick. However, with the help of spiritual knowledge we have to excavate these layers so as to find the ancient wisdom which, like the ancient pagan altars, has been so thoroughly swept away.

The Egyptian priests determined that Plotinus was not possessed by a devil, a demon, but by a God. In Western Europe, however, it was determined that it was a demon after all. You can look all this up including Brentano's *What Kind of Philosopher Sometimes Makes the Epoch?* in which you will find that the Egyptian temple priests determined that in Plotinus, the philosopher of the third century CE, it was not a demon which possessed him but a God; Brentano determines that it was not a God but a demon.

And this is what happened in the nineteenth century: Gods were seen as demons and demons as Gods and it was no longer possible to differentiate in the universe between Gods and demons. This is what lives on in the chaos of our civilization.

It really does make you think when you look at these things in the right way. Today I just wanted to describe a chapter of history to you, quite objectively, because of course all that happened historically was necessary. But it is also necessary that when people had to lose sight of certain things for a certain time, that they rediscover them and really take them to heart.

Twelfth Lecture

DORNACH, 21 JULY 1922

THE last few lectures here were dedicated to a discussion of how we should conceive of modern consciousness. In the last one I tried to reach back to earlier times and to point out how what now lives in people's souls has been in preparation for a long time within Occidental civilization. Today I would like to pick out various episodes from the immediate present to draw your attention to how a spiritual life has of necessity to develop out of the general consciousness of our times—a necessity emerging from the evolution of humanity. We can say that wherever we observe human beings in modern civilization, whether in the West, in the middle or in the East, wherever we look more closely it becomes clear that without the introduction of a spiritual impulse things cannot move on.

Today we want to look at the last fifty years of intellectual/spiritual development in Central Europe through what characterizes the beginning and the end of this period and thus to prepare for the lectures tomorrow and the day after. I want to do this symptomatically. I want to characterize various points for the beginning and for the end of these fifty years.

If we go back to approximately the start of the eighteen-seventies, then we find various intellectual/spiritual phenomena, which show us the state of the human soul at the time. I want to highlight some of these phenomena. Around 1872, 1873 we have a sensational work of fiction, which closely reflects the times. Younger people now will have forgotten all about this, but the novel that I mean is in fact one that fifty years ago seized people's attention in a quite drastic way. I mean *Children of the World* by *Paul Heyse.*[69] Paul Heyse was a famous novelist of the time and with this book he wanted to depict the lives of a number of characters who are all steeped in a certain indeterminate religiosity, but at the same time are all lapsed from any formal religious denominations. So Paul Heyse wanted to contrast what he calls in rather old-fashioned terminology to my mind, the children of God with the children of the world, who belonged to no particular confession, who were as they expressed it at the time 'non-denominational', but who still tended to be drawn to the religious. Now I do not intend to speak much about the novel itself, but to point out how such a work, portraying non-religious people, made such an impression at the time.

I have often spoken to you about my old friend and teacher *Karl Julius Schröer*.[70] One of his interests was the study intellectual phenomena as they affected social life in general. And so Karl Julius Schröer characterized the influence of Paul Heyse's *Children of the World* by saying that it was extremely odd how at the time, fifty years ago, this novel did the rounds, how everyone was interested in it and how through this novel people noticed something they would never have thought about before: that they also had distanced themselves from a positive religious commitment, that even though they might still be searching for a religious faith, this was not restricted to any religious denomination. And what was especially interesting was Schröer's observation at the time that people who had taken part in the religious rituals of their Church up until then, who out of habit had joined in the old rituals and customs of their Church, these people discovered that the novel expressed their inner convictions. And Schröer added that in the face of such a phenomenon religious controversies seemed like an anachronism, like something which was no longer part of the present—meaning the beginning of the eighteen-seventies— because people had already gone beyond this in their thinking. But even though all this is valid, we still have to say that despite having lost all connection to established faiths, the people described in the novel nevertheless have the tendency to search for some kind of religiosity. However, they cannot find anything. They go about the world with no faith; they are unable to find any connection to the spiritual world through religious feeling.

If we now move on from this fictional-literary phenomenon to the lecture theatres, then we find that at just about the same time the opinions of many people in scientific life were expressed by *Du Bois-Reymond* in the lecture I have often mentioned: *Limits of our knowledge of nature*. In this famous lecture, given by Du Bois-Reymond in 1872, he argues that a fact is only proven when we examine nature through experiment and observation and come to a kind of mathematical, mechanical thinking about the edifice of the world, a kind of mechanism, an atomic mechanism of the edifice of the world. Science cannot go beyond this perception of the world; all else must be left to faith. However, if we had asked someone, who spoke like this at the beginning of the eighteen-seventies, someone like Du Bois-Reymond in his *Limits of our knowledge of nature*, if we had asked them how people should search for a religious way to the spiritual world, there would have been no answer. They would just have said something similar to the characters in Paul Heyse's *Children of the World*, who were portrayed as non-denominational.

Now it has to be said that the people of those times who took part in what is called cultural life, who had absorbed some of the scientific world view and adopted some of the ideas permeating the age, all had more or less the same kind of mood. Whether or not they practised their old religious faith depended on their customary way of life, on their prejudices and so on; it was not dependent on strict adherence to what their souls had absorbed through the culture of the age. The people of these last fifty years lived in an uncertain, unstable relationship with the spiritual world. We can also find this uncertainty in other areas of life. A few years before the publication of Heyse's *Children of the World* and Du Bois-Reymond's *Limits of our knowledge of nature*, the well-known writer *Herman Grimm*[71] published *Invincible Forces*, also a novel. He depicts class prejudices and class differences within Occidental civilization as invincible forces. And interestingly in this novel he contrasts the class differences of Occidental civilization with what has developed out of a certain ahistorical and unusual situation in America as a life not having to contend with these class differences and prejudices. And it is interesting how at the end of the eighteen-sixties, also just about half a century ago,

Herman Grimm describes how, despite all their liberalism and all their humanism, the European people lack the strength to overcome these class differences. These are for him invincible forces.

If we go deeper and ask ourselves why such things are invincible forces for Europeans, then the answer must inevitably be that their thinking has become passive, this thinking that I have characterized for example as I spoke about *Richard Wahle*, as reaching only as far as 'events' and refusing to look into the determining factors behind them, which means wanting to apprehend only the phenomena, not the forces. This thinking has dominated the leading minds of the last fifty years. With such a thinking which contains no forces, but is merely thinking in feeble thought images, with such a thinking we are simply not able to overcome what exist in reality as class differences and class prejudices. To be able to overcome them we would need a thinking steeped in reality, a thinking permeated by reality. And this thinking permeated by reality, which actually created class differences in the old days, which created all of our society in the old days, this dynamic thinking, in contrast to mere descriptive thinking, has declined in the last fifty years within European civilization. It has declined in science, which is why it is now based only on observation and experiment; it has also declined in life so that people just continued to think in the old conventions deriving from class prejudices. They did not bother to think any further. For if they had tried to think further, they would have needed an active form of thinking. And as the proletarian class began to think about class differences, class distinctions, even this feeble thinking which has no dynamism was abandoned. They said that class differences have nothing to do with the forces in human thinking, they are completely dependent on economic, physical forces. They just drew the obvious conclusion.

So there you have what fifty years ago was the starting point of modern intellectual/spiritual life. And now I would like to show you a work that appeared just recently and which again is typical of our times; *Mirror Man* by *Werfel*.[72] Here you have something born out of the forces of our times, in a similar way to how *Children of the World* or *Invincible Forces* were born out of their times fifty years ago.

Now what is the situation today confronting people such as Werfel? In the last decades this feeble, impotent thinking has been in the ascendant. People had been searching for a connection to the religious, to the spiritual world, but there was nothing. However, human nature cannot remain so one-sided. It can remain so for about fifty years in the development of the world, but then human nature starts to react. So if we confine ourselves to the last fifty years we see that people struggled to find something more powerful than the feeble, impotent thinking of the times. Now many works of the present day are evidence of the striving for a more powerful understanding of reality, particularly, however, this *Mirror Man* by Werfel.

This *Mirror Man* by Werfel forces you to speak about the present as follows. People have sought long enough in a feeble and impotent way to find something that makes a human being fully human. Now a vague inner sense is making itself felt, a sense that along those paths where people have been searching for the last fifty years and which are not really paths at all but slippery slopes, where you are always falling over, that on these slippery slopes there is nothing to be found. We have to get more iron into our blood again. *Mirror Man* is a result of this kind of aspiration. I will just describe in a few words what this *Mirror Man* is all about. It is not my intent to criticize the artistic aspect. But that is not the point and as we will see, what I have to say also applies to this artistic aspect.

We see an immature human being, who has grown tired of the life of the world as it is now lived. He takes his leave of this outward life and his aim now is to become a human being. He admits to himself that in ordinary life as people lead it nowadays, in Asian, in European and in American civilization, it is not possible to become a human being. You get up in the morning, eat breakfast, then you go about some task that maintains your position in the social order, then you have lunch or you receive guests and talk about things which really do not need to be talked about and the only purpose of which is to move your lips, so that they have something to do; then you go for a walk with your guests and do whatever else it is you do nowadays. You cannot become a human being in such a social context. I am not relating this word for word; it is just a characterization. Thus if you want to become a human being you will have to try a different way of living. So now the hero—to use the old aesthetic style of referring to them—attempts to find a new way by applying to a monastery. He is told that this is an extremely difficult path. I will not go into details here, but only point out what is important for us today. He is told that it is a difficult path and that above all he must be quite aware that he will have to go through three stages of cognition. In the first stage of cognition he will have to become clear about the position of the human being in relation to the world insofar as this position is part of the human ego itself. So this life in the ego and the quest to overcome the ego is the first stage of cognition. After having begun in a sense to peel off the ego, the second level of world cognition would consist of no longer seeing the world from the point of view of his own advantage as he had done before he began to peel off the ego. The third stage would be that he would really understand the world and reality and not as someone does who lives in their ego. He is told all this. And he is warned not to be too vehement in this striving to become a human being. He is warned of the difficulties he will face. But he does not give up.

So then he is allowed to enter the Order. I only want to touch on the essentials. The initiation consists of him being alone in the night in a room where only one monk keeps watch over him. And there at first he is lost in thought, but then he falls asleep and after a short time he believes he has woken up. And now he finds himself in a room, on one wall of which is a mirror. He sees himself in this mirror and is astounded at what this means. What it means is that when a person orders their thoughts and reaches a strong decision such as he has done and then looks at their own mirror image, they will see themselves differently. We are shown that the hero is just beginning to see himself. The mirror image looks like him but somehow different. And then he does what must follow such an astonishing experience and smashes the mirror, believing that he has injured himself. But then out of the shards he finds himself confronted by the mirror man, who is both himself and in another way is not himself.

Now this person has attained the first level of cognition. He must get used to not only being in the world as an ego person—however, without ego consciousness—but to being in the world accompanied by the mirror man, which he is and also is not. Now this mirror man, who leads him on to all kinds of deeds in the outer world, is the embodiment of the encounter with the phenomena of the world and his own deeds in a completely new way, the confrontation with his own ego.

Now I will not go into great detail. In reality the person concerned is actually still lying in bed, but is going through all that he is able to go through according to his previous experiences of life in the outside world and his own deeds in it. This is not always pleasant. However, how someone describes it depends on their own personal taste. In the way the author describes it we can see what he thinks of it. Each person experiences events in the world in their own way. So we are guided through the events of the world. Just as Mephisto is the driving force in *Faust*, so this mirror man is here the driving force and the protagonist is led from one incident to the next and in some cases to do wrong. Everything appears to him in a new light, because he has looked in the mirror and seen himself. He sees all sorts of things in the world. Sometimes he sees things as they appear to him as an ego person and sometimes as they appear to him who has faced himself in the mirror. He continues to experience the world and in so doing leaves his ego ever more behind. The mirror man, who is at first quite thin, grows fatter and fatter. This is a polar-parallel phenomenon which is quite well described. And so this person lives on in the world and now that he has confronted his own ego he experiences what he would have experienced before in a completely different way. In the end he is so involved with events in the world that he becomes his own judge and sentences himself to death; again this is characteristic. He discovers that he cannot really live in the world.

When he entered the monastery, he was already aware that it is not possible to live in modern society if you want to become a human being. Now this has escalated to the point where he has become his own judge and has condemned himself to death. And now he wakes up. In a sense he wakes up at the moment of his death sentence. He is still in the same room. Now he looks at the mirror. However, as he does this, he notices that the mirror does not reflect a procession of monks who are just passing. Previously when he looked in the mirror it showed him himself and all else in front of it. But now a procession of monks is passing by and they are not reflected. Now he notices that he is not standing in front of a mirror, but that the mirror has become a window. He is looking through it and out into the world, into the countryside. He has attained the third level of cognition. After having seen only what the mirror offers, now he sees the whole world. By having had the mirror man at his side he saw what he had seen before but in a different way. Now, however, he is looking in a sense through the surface of things—this is how it is described—and into free reality. And of course it is hinted at that now he is seeing spiritual reality.

So here we have a trilogy. The first part is the mirror, the third is, let us say, the window. The mirror has become a window. Here are two world views which are polar opposites to one another. At first each person sees in the other person their own mirror image, sees in the other only what they have in themselves; when they are trapped in their ego they can only see in the next person or in some aspect of nature their own mirror image. At the end when they have broken through the mirror, they no longer see their reflection but see through the surface of things into the spiritual. And in between there is the stage where they both flow into each other.

1. The mirror;
2. one flows into the other;
3. the window.

Now I would like to point out two characteristics of this drama. The first is that we see the author's desire to depict a person rising up to a certain religious connection with another world. We can forgive the fact that the first part with the mirror is quite short, because it is interesting to see how the person finds their way into a vision of their own ego, so that this ego becomes so real that it accompanies them through the world. The middle part is more extensive and the author describes a number of experiences. To find this appealing you have to have a taste for it or not, as is the case. But as I said before, each person has to take it according to their personal taste. In any case this part where the protagonist is looking into his experiences in the world is rather long. The third part is quite short and what he sees outside is in a way only hinted at symbolically by looking through the window; it is not really described any further. As I said it is quite short. This is the one characteristic I would like to bring out. The other is that we have to recognize that here someone is striving in the nicest way to bring some juice, some power into thinking. And we see that a modern human being such as Werfel is not able to do so. Why not? That is rather strange. I have to say I read this drama with great interest because it seems to me symptomatic for our present intellectual life as represented by various individuals; but when I had finished reading I had to say to myself: The progression is firstly the mirror, secondly one flows into the other, then thirdly the window. However, we could just as well reverse the order and read it from back to front. And why? Because it is quite possible that we look at it in another way and then we could say that a person's attitude towards the world determines how things appear to them. The person is no different than the phenomena. They have not woken up to ego consciousness. So our protagonist stands at the window and looks out into the world. Now he has turned for help to the old monk, unable to stand any longer always just looking at things through the window; he wants to find himself. We could say that the old monk tells him that he will have to go through three stages of perception. The first one is the world but we cannot find ourselves, our ego in it. We lose ourselves in the world. The second stage is when we are just developing our ego and we see in the world a great multitude of beings. The world comes alive, becomes spiritualized. Before we saw it without spirit, now it becomes full of spirits. Everywhere, in every being, plant, animal, cloud and so on we see something spiritual. Numerous spiritual beings appear before us in this second stage of cognition. In the third stage we wake up. We go to the window and look out. We see everything anew; we see the real world for the first time. The window has turned into a mirror; the human being has become conscious. We encompass all these mirror beings, which appear to us in the world as plants, animals, clouds and so on within ourselves; in us they become our own self, that has now become cosmic. And so by perceiving our true selves we first perceive the cosmos.

So we could rewrite the whole thing from back to front: the last part of the trilogy first, then the middle part, then the part with which it began. This is extremely interesting, because it is exactly this which makes this drama so typical for our present age. What is so typical of intellectualism?

It is typical of intellectualism that you can start your thinking at any point and end it at any point as well, quite arbitrarily. You can argue in one direction and then in the other. I have often pointed this out. With thinking you can prove anything or disprove anything. Intellectualism is nothing but a system of feeble, impotent thoughts, which lets you start anywhere, move along to a certain point and then finish. However, we could just as well start at the point where we finished and move in the opposite direction.

Nowadays you can be quite an intelligent person and at the same time the crassest of materialists, because it is relatively easy to prove materialism. And if you are merely an intellectual then you can wage war intellectually from the point of view of monism against the spirit, as happened after a meeting in the wake of the anthroposophic congress in Vienna. You can easily prove that materialism is right. You can just as well be a spiritualist and easily prove that too. As long as you stick to the intellectual you can prove all these things and all these intellectual discussions appear to be completely conclusive.

This is the way it is in our times. People really have no idea how they weave a reality out of spiritualism, materialism, realism, idealism and how they are deluding themselves with this intellectual spirit. They think and rightly so: we can prove all this conclusively. They are creatures of materialism. And because it is true that we can prove all this conclusively, it becomes very bleak when we are forced to seriously discuss some aspect of reality and then to open the debate for 'general discussion'. Then one person says this, another that, the third something else. Basically if we are even only slightly awake, we can say that they are all right. By the same token they are also all wrong. All this chatter really only has one function: that perhaps one person or other notices how we are all deceiving ourselves by relying on intellectualism, because we can prove absolutely anything with it. It is just a question of settling into a particular belief or orientation, a sect or a party for example, and then you can say with complete conviction that it is all perfectly clear and anyone who thinks differently is an ass. Yes, but another person can just as well prove that the first one is an ass and they themselves are right. This is quite possible today for intellectual life has reached the point where such things are completely normal. And so it is also completely normal for someone to write such a piece without coming anywhere near any real spiritual knowledge. Werfel shows us that he comes nowhere near real spirituality by the fact that nothing of real value is seen through the window; spiritual knowledge would begin there where something significant is seen through the window. Only the three stages are depicted and then our protagonist awakes and looks out, but what he sees is not described. So that even after having made so many concessions to ordinary consciousness and actually writing this *Mirror Man,* the author stalls when he could really get to the point and reveal something of importance. And for example when confronted with my *Knowledge of the Higher Worlds—How is it Achieved?* or *Occult Science—An Outline* then all people can say is that if you really believe in such things then you are not in your right mind. So that if all we can allow is that the protagonist has arrived at the window, but we will be careful not to let him see anything through it, then we are not ready to truly enter into spiritual life, then we are really completely stuck in intellectualism.

This is why it is possible for me to say these things. Obviously, it is not legitimate to criticize a work of art from a philosophical point of view. However, my critique is not philosophical; what I have said is from an artistic viewpoint. Because what happens is that you read the trilogy with great interest, but at the end of it everything is upside down! This is an uncomfortable feeling, so in order to get back on your feet, you would have to rewrite the whole story from back to front. It would take quite a while to work your way back on to your feet. In fact it becomes absolutely clear that we are being cheated artistically, that behind this story the wheel of intellectualism is turning. A real work of art makes a different impression. A real work of art cannot be turned around. Just try to rewrite Goethe's *Faust* from back to front. You cannot do it! A work of art cannot be turned backwards. You can do it with this trilogy because the intellectualistic aspect dominates; it falls short of attaining a real vision. Now intellectualism has the vague, indeterminate feeling that thinking needs more juice and vitality, but in reality, it completely lacks juice and vitality; it is empty. There is only a kind of formula of a real inner experience. And so from this example, which shows us what the spirit of our times produces, we can see where the true path lies.

For fifty years now people have had the feeling that we have to move towards the spiritual, but they want to avoid the real path. They take up all sorts of old traditions such as the threefold path and so on. This threefold path is quite typical these days; you can find it in all kinds of books describing the old paths of atavistic clairvoyance.

As long as they forgo any presentation of what you can see through the window, the story can easily describe the mirror, the one flowing into the other and then the window and be a part of the intellectual life of the times. It is quite easy to describe if you only use these general terms. However, if we just stop there, we will never overcome this intellectualism, which has for so long fascinated modern society.

I have often pointed out this intellectualistic element in various contexts. For example when you go into some branch office of the Theosophical Society and find diagrams of all sorts of things hanging up: cultures, rounds, whole world systems, all sorts of wonderful intellectual constructions—all completely intellectualistic! And when they want to describe the structuring of the human being, there is a diagram: physical human being: dense physical matter; etheric body: finer matter; astral body: even finer; Kama-Manas: even finer; Manas: even finer, finer and finer. But all only grasped with the intellect! This 'finer, finer and finer' has no end! But it is all just intellectualistic. Just as we can keep on turning a wheel, when we stick to the intellectualistic we can keep making matter ever thinner and thinner. And so we had an intellectualistic theosophy. And here we have an intellectualistic piece of fiction, which even goes as far as mysticism, celebrated by many of our contemporaries and rightly so, because we can see in it the state of the search for the spiritual in our times.

My assessment is not unartistic. I look at the mirror man who accompanies the hero through all his evolution and this mirror man is something completely different from what we see in Mephisto towards Faust. There is life in *Faust*. As you know I have described how Mephisto is ultimately the other side of Faust, just as Wagner is. 'Thou art like the spirit thou dost know. Not me!'[73] You are like Wagner, you are like Mephisto and so on. But here there is life. There is no life when the self jumps out of the mirror, at first thin, then ever plumper and plumper as the hero's life diminishes.

The unalive, the abstract in other words, is what dominates this work from beginning to end. The abstract can always be turned on its head. And since we find no artistic vision, intense and full of juice, but only thought templates exaggerated into images, we sense something unartistic. And it is curious that such things are often defended by people saying that anthroposophy is just a striving for ideas and therefore unartistic. In reality anthroposophy strives for real vision, only of course people have to be ready for such a vision. We have to look through the window and see something. Here people are calling something artistic which has not really hatched, something just on the verge of being hatched, but which then prefers to remain inside the egg. You will understand what I mean with this image of the chicken which does not really want to come out of the egg and live in the world. It is as if a person wants to go down the path of knowledge but to avoid the spiritual world in all its actuality and realness. I will refrain from describing how the egg feels when the chicken does not hatch properly! But this is a fair description of what such minds produce when they refuse to see reality and hatch properly.

I do not intend to detract from the value of such works in any way. In this *Mirror Man* I see something of great worth for our present times. However, something like this has to be characterized from a higher point of view so that it can be situated accordingly in contemporary intellectual life, in contemporary cultural life, as I have here tried to do.

Thirteenth Lecture

DORNACH, 22 JULY 1922

Today I would like to bring another aspect of the cosmic view to our deliberations. As humans we have to be aware that in the time between birth and death we are on the earth and we perceive all the impressions we have through our senses and our intellect from the point of view of our situation on the earth. Often we become all too conscious of how closely we are bound to our external physical corporeality during our stay on earth. Nowadays we learn in school how human beings can only survive if we breathe the air, which consists of a specific combination of nitrogen and oxygen. Human earthly life is completely dependent on this air. We only have to consider how different our physical life would be if for example the air around us contained more oxygen than it already does.

If there was more oxygen mixed into the air then we would live faster, which means we would have a shorter lifespan reckoned in years on the earth. Time would be in a sense compressed and our lifespan would be shorter. This is basically just one rough example. We can imagine what would happen if any of the elements in our environment that affect us were changed only slightly and how our whole organism would be different. Nowadays people think more often about such things and are becoming more aware of the physical dependence of human beings on their environment. But people are at best only abstractly aware that humans have a soul-spiritual being and they never have such a clear idea about this soul-spiritual as they do about the physical. We know so much about the physical bodily aspect of our organization that we can say how a rise in oxygen saturation in the air would affect us. We do not think about our soul-spiritual being with the same intensity and consider for example that if the soul-spiritual were to be in some way different would it be able to exist on the earth between birth and death?

However, just as our physical body is adapted to the amount of oxygen in the air, just as many other aspects of our bodies are adapted to conditions on or near the surface of the earth, so between birth and death our soul-spiritual is adapted to what is directly on the surface of the earth. And if we become quite conscious of this then we have to say that just as a physical human body could not survive only a few miles above the surface of the earth, so the human soul with its thinking, feeling and willing could not survive if earthly conditions were different. The soul-spiritual would have to be organized in a different way in a different relationship to the earth. The physical human body would have no use for the lungs, as they are now organized, if it were to be lifted up miles above the surface of the earth and in the same way under other conditions the human soul would have no use for thinking, feeling and willing as they have developed on the earth.

Now we would not be able to attain any clear ideas about these things if it were not possible that people searching for inner soul development could achieve other soul experiences than those possible for normal thinking, feeling and willing. You all know from what I have described in my book *Knowledge of the Higher Worlds—How is it Achieved?* that you can achieve quite different soul moods, soul states and soul content. You can achieve a soul state which not only has ordinary thinking but also imagination, so that instead of in thoughts it lives in images. Then you can go further and reach inspiration. This is comparable to how our lungs breathe in air; the soul breathes in or inspires the soul-spiritual, the substance of the soul-spiritual, which permeates the world. And just as when the lungs breathe in oxygen, this gives them life, gives the whole body life, when the soul achieves higher knowledge and reaches inspiration, this gives it life. And it is the same with the next level of cognition, which is intuition.

Here the soul rises up to a completely different state and has a quite different experience. However, this different experience as you know is connected to what is tantamount to the soul leaving the body. When we achieve imagination, inspiration and intuition we have the feeling of no longer being inside the body in the way we are in our normal earthly life. Then the soul-spiritual is like a lung which has converted from breathing air to breathing light. And with such an organism it could live several miles beyond the earth. Now of course this is not possible in the physical, not for human beings, but for the soul-spiritual in us it is possible that when we leave the body and experience imagination, inspiration and intuition in our souls we leave the earthly view of the world and ascend to that view we had before we descended into the physical body, the cosmic view. Then we are simply no longer on the earth, but are looking at the earthly from another point of view. This is not really important when we are looking at human souls. But it is very significant when we are to get to know the spiritual in the cosmos itself. I will try to make this clear in a diagram.

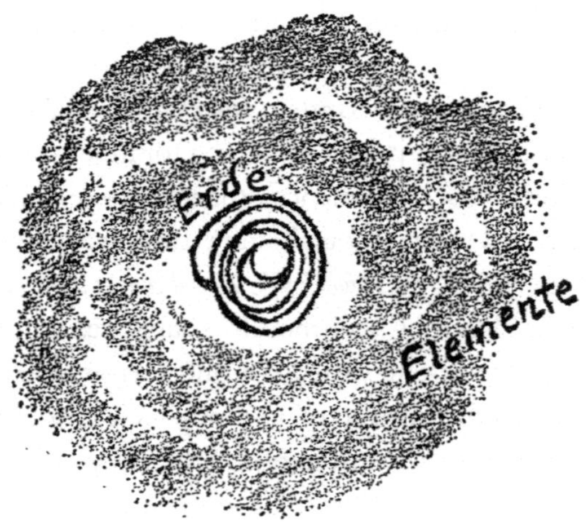

Erde = earth, Elemente = elements

Imagine that here is the earth, the human being on the earth. The human being sees the elements in the earthly environment—we can call them the solid, the fluid, the aeriform. They perceive the fiery, the warmth. Then, however, what belongs to the surface of the earth is at an end. By perceiving the fiery, the warmth, the person has already risen to the perception of the periphery of the earth.

They have reached the light, what we call the light ether. It is one of our peculiarities that by seeing, by looking, we can perceive the light ether. When, however, a person has achieved imaginative cognition then they feel as if they are no longer on the earth looking out into the light ether, but they have the feeling as if they are looking at the whole thing from outside [see diagram, below, red].

Now with regard to what I am discussing here we can explain relatively clearly how this happens. When you are standing somewhere on the earth and you let your gaze wander freely out into the cosmos then in the daytime you are always looking into the light. At night you see the stars in the sky. You are using what we might call the perceptive faculty of your eyes. But this perceptive faculty is always based on the power of the will. In the earthly act of seeing you actually only utilize this faculty of the will to adjust the focus of the eyes. When, however, you reach imaginative cognition then this faculty of will develops more and more for the individual senses. You can feel how in a way you ascend through the eyes out into space and how you can increasingly look at the cosmos from outside.

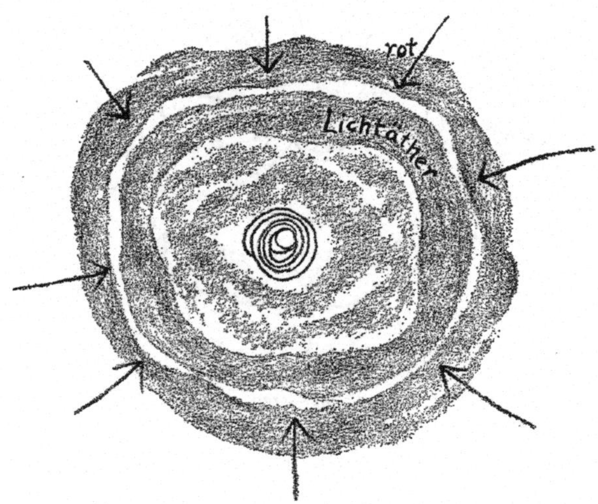

rot = red, Lichtäther = light ether

Now you must not think that what I am describing here means that your eye becomes enormous and grows out into space, so that you look at the cosmos from outside just as you now look at it from inside. It is not the faculty of perception which lets you do this, but the faculty of will, which becomes clairvoyant. It is an experience in the spreading out of the will and you are yourself inside this spreading out. In this case you are also looking at the stars from outside, just as someone who is in the spiritual world as a soul being also sees the stars from outside, from where there are no longer any stars, not from the realm of the etheric but from the astral realm, of which we can say space exists there but at the same time space no longer exists there. From what I have described, it is not really meaningful to speak as if space still existed there. You feel as if space were actually inside you. There you see no stars. You know you are looking at the stars but you see no stars, you see images. You actually see images all over the starry heavens. Suddenly it becomes clear why in ancient times when people depicted the spheres, they painted not just stars but images.

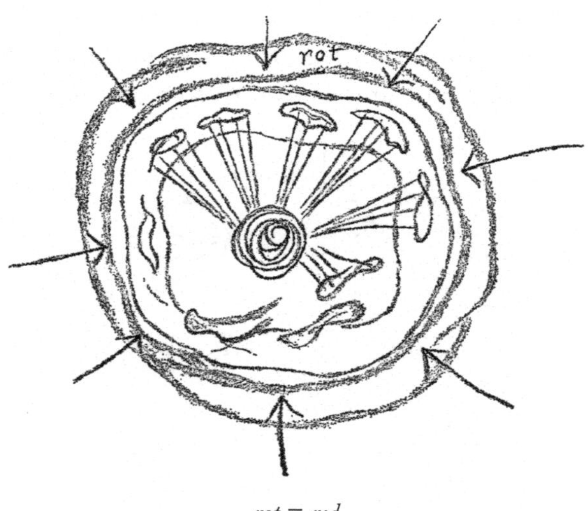

rot = red

Now imagine you are looking through these images. Then you notice that all these images are radiating forces down to the earth and that these radiating forces are bundled. When you look up at a shining star from down here on the earth, then you have the feeling that the rays are diverging. But when you look from outside you have the feeling that the rays, the light effects radiating from the images—they are not just light effects but also forces—are actually converging. They go down to the earth, these forces. And what do they do there? You see that they shape for example the plant forms. And someone who has imaginative vision would say that the lily is a plant form on the earth whose gestalt has been shaped by a particular group of stars. Another plant, a tulip for instance, has been formed by another group of stars.

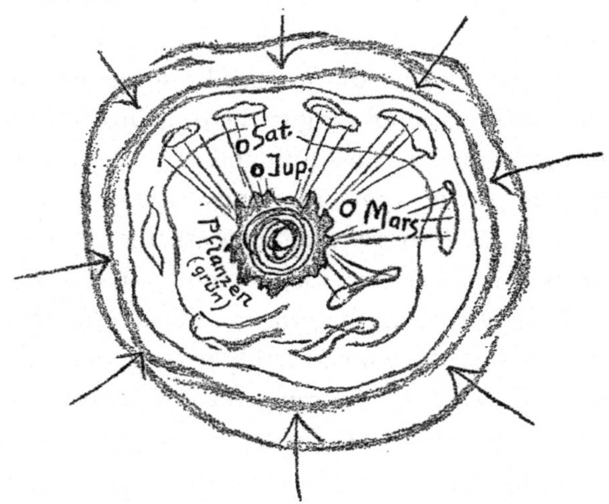

Pflanzen (grün) = plants (green), Sat. = Saturn, Jup. = Jupiter, Mars = Mars

So you see the plant cover on the earth [green] has actually been painted by the stars in the heavens. The actual shape of the physical body of the plant is determined by the cosmos, shaped by the cosmos. And now you can easily understand something more when you look further, when you look at the fixed stars and then you look at the planets, Saturn, Jupiter, Mars and so on, closer to the earth. They are moving. The fixed stars show you stationary constellations, which give the plants their form. But the moving planets send down moving forces. And it is these which draw the plants up out of their roots and let them grow higher and higher. Just as the form of the plants is shaped by the fixed stars, so their movement is shaped by the movements of those heavenly bodies closer to the earth. Only what goes on in the plant itself, the metabolism for example, by which the plant absorbs and assimilates carbon dioxide and then gives off carbon so that it can form the body of the plant, this comes from the earth itself. So we can say that if we look at the plant as a whole its form comes from the stars, its growth from the movement of the planets and its metabolism from the earth. Those who see themselves as the guardians of scientific thinking would think what I have said complete folly despite it being the actual truth. Such people who look at the form and growth of the plant as it is seen today resemble—and here I must offer an analogy I have often used—someone who looks at the needle of a compass pointing in the one direction towards the north and in the other to the south and says that it is inherent in the needle itself that it points as it does. It is not inherent in the needle, rather as modern research also assumes it is because the earth itself is an enormous magnet and attracts one end of the needle to the north and the other to the south. Here scientific research accepts that the whole earth participates in the direction of the compass needle. In the same way we have to assume that the whole of the cosmos participates in the gestalt of the plant. The plant is formed by the whole universe. It is just ridiculous that the same people who take the whole earth as participating in the direction of the compass needle want to explain the form of the plant as being inherent in the cells and forces within itself. Just as we can only understand the compass needle by including the whole context of the magnetic earth, so we can only understand the plant when we include the whole context of the cosmos. Then we can say for example here I am in Central Europe and here certain constellations are significant for the blossoming of the plants. This is why these plants grow here because the heavens let certain plants grow in certain regions.

If we want to look at plants from this point of view, meaning right down to their gestalt, then we have to look at the whole cosmos. With animals we only need to go as far as the constellations of the zodiac. I have already spoken about this. The stars beyond the zodiac have no influence on the animal kingdom. Thus in their organic development animals are already more autonomous and less dependent on the whole of the universe but only on what is in and within the zodiac.

Humans are even more autonomous, because they are influenced not as soul beings but as physical beings only by the planets. Only where they are moral or soul beings do we have to look further than the influence of the planets, as was the case in the ancient valuable forms of astrology, not, however, in the modern, amateurish forms that are left. From all this you can see that in as far as we are dealing with the external certain aspects are true for the plant. For animals their form is connected with the zodiac, their growth with the movement of the planets and their metabolism with the earth.

If we now come to human beings then we are no longer able to assign their form to any particular constellations, but only to the universe as a whole, not to individual groups of stars, but to the whole sphere. This is why I have said—and this is already being published—that in a certain way the human brain is an imprint of the whole starry sky,[74] not of any individual constellation of stars. So the whole sphere is for the form. Human growth, however, is in a sense also connected to the movements of the planets, but to all the movements of all the planets and not just to individual ones as is the case for plants and animals. And human metabolism is again connected to the earth.

> Plant: form, starry heavens; growth, planets; metabolism, earth.
> Animal: form, zodiac; growth, planets; metabolism, earth.
> Human beings: form, star sphere; growth, planets; metabolism, earth.

So where is the development in cognition? Basically up until the time of the Mystery of Golgotha nobody concerned with human knowledge had any doubts about what I have just explained to you. Even though this ancient knowledge was not the completely conscious knowledge that we strive for today in anthroposophy, still there was in those days a kind of dreamlike, clairvoyant cognition right up until the Mystery of Golgotha. And those people who were recognized as knowing about the world did not for a moment doubt when they looked at a flowering plant that they should connect it to a particular configuration in the star-studded sky. And it was the same with the other aspects.

Then this knowledge slowly disappeared in the first four centuries after the Mystery of Golgotha and after the old wisdom had been eradicated—I have often spoken about this—only that knowledge remained which was carried over into the Middle Ages and was already completely corrupt. We can find all this in the cheap books that those people, who refuse to concern themselves with new forms of cognition and want to stick to the old ways, love to read.

The knowledge that we are striving for in full consciousness today, cosmic knowledge whose images appear as phenomena on our earth, this did not appear in the form of conscious clairvoyance, but it did exist in a certain form nevertheless. Then its light dimmed more and more. Then for a long time human beings were preoccupied with what emerged from within them as artistic expression in drama, in dialectical thoughts, in the sounds and context of rhetoric, in the numbers of arithmetic, in the forms of geometry. After human beings had occupied themselves for several centuries with these artistic expressions of the forces in their souls the world view developed which no longer looked out into the cosmos, no longer asked what it is out there which enables the development of a lily flower, of a tulip. On the contrary that world view developed which when looking at the extraterrestrial only calculates the present position of the stars and only recognizes mathematics and at most mechanics and astrophysics as legitimate in this regard.

If the earth is here and there is a mole in the earth, then the mole has a certain view of the world. However, there is not much of a sun-like quality to this world view. In modern times human beings have lost the possibility of looking from a lily flower, from a tulip out into the heavens, just as a mole does not have the possibility of looking out beyond the darkness of the earth. Thus people are stuck in earth, water, air and fire. At the most they look out into the light as does an earthworm coming to the surface when it rains and perhaps seeing something of the light outside. Humans have gradually spun themselves into a life like that of a mole with regard to the spiritual world. Like a mole it is only what a person can find inside themselves, mathematical relationships for example, that they look for out in the cosmos. But they do not look for actual, spiritual reality out there in the cosmos. We could say that people can only attain an experience of freedom if they have for a while lived like a mole and looked at the lily without knowing that it is an image of the heavens, looked at the tulip without knowing that it is an image of the heavens. In so doing human beings have turned their faculties more towards the inside and so have attained an experience of freedom. However, now we are at a point when we must turn our attention towards the spiritual universe. What for centuries has appeared to us as a mathematical, mechanical structure in space we must now perceive with our soul-eye as a spiritual cosmos. We can even say that for centuries civilized humanity has led the spiritual life of a mole in order to develop human freedom; what humanity experiences is always meaningful. However, we have to understand this meaning and not get stuck at any one level of development, but move on with it and be clear that once humanity has developed the experience of freedom in their earthly mole-existence then they must again go beyond this mathematical world and into the spiritual cosmos.

Now try to envision what I have just explained to you. It is really the case that during the first four centuries CE the life of the soul became darker, that earlier people had looked out into the cosmos and seen the light of the spirit. In the first four centuries after the Mystery of Golgotha people still had this ability to see the spirit even though it was becoming darker and darker, but still they were able to perceive the Mystery of Golgotha, the Christ event, spiritually. The literature concerning the spiritual perception of this Christ event, however, was being destroyed. There is nothing left of this literature but what its opponents have written. Thus in relation to the Mystery of Golgotha human beings have only the seemingly simple descriptions of the Gospels, since the great depictions that the spiritualists of the first four centuries have given us are gone. We only have the descriptions of the opponents. We only have as much of the great descriptions of the Mystery of Golgotha as posterity would have of anthroposophy if they only read the writings of *Kully*.[75] I think people would not get an adequate idea from him. We should not forget how these four centuries have tried to eradicate all the most intensive knowledge that was still available when people could see into the cosmos and knew that Christ has come to the earth from the spiritual cosmos. We had to understand the spiritual cosmos in order to understand that the Christ had come from the spiritual world onto the earth and had incarnated in a human being. As it was, because humanity immersed itself in the earthly, all that was left were the memories of the Mystery of Golgotha. The memories were passed from generation to generation. And what were passed on as memories were then called revelations and people tried to understand them with the intellectualism that was already gaining ground.

So what is our responsibility towards all this? It is up to us to learn to look out into the cosmos and see spirit everywhere; not that we just immerse ourselves in ourselves and experience spirit inside us, but that we experience the spirit in all the formations of the cosmos out there. This is our task and must be undertaken. We must enter into the bright spirit of the whole cosmos, then we will see the Mystery of Golgotha in a new light.

I have described how in the last third of the nineteenth century this holding on to the Mystery of Golgotha in a mere confessional way had all but disappeared. I also said that at the beginning of the eighteen-seventies *Karl Julius Schröer* had already said that the religious controversies are really an anachronism. He thought that people were already striving for something completely different, a different kind of piety, a different kind of connection to the spiritual world. And basically it took these last fifty years to create such feeble attempts as the one I have shown you in *Mirror Man* by Werfel. Now other individual human beings are striving to find a connection to the spiritual world. However, you must not think that such a connection to the spiritual world is easy to find. The reason it is not easy to find is that nowadays we have a formidable authority in formalized science, in what is now practised officially everywhere as science. This is what has developed out of the activities of the mole. This is not meant in a derogatory way. I just want to characterize the situation and really not be derogatory, because essentially there has been much great work done since the fifteenth century by these cosmic moles that we call human beings.

Now if you cannot believe this then study for example the geography of the earthworms from the point of view of spiritual science. Of course this is a dreamlike geography but still it is marvellous; but it is not appropriate for human beings. And then examine the geography of the plants! In its etheric body a plant is not even able to dream, but what we can discover in this same etheric body is truly greater than anything that you can learn today in the various university departments. So I really do not mean it in a derogatory sense when I speak of the life of a mole, because I actually hold it in the highest esteem.

However, the world is evolving and now is the time when we have to engage again with the cognition of the soul, with the perception of the spiritual. Human beings will not be able to continue living without developing this soul-spiritual perception of the spiritual world. So we have to be completely clear about how this has affected us in the last fifty years. Here I would like to introduce another person who is typical for their times. With regard to human culture and its progress we can sometimes study how things have developed better by looking at the actual life of a person rather than describing things impersonally and in the abstract.

Now previously I have talked about *Brentano* and *Nietzsche* in order to show you what human souls went through in historical development. Today I want to show you something from the other side, namely how a person was perceived by other people.

In the eighteen-twenties, on 22 July 1822—today we celebrate his hundredth birthday—a certain *Gregor Mendel*[76] was born. I mentioned him recently because while we were in Vienna many articles about him were published as his hundredth birthday approached. This Gregor Mendel was born as the son of a farmer in Silesia and with great effort he managed to study and make good progress so that he was ordained as a priest at the age of twenty-four in Moravia. He became a Catholic priest. As a pupil at the grammar school and later at the

Catholic seminary Gregor Mendel was a good, even an exceptional student. In Austria in those days—the eighteen-forties or fifties—it was customary for an especially good and diligent student to receive a scholarship from their abbey or monastery. They would then be sent to university to train as secondary school teachers or grammar school teachers. Then almost all the teaching posts in grammar and secondary schools were filled with monks or priests—I mentioned this recently in my description of the trip to Vienna. In Austria priests were teachers at those schools that we call here the higher schools, right up to the universities.

Then Mendel was sent to Vienna to study mathematics and the exact sciences. After having studied for three years students were expected to take the State examination for teachers. Mendel came to the exam thinking that it would be no problem as he had always had excellent results. But he failed the State exam, had to take it again and failed again; a third try was not allowed, because if you had failed twice in such an important exam, you could not continue.

Then through all sorts of short cuts that were possible in the Austria of the times, a headmaster of a school in Moravia who was looking for a teacher, decided that as there was no one with good results and they needed a teacher, they would take Gregor Mendel. So for fifteen years he was a teacher in the secondary school there. We cannot dispute it: he became one of those priests who are secondary school teachers.

Then, however, he immersed himself in his passion for natural science and made numerous experiments on the subject of how inheritance functions especially in plants. He collected plants, for example some with a reddish flower and some with a white one. Then he pollinated those with the reddish flowers by those with the white flowers, with the result that the daughter plants all had reddish flowers. However, in the second generation it was different. There was a certain number of reddish flowers, white flowers and also mixed ones. In short Gregor Mendel said: I must look for the atomic, the atomistic in the plant world, in the organic world in general. Anyone who knows the history of intellectual life knows how much this subject of heredity occupied people's minds at that time. There were a great many theories of inheritance. But Gregor Mendel was not interested in all these theories; instead he planted his pea plants and observed how inheritance functioned when he pollinated a plant with a white flower by one with a reddish flower and looked at whether he got a reddish flowering plant, a white flowering one or a mixed one. Then he could determine the effects through generations, for example how the colours were inherited, how the inheritance in the pea plants changed under certain conditions and according to the scale of the experiment and so on.

Yesterday I described the times—the eighteen-sixties—when all this emerged that I have already discussed: what was in for example *Invincible Forces* by *Herman Grimm*, in *Children of the World* by *Paul Heyse*, in *Limits of our knowledge of nature* by *Du Bois-Reymond* and so on. Mendel's contribution was the determining of the principles of inheritance.

The learned examiners at the State examinations took the trouble to have him fail twice, so that they certified him twice as being entirely unsuited to teach grammar or secondary school pupils about science! And later on people just ignored him—in the library you will find the books he wrote about the laws of heredity practically covered in mould. Nobody was interested in them.

However, in the last twenty or twenty-five years you will find that people have started to be interested in Gregor Mendel. They unearthed his laws of heredity. Now we are on the brink of a very special phase of science. At the time when Herman Grimm tried to show that because it is not powerful enough the human intellect is unable to overcome class prejudice, at the time when Du Bois-Reymond uttered the word *ignorabimus* and Paul Heyse wrote *Children of the World*, the time when reason or intellect was becoming less and less juicy and powerful, but when people without formal religion were increasingly looking for a new piety and when scientists were at pains to develop a dehumanising atomism, in this time which lasted about fifty years, Gregor Mendel was attempting to develop a botanical and zoological atomism. He aimed to classify each plant according to its inheritance of reddish and white flowers, large and small, thicker and thinner blossoms and to study how existing thick or thin, reddish or white flowers are immutable, just as atoms are immutable. Then people would say that in carbon dioxide we have carbon and in hydrocarbon we also have carbon. Carbon dioxide is something completely different from hydrocarbon but we have carbon in both. The atoms that make up carbon are in carbon dioxide and in hydrocarbon the same.

Mendel said that he had here a reddish pea blossom and there a white one. Now they have children which are perhaps reddish. Then the children have children and some of them are reddish, some of them are white, some of them are mixed red and white. And then it continues. They too have children and among these are reddish ones, white ones, mixed ones and so on. Here we have the atomistic view of plants. If we only look at the colour, reddish or white, then in those plants where the flowers are red, the white is concealed; white is also there but is hidden inside. In the next generations of children it will come out, just as carbon is in carbon dioxide and in hydrocarbon, which are completely different from each other. This is the essential aspect of atoms, carbon is here and it is there; atoms are the same wherever they are, constant and eternal. The eternal atoms in the plant which pass on through heredity, are for example the colours, or whether the plant is thick or thin, large or small. The white remains; it is just sometimes concealed. Just as in water there is oxygen, so here in the children with reddish flowers the white is hidden and will re-emerge when there is an opportunity.

Gregor Mendel was really a great man; he discovered atomism, which had until then been applicable only to the world of inanimate objects, in the living world of plants; this was completely in accord with the spirit of the times. He also made very interesting observations in the animal realm even though he had twice failed the State exams. He did all this but at the time it was largely ignored.

Then came the time when, through the discovery of radium and so on, atomism in the world of objects was blown apart. Recently there was a lecture in Berlin[77] which seems to have explained this clearly; nowadays we can no longer hold on to this old idea of atomism. But people are unable to catch their breath quite so fast. Now, no longer being able to hold on to atomism, they are caught in a kind of breathlessness. Physics cannot go on as it was, chemistry also up to a point. So now after having let Gregor Mendel's work become covered in cobwebs, they have to dig out his laws of heredity and today you will find people discussing Mendelism everywhere; his principles of inheritance are a top priority one hundred years after he was born. In all the great academic institutions there are now centenary celebrations for Gregor Mendel.

It is an interesting life: the priest, who was completely ignored during his life and who failed the State exam twice, did manage to accomplish something that today is celebrated by academics the world over as an intellectual achievement of the first order. With Brentano I showed you the person from the inside, how he viewed the world, what he thought of the Vatican and the dogma of infallibility. With Nietzsche I tried to show you something similar. With Gregor Mendel, however, I wanted to show you how others regarded him. It is really interesting that the scholarly world had him fail the exams twice in a row, that at first he remained unknown and now he leads the world in relation to the so-called laws of heredity. What is this? Basically it is just the last stage of the development of intellectualism and also something else that I will talk about tomorrow.[78] We can see this last stage of intellectualism, the dying breaths of intellectualism so closely connected to atomism, in the relationship of Gregor Mendel to the world during his lifetime and also at the present time.

To be quite clear: I do not have the least desire to take any of this glory away from Gregor Mendel. On the contrary I used the occasion today to introduce you to a really great man, so that you are aware of who he was. He *is* a great man. But it is just by studying these great human beings and their inner and external destinies that we can study the evolution of humanity. We have to study this by means of the great individuals not the smaller ones, and Gregor Mendel is such a great one. You can be sure that I am more pleased that he is celebrated in many scientific institutes than I am that he failed his exams twice. You can be sure of that. The fate of Gregor Mendel is extremely interesting. And I would say that this clinging to atomism in the organic world is extremely typical for our times and belongs to all those phenomena that I have described to you these last few days and which I depicted yesterday from another point of view. Today I have described it from the point of view of Mendelism on the occasion of Johann Gregor Mendel's centenary.

NOTES

The lectures collected in this volume first appeared in this form in the first (German) edition of 1969. Rudolf Steiner did not intend the lectures to be printed, and he did not read them through himself.

The title of the volume goes back to Marie Steiner, who chose it for the first publication of the lecture from 25 June 1922.

Textual basis: The lectures were written down and transcribed in plain text by the professional stenographer Helene Finckh, who recorded most of Rudolf Steiner's lectures from 1916. The stenographs have been preserved and were taken into account in the publication.

1 spiritualistic fallacies: Rudolf Steiner on spiritualism, see the lectures 'History of spiritualism' and 'History of hypnotism and somnambulism' in GA 52, *Spiritualism, Madame Blavatsky and Theosophy*, and *The Occult Movement in the Nineteenth Century*, GA 254.

2 psychophysical parallelism: in this regard Rudolf Steiner liked to refer to the psychologist Hermann Ebbinghaus (1850–1909) (*An Outline of Psychology*, Leipzig, 1908).

3 Arthur Schopenhauer, 1788–1860. *The World as Will and Representation* was Schopenhauer's most important work (1819).

4 Herder on the dawn: Johann Gottfried Herder (1744–1803) *The Spirit of Hebrew Poetry* and *The Oldest Document of Humanity*, Vol I, Part IV: *Teachings at Dawn*, Riga, 1774.

5 Jacob Boehme, 1575–1624. *Aurora or the Dawning of the Day in the East*, Amsterdam, 1682.

6 From Goethe's *Faust*: 'Disciple, up!', Part I: 'Night', line 445/446.

7 Julian the Apostate, 332–363, Roman emperor 361–363.

8 in the days: The lecture was given at a time when there was a severe economic crisis after WW1.

9 small volume about the Lord's Prayer: *Das Vaterunser. Eine esoterische Betrachtung,* supplement to the GA Bibl., Nr. 95.

10   Novalis on mathematics: Novalis (Friedrich von Hardenberg, 1722–1801) *Mathematical Fragments* (many editions).

11   *Theosophy, An Introduction to the Supersensible Knowledge of the World and the Destination of Man* (1904) GA 9.

12   *Philosophy of Freedom, The Basis for a Modern World Conception* (1894), GA 4.

13   *Theosophy*, op. cit.

14   *Occult Science, An Outline* (1910), GA 13.

15   *How to Know Higher Worlds* (1904–1905), GA10.

16   aphorism that materialism: 'Psychological Aphorisms' in the journal *The Goetheanum*, Vol.1, 1921–22, nr. 47.

17   next time: see *Man and the World of Stars*, GA 219.

18   *Riddles of the Soul*, (1917) GA 21.

19   Franz Brentano, 1838–1917. *The Teaching of Jesus and its Enduring Significance.* Published posthumously by Alfred Kastil, Leipzig, 1922.

20   in the journal *The Goetheanum*: *The Teaching of Jesus* by Franz Brentano, 'Understanding Human Beings (Brentano and Nietzsche)', in GA 36, *Der Goetheanumgedanke inmitten der Kulturkrisis der Gegenwart*.

21   Clemens Brentano, 1778–1842, poet of the Romantic school. His mother, Maximiliane, 1757–1793, was a daughter of the writer Sophie La Roche, 1731–1807.

22   Thomism: *The Redemption of Thinking* , three lectures, Dornach 22–24 May 1920. GA 74.

23   Wilhelm Emanuel Baron Ketteler, 1811–1877, from 1850 on Bishop of Mainz.

24   Thesis of Franz Brentano: 'The true method of philosophy is none other than that of the natural sciences'. Published in: *On the future of Philosophy Posthumously* by Kramer, Leipzig, 1929.

25   about which I have spoken here recently: On 18 June 1922 in Vienna in *The Tension Between East and West*, GA 83.

26   Adolf Wilbrandt's *Guest of the Evening Star:* Adolf Wilbrandt (1837–1911); see also the volume in the library of Rudolf Steiner: Oskar Kraus: *Franz Brentano, Towards an Understanding of his Life and Teachings.* Munich, 1919, p. 13f.

27   a study of the soul without the soul: Friedrich Albrecht Lange coined the expression in his *History of Materialism,* Reclam edition, Vol. 2, p. 474. ('A Critique of Herbart and his School').

28   *Riddles of the Soul* (1917), GA 21.

29 Brentano: writings appearing after his death: *The Teaching of Jesus and its Enduring Significance* with the Appendix: 'A brief description of the Christian doctrine', Leipzig, 1922.

30 David Friedrich Strauss, (1808–1874), Protestant theologian and author.

31 modernism: a reform movement in the Catholic Church aiming at harmonising the Catholic faith with modern life at the end of the nineteenth century. Frowned upon by both Leo XIII (1899) and Pius X.

32 'Are we still Christians?', 'Do we still have religion?' These are the titles of Chapters 1 and 2 in Strauss's book *The Old Faith and the New, A Confession.* 1872.

33 *How to Know Higher Worlds,* op. cit.

34 Quotations from Brentano: from *The Teaching of Jesus and its Enduring Significance,* Leipzig 1922, p. 19, p. 37, p. 39.

35 *Occult Science, An Outline* (1910), GA 13. Op. cit.

36 Kant, who wanted to express this separation of knowledge and faith philosophically: In the Preface to the 2ⁿᵈ edition of *Critique of Pure Reason:* 'I had to deny knowledge in order to make room for faith.'

37 It is a lovely idea that Hegel gives us, when he says: 'Raising thinking above the sensible, going beyond the finite to the infinite, the leap which abandons the sensible for the supersensible, all this is thinking itself.' *Encyclopaedia of the Philosophical Sciences, An Outline.* Part 1. §50.

38 a great antipathy towards Fichte, Schelling and Hegel: 'Perhaps our most recent times are such an age of decadence in which all ideas flow murkily the one into the other and there is not even a trace of a skilled methodology. This being the case, the rapid rise and fall of opposing systems can no longer disconcert us.' Brentano, *On the Reasons for Discouragement in the Field of Philosophy,* Vienna, 1874, p. 18.

39 yet Hegel says: 'Hence logic is to be understood as the system of pure reason, as the realm of pure thought. This realm is truth unveiled, truth as it is in and for itself. It can therefore be said that this content is the exposition of God as he is in his eternal essence before the creation of nature and of a finite spirit.' In *Science of Logic,* Introduction.

40 that I have publicly mentioned an important fact: in *The Spiritual Guidance of the Individual and Humanity,* GA 15.

41 Adolf Fick, 1829–1901, physiologist. *The Forces of Nature and their Interdependence.* Popular lectures. Wuerzburg, 1869.

42   Julius Robert Meyer, 1814–1878, founder of the mechanical theory of warmth.

43   Hermann von Helmholtz, 1821–1894, natural scientist.

44   Rudolf Clausius, 1822–1888, physicist.

45   James Prescott Joule, 1818–1889, physicist.

46   I am only quoting Adolf Fick himself: see note 41 above, sixth lecture: 'Conclusions as to the fate of the universe'.

47   Carl Vogt, 1817–1895, zoologist and physiologist.

48   Ernst Wilhelm von Bruecke, 1819–1892, physiologist.

49   Richard Wahle, 1857–1935, philosopher. *The Whole of Philosophy and its End, its Legacy for Theology, Physiology, Aesthetics and Public Education,* Vienna, 1894, p. 538 (Conclusion).

50   first lecture in Vienna: 'Anthroposophy and Natural Science', 1 June 1922 in *The Tension Between East and West,* GA 83.

51   *Riddles of Philosophy,* (1914), GA 18.

52   Brentano on Meditation: *Memories of Franz Brentano by Carl Stumpf* in *Franz Brentano: Notes on his life and teachings* by Oskar Kraus, Munich, 1919. In the Appendix: 'Who does not meditate', Brentano wrote to me in Goettingen on New Year's Eve '67, 'seems to me not really to live and a philosopher who does not cultivate and practise meditation, does not earn the name, he is no philosopher but a scientific artisan and of all the philistines the most philistine. For the Lord's sake do not allow yourself to be diverted from your decision to devote a little time every day to meditation. Disloyalty to the resolutions that God has given you would come back to haunt you. Then perhaps the most precious of life's incipient blossoms would wither and die. If I could only make it clear how terrible this loss would be! I am not able but I can say this most truthfully: I would rather throw all my scholarly life to the wind and would rather die than to relinquish meditation.'

53   last edition of *The Goetheanum,* Vol. 1, Nr. 49.

54   Friedrich Nietzsche, 1844–1900. *The Birth of Tragedy out of the Spirit of Music,* 1872; *Philosophy in the Tragic Age of the Greeks,* 1873, a fragment; *Richard Wagner in Bayreuth,* 1876 inter alia.

55   *Twilight of the Idols or How to Philosophize with a Hammer,* 1889.

56   Emil Du Bois-Reymond, 1818–1896. 'Limits of our Knowledge of Nature'—a lecture in the 2nd public session of the 45th Assembly of German Natural Scientists in Leipzig on 14 August 1872, 1st edition 1872; the quotation from page 26 word for word: 'It is absolutely and

forever inconceivable that a number of carbon, hydrogen, nitrogen, oxygen etc atoms should not be indifferent as to their own position and motion, past, present, or future.'

57   congress in Vienna: Second international congress of the anthroposophic movement in Vienna, 1–12 July 1922, see also note 50.

58   the opponents called a meeting: In a room in the town hall a few weeks after the West-East Congress. There was a discussion between the opponents and the supporters of anthroposophy (information from Dr H. E. Lauer who took part in the meeting).

59   book about natural history: Probably means the work *De Vegetabilibus* by Albertus Magnus.

60   Albertus Magnus, 1193–1280, Dominican, known as 'Doctor universalis'.

61   Du Bois-Reymond called this the head of Laplace: In the lecture cited above (note 56) on page 13f. it says: 'But the spirit Laplace was thinking of, who knew the world formula, could have said this.'

62   Plotinus, 205–270, main representative of Neoplatonism.

63   Brentano on Plotinus: *What Kind of Philosopher Sometimes Makes the Epoch?* Brentano, Vienna, 1876.

64   Paul Deussen, 1845–1919, philosopher, Indologist. *Philosophy of the Greeks*, 2nd edition, Leipzig 1919, p. 272: 'In the platonic system there is no room for a personal God as the creator of the world, for as we have seen ideas exist through themselves, but would no longer do so and would need a whole new system with a different structure if we were to assume a personal God as the highest principle. That all ideas are dependent on the idea of the good makes no difference to their glory, since the idea of the good is, as we have shown on page 263, none other than the expediency of a common family type of all ideas, which seems to Plato to be special and to dominate all other ideas.' Page 263: '…this highest peak of the world of ideas is the idea of good. Plato compares it to the sun'.

65   Ammonius Saccas (=carrier of the sack), 175–242, founder of Neoplatonism, teacher of Plotinus. With regard to what Rudolf Steiner says about the Neoplatonists see also lectures from 6 November 1921 in GA 208; 24 April 1922 in GA 211; 23 July 1922 in GA 214; 1 October 1922 in GA 216 as well as Emil Bock: *The Life and Times of Rudolf Steiner*, Stuttgart 1961.

66   Iamblichus, died ca. 330, continued the teachings of Plotinus.

67   supposed to be a sermon of the Apostle Peter: The so-called mission sermon of Peter. See also *New Testament Apocrypha*, edited by Edgar Henneke, Tuebingen 1924, p. 145.

68   Henrick Ibsen, 1828–1906. *Emperor and Galilean*, two parts, 1873.

69   Paul Heyse, 1830–1914. *Children of the World*, 3 volumes, 1873.

70   Karl Julius Schröer, 1825–1900, literary researcher and linguist. Taught Rudolf Steiner at the Institute of Technology in Vienna; see also *Autobiography*, GA 28.

71   Herman Grimm, 1828–1901. *Invincible Forces*, 3 volumes, 1867.

72   Franz Werfel, 1890– 1945. *Mirror Man. A Magical Trilogy*, 1920. See also the essay by Rudolf Steiner in *Das Goetheanum*, 30 July 1922, now in GA 36, *Der Goetheanumgedanke inmitten der Kulturkrisis der Gegenwart*.

73   'Thou art like the spirit thou dost know. Not me!' *Faust*, Part 1: 'Spirit of the Earth'. Line 512.

74   the human brain is an imprint of the whole starry sky: in *The Spiritual Guidance of the Individual and Humanity*, GA 15.

75   Max Kully, 1878–1936, Catholic vicar of Arlesheim, writer of pamphlets attacking Rudolf Steiner and anthroposophy.

76   Gregor Mendel, 1822–1884. So-called 'Mendel's laws' = crossbreeding experiments on pea varieties. Writings: *Experiments on Plant Hybrids*, 1865; *On Some Bastards of Hieracium*, 1865.

77   lecture in Berlin: Walther Nernst, 1864–1941, *On the Validity of Natural Laws*, Berlin, 1921.

78   something else that I will talk about tomorrow: see lecture 1 in *The Mystery of the Trinity*, GA 14.

Rudolf Steiner's Collected Works

The German Edition of Rudolf Steiner's Collected Works (the *Gesamtausgabe* [GA], published by Rudolf Steiner Verlag, Dornach, Switzerland) will be completed in the year 2025. The works are organized either by type of work (written, spoken, artistic creations), chronology, audience (public or other), or subject (education, art, etc.). For ease of comparison, the Collected Works in English (CW), listed below, follows the German organization and numbering.

The volumes that have so far been published in the English Collected Works edition appear *in italics with their published titles*; all other volumes, including those that have appeared in editions other than the CW, are set in Roman type with *literal translations* of the German titles. Published English titles are not necessarily the same as the German.

This list is current as of the date of this volume's publication.

A. Written Works

I. Writings 1884–1925

CW 1	Introductions and Selected Commentary on Goethe's Natural-scientific Writings
CW 1a–e	Goethe's Natural-scientific Writings
CW 1f	Editorial Afterwords to Goethe's Natural-scientific Writings in the Weimar Edition (1891–1896)
CW 2	*Goethe's Theory of Knowledge: An Outline of the Epistemology of His Worldview*
CW 3	Truth and Science
CW 4	The Philosophy of Freedom
CW 4a	Documents to "The Philosophy of Freedom"
CW 5	Friedrich Nietzsche, A Fighter against His Own Time

CW 6	Goethe's Worldview
CW 7	Mysticism at the Dawn of Modern Spiritual Life and Its Relationship with Modern Worldviews
CW 8	*Christianity as Mystical Fact and the Mysteries of Antiquity*
CW 9	Theosophy: An Introduction into Supersensible World Knowledge and Human Purpose
CW 10	How Does One Attain Knowledge of Higher Worlds?
CW 11	From the Akasha-Chronicle
CW 12	Levels of Higher Knowledge
CW 13	Occult Science in Outline
CW 14	*Four Modern Mystery Dramas*
CW 15	The Spiritual Guidance of the Individual and Humanity
CW 16/17	*A Way of Self-Knowledge & The Threshold of the Spiritual World*
CW 18	The Riddles of Philosophy in Their History, Presented as an Outline
CW 18a	Views of the World and of Life in the Nineteenth Century
CW 19	Thoughts during the Time of War (1915) and Further Texts on the Events of the World War (1917–1921)
CW 20	The Riddles of the Human Being: Articulated and Unarticulated in the Thinking, Views and Opinions of a Series of German and Austrian Personalities
CW 21	The Riddles of the Soul
CW 22	Goethe's Spiritual Nature and Its Revelation in "Faust" and through the "Fairy Tale of the Snake and the Lily"
CW 23	The Central Points of the Social Question in the Necessities of Life in the Present and the Future
CW 24	Essays Concerning the Threefold Division of the Social Organism and the Period 1915–1921
CW 25	Three Steps of Anthroposophy. Philosophy – Cosmology – Religion
CW 26	Anthroposophical Leading Thoughts
CW 27	Fundamentals for Expansion of the Art of Healing according to Spiritual-Scientific Insights
CW 28	*Autobiography: Chapters in the Course of My Life: 1861–1907*

II. Collected Essays

CW 29	Collected Essays on Dramaturgy, 1889–1900
CW 30	Methodical Foundations of Anthroposophy: Collected Essays on Philosophy, Natural Science, Aesthetics and Psychology, 1884–1901
CW 31	Collected Essays on Culture and Current Events, 1887–1901
CW 32	Collected Essays on Literature, 1884–1902
CW 33	Biographies and Biographical Sketches, 1894–1905

CW 34	Lucifer-Gnosis: Foundational Essays on Anthroposophy and Reports from the Periodicals "Luzifer" and "Lucifer-Gnosis," 1903–1908
CW 35	Philosophy and Anthroposophy: Collected Essays, 1904–1923
CW 36	The Goetheanum-Idea in the Middle of the Cultural Crisis of the Present: Collected Essays from the Periodical "Das Goetheanum," 1921–1925
CW 37	Writings on the History of the Anthroposophical Movement and Society 1902–1925

III. Publications from the Literary Estate

CW 38/1	Complete Letters, Vol. 1: Weimar Period 1879–1890
CW 38/2	Complete Letters, Vol. 2: Weimar Period 1890–1897
CW 38/3	Complete Letters, Vol. 3: Early Berlin Period 1897–1905 [forthcoming]
CW 38/4	Complete Letters, Vol. 4: Activity within the Theosophical Society 1905–1912 [forthcoming]
CW 38/5	Complete Letters, Vol. 5: From the Founding of the Anthroposophical Society to the Opening of the Goetheanum 1913–1920 [forthcoming]
CW 38/6	Complete Letters, Vol. 6: The Last Years 1920–1925 [forthcoming]
CW 40	Truth-Wrought Words
CW 40a	Sayings, Poems and Mantras; Supplementary Volume
CW 41a	Translations and Free Renderings from the Old and New Testaments
CW 41b	Translations and Free Renderings of Various Works
CW 42	Stage Adaptations I: Dramas by Edouard Schuré
CW 43	Stage Adaptations II: The Oberufer Christmas Plays
CW 44	Sketches, Fragments and Paralipomena on the Four Mystery Dramas
CW 45	Anthroposophy: A Fragment from the Year 1910
CW 46	Posthumous Essays and Fragments 1879–1924
CW 47/48	Notebooks and Notepads (digital edition)
CW 49	Notes for and about Helmuth and Eliza von Moltke and Relatives, 1904–1924 [forthcoming]
CW 50	[Blank number]

B. Lectures

I. Public Lectures

CW 51	*On Philosophy, History, and Literature: Lectures at the Worker Education School and the Independent College, Berlin, 1901–1905*
CW 52	Spiritual Teachings Concerning the Soul and Observation of the World

II. Lectures to the Members of the Anthroposophical Society

The Theosophy in the Gospel of John

III. Lectures and Courses on Specific Realms of Life Lectures on Art

CW 273	*Goethe's* Faust *in the Light of Anthroposophy: Volume Two of Spiritual-Scientific Commentaries on Goethe's* Faust
CW 274	Addresses for the Christmas Plays from the Old Folk Traditions
CW 275	Art in the Light of Mystery Wisdom
CW 276	*The Arts and Their Mission*
CW 277a	The Origin and Development of Eurythmy 1912–1918
CW 277b	The Origin and Development of Eurythmy 1918–1920
CW 277c	The Origin and Development of Eurythmy 1920–1922 [forthcoming]
CW 277d	The Origin and Development of Eurythmy 1923–1924 [forthcoming]
CW 278	Eurythmy as Visible Song
CW 279	*Eurythmy as Speech Made Visible: Speech Eurythmy Course*
CW 280	The Method and Nature of Speech Formation
CW 281	The Art of Recitation and Declamation
CW 282	Speech Formation and Dramatic Art
CW 283	The Nature of the Musical Element and the Experience of Tone in the Human Being
CW 284	*Rosicrucianism Renewed: The Unity of Art, Science & Religion: The Theosophical Congress of Whitsun 1907*
CW 285	[Blank number]
CW 286	Paths to a New Style of Architecture. "And the Building Becomes Man"
CW 287	*Architecture as Peacework: The First Goetheanum, Dornach, 1914*
CW 288	*Architecture, Sculpture, and Painting of the First Goetheanum*
CW 289	The Building-Idea of the Goetheanum: Lectures with Slides from the Years 1920–1921
CW 290	*Toward a New Theory of Architecture: The First Goetheanum in Pictures [no longer in the German GA]*
CW 291	The Being of Colours
CW 291a	Knowledge of Colours. Supplementary Volume to "The Being of Colours"
CW 292	*Art History as a Reflection of Inner Spiritual Impulses*

Lectures on Education

CW 293	General Knowledge of the Human Being as the Foundation of Pedagogy
CW 294	The Art of Education: Methodology and Didactics
CW 295	The Art of Education: Seminar Discussions and Lectures on Lesson Planning
CW 296	The Question of Education as a Social Question
CW 297	The Idea and Practice of the Waldorf School

Lectures on Medicine

Lectures on Natural Science

CW 320   Spiritual-Scientific Impulses for the Development of Physics 1: The First Natural-Scientific Course: Light, Colour, Tone, Mass, Electricity, Magnetism

CW 321   Spiritual-Scientific Impulses for the Development of Physics 2: The Second Natural-Scientific Course: Warmth at the Border of Positive and Negative Materiality

CW 322   The Borders of the Knowledge of Nature

CW 323   *Interdisciplinary Astronomy: Third Scientific Course*

CW 324   Nature Observation, Mathematics, and Scientific Experimentation and Results from the Viewpoint of Anthroposophy

CW 324a   The Fourth Dimension in Mathematics and Reality

CW 325   Natural Science and the World-Historical Development of Humanity since Ancient Times

CW 326   The Moment of the Coming Into Being of Natural Science in World History and Its Development Since Then

CW 327   *Agriculture: Spiritual-Scientific Foundations for Agricultural Renewal*

Lectures on Social Life and the Threefold Arrangement of the Social Organism

CW 328   The Social Question

CW 329   The Liberation of the Human Being as the Foundation for a New Social Form

CW 330   The Renewal of the Social Organism

CW 331   Work-Council and Socialization

CW 332a   The Social Future

CW 332b   Lectures and Speeches on Social and Economic Issues

CW 333   *Freedom of Thought and Societal Forces: Implementing the Demands of Modern Society*

CW 334   From the Unified State to the Threefold Social Organism

CW 335   The Crisis of the Present and the Path to Healthy Thinking

CW 336   The Great Questions of the Times and Anthroposophical Spiritual Knowledge

CW 337a   Social Ideas, Social Realities, Social Practice, Vol. 1: Question-and-Answer Evenings and Study Evenings of the Alliance for the Threefold Social Organism in Stuttgart, 1919–1920

CW 337b   Social Ideas, Social Realities, Social Practice, Vol. 2: Discussion Evenings of the Swiss Alliance for the Threefold Social Organism

CW 338   *Communicating Anthroposophy: The Course for Speakers to Promote the Idea of Threefolding*

CW 339   Anthroposophy, Threefold Social Organism, and the Art of Public Speaking

CW 340/41   *Rethinking Economics: Lectures and Seminars on World Economics*

Lectures and Courses on Christian Religious Work

CW 342   *First Steps in Christian Religious Renewal: Preparing the Ground for The Christian Community*

CW 343   Lectures and Courses on Christian Religious Work, Vol. 2: Spiritual Knowledge – Religious Feeling – Cultic Doing

CW 344   Lectures and Courses on Christian Religious Work, Vol. 3: Lectures at the Founding of The Christian Community

CW 345   Lectures and Courses on Christian Religious Work, Vol. 4: Concerning the Nature of the Working Word

CW 346   Lectures and Courses on Christian Religious Work, Vol. 5: The Apocalypse and the Work of the Priest

Lectures for Workers at the Goetheanum

CW 347   The Knowledge of the Nature of the Human Being According to Body, Soul and Spirit. On Earlier Conditions of the Earth

CW 348   On Health and Illness. Foundations of a Spiritual-Scientific Doctrine of the Senses

CW 349   On the Life of the Human Being and of the Earth. On the Nature of Christianity

CW 350   Rhythms in the Cosmos and in the Human Being. How Does One Come To See the Spiritual World?

CW 351   The Human Being and the World. The Influence of the Spirit in Nature. On the Nature of Bees

CW 352   Nature and the Human Being Observed Spiritual-Scientifically

CW 353   The History of Humanity and the World-Views of the Folk Cultures

CW 354   The Creation of the World and the Human Being. Life on Earth and the Influence of the Stars

C. Artistic Works

CW A 1–10; 57 The Architectural Work I: The Goetheanum and Its Predecessors

CW A 11   The Sculptural Work

CW A 12   The Goetheanum Windows. The Speech of Light. Sketches and Studies

CW A 13–16;
52–56   Painting Work
CW A 14   Sketches for the Painting of the Small Dome of the First Goethe-
               anum
CW A 27–43 The Architectural Work II: Commercial and Residential Buildings
               in Dornach and Other Places [forthcoming]
CW A 45   The Graphic Work
CW A 48   The Drawing Work
CW A 51   The Art of Jewellry as a Goethean Language of Form
CW A 54.0   A Path of Training in Painting. Pastel Sketches and Watercolours
CW A 54.1   Nature Moods. Nine Training Sketches for Painters

Eurythmy Figures

CW A 26   Skectches of the Eurythmy Figures
CW A 26a   The Eurythmy Figures of Rudolf Steiner, Artistically Executed by
               Annemarie Bäschlin
CW A 26b   Eurythmy Figures from the Time When They Were Created

Eurythmy Forms

CW A 23/1   Volume I: Eurythmy Forms for Poems by Rudolf Steiner
CW A 23/2   Volume II: Eurythmy Forms for the Calendar of the Soul by
               Rudolf Steiner
CW A 23/3   Volume III: Euythmy Forms for Poems by J. W. von Goethe
CW A 23/4   Volume IV: Eurythmy Forms for Poems by Christian Morgen-
               stern
CW A 23/5   Volume V: Eurythmy Forms for Poems by Albert Steffen
CW A 23/6   Volume VI: Eurythmy Forms for German Poems by Fercher von
               Steinwand, Hamerling, Hebbel, C. F. Meyer, Nietzsche, among oth-
               ers
CW A 23/7   Volume VII: Eurythmy Forms for English Poems
CW A 23/8   Volume VIII: Eurythmy Forms for French and Russian Poems
CW A 24   Volume IX: Eurythmy Forms for Tone Eurythmy

Blackboard Drawings from Lectures

CW A 58/1   Volume I: 20 Plates from Public Lectures 1920–1924 in CWs 73a,
               74, 76, and 84
CW A 58/2   Volume II: 38 Plates from Lectures in 1919 in CWs 191 and 194
CW A 58/3   Volume III: 34 Plates from Lectures in 1920 in CWs 196 and 198
CW A 58/4   Volume IV: 33 Plates from Lectures in 1920 in CWs 199 and 200
CW A 58/5   Volume V: 31 Plates from Lectures in 1920 in CW 201
CW A 58/6   Volume VI: 46 Plates from Lectures 1920–1921 in CWs 202–204

SIGNIFICANT EVENTS IN THE LIFE OF
RUDOLF STEINER

1829: June 23: birth of Johann Steiner (1829–1910)—Rudolf Steiner's father—in Geras, Lower Austria.

1834: May 8: birth of Franciska Blie (1834–1918)—Rudolf Steiner's mother—in Horn, Lower Austria. 'My father and mother were both children of the glorious Lower Austrian forest district north of the Danube.'

1860: May 16: marriage of Johann Steiner and Franciska Blie.

1861: February 25: birth of *Rudolf Joseph Lorenz Steiner* in Kraljevec, Croatia, near the border with Hungary, where Johann Steiner works as a telegrapher for the South Austria Railroad. Rudolf Steiner is baptized two days later, February 27, the date usually given as his birthday.

1862: Summer: the family moves to Mödling, Lower Austria.

1863: The family moves to Pottschach, Lower Austria, near the Styrian border, where Johann Steiner becomes stationmaster. 'The view stretched to the mountains . . . majestic peaks in the distance and the sweet charm of nature in the immediate surroundings.'

1864: November 15: birth of Rudolf Steiner's sister, Leopoldine (d. November 1, 1927). She will become a seamstress and live with her parents for the rest of her life.

1866: July 28: birth of Rudolf Steiner's deaf-mute brother, Gustav (d. May 1, 1941).

1867: Rudolf Steiner enters the village school. Following a disagreement between his father and the schoolmaster, whose wife falsely accused the boy of causing a commotion, Rudolf Steiner is taken out of school and taught at home.

1868: A critical experience. Unknown to the family, an aunt dies in a distant town. Sitting in the station waiting room, Rudolf Steiner sees her 'form', which speaks to him, asking for help. 'Beginning with this experience, a new soul life began in the boy, one in which not only the outer trees and mountains spoke to him, but also the worlds that lay behind them. From this moment on, the boy began to live with the spirits of nature . . .'

1869: The family moves to the peaceful, rural village of Neudorfl, near Wiener Neustadt in present-day Austria. Rudolf Steiner attends the village school. Because of the 'unorthodoxy' of his writing and spelling, he has to do 'extra lessons'.

1870: Through a book lent to him by his tutor, he discovers geometry: 'To grasp something purely in the spirit brought me inner happiness. I know that I first learned happiness through geometry.' The same tutor allows him to draw, while other students still struggle with their reading and writing. 'An artistic element' thus enters his education.

1871: Though his parents are not religious, Rudolf Steiner becomes a 'church child', a favourite of the priest, who was 'an exceptional character'. 'Up to the age of ten or eleven, among those I came to know, he was far and away the most significant.' Among other things, he introduces Steiner to Copernican, heliocentric cosmology. As an altar boy, Rudolf Steiner serves at Masses, funerals, and Corpus Christi processions. At year's end, after an incident in which he escapes a thrashing, his father forbids him to go to church.

1872: Rudolf Steiner transfers to grammar school in Wiener-Neustadt, a five-mile walk from home, which must be done in all weathers.

1873–75: Through his teachers and on his own, Rudolf Steiner has many wonderful experiences with science and mathematics. Outside school, he teaches himself analytic geometry, trigonometry, differential equations, and calculus.

1876: Rudolf Steiner begins tutoring other students. He learns bookbinding from his father. He also teaches himself stenography.

1877: Rudolf Steiner discovers Kant's *Critique of Pure Reason,* which he reads and rereads. He also discovers and reads von Rotteck's *World History.*

1878: He studies extensively in contemporary psychology and philosophy.

1879: Rudolf Steiner graduates from high school with honours. His father is transferred to Inzersdorf, near Vienna. He uses his first visit to Vienna 'to purchase a great number of philosophy books'—Kant, Fichte, Schelling, and Hegel, as well as numerous histories of philosophy. His aim: to find a path from the 'I' to nature.

October
1879–1883: Rudolf Steiner attends the Technical College in Vienna—to study mathematics, chemistry, physics, mineralogy, botany, zoology,

biology, geology, and mechanics—with a scholarship. He also attends lectures in history and literature, while avidly reading philosophy on his own. His two favourite professors are Karl Julius Schröer (German language and literature) and Edmund Reitlinger (physics). He also audits lectures by Robert Zimmermann on aesthetics and Franz Brentano on philosophy. During this year he begins his friendship with Moritz Zitter (1861–1921), who will help support him financially when he is in Berlin.

1880:   Rudolf Steiner attends lectures on Schiller and Goethe by Karl Julius Schröer, who becomes his mentor. Also 'through a remarkable combination of circumstances', he meets Felix Koguzki, a 'herb gatherer' and healer, who could 'see deeply into the secrets of nature'. Rudolf Steiner will meet and study with this 'emissary of the Master' throughout his time in Vienna.

1881:   January: '... I didn't sleep a wink. I was busy with philosophical problems until about 12:30 a.m. Then, finally, I threw myself down on my couch. All my striving during the previous year had been to research whether the following statement by Schelling was true or not: *Within everyone dwells a secret, marvellous capacity to draw back from the stream of time—out of the self clothed in all that comes to us from outside—into our innermost being and there, in the immutable form of the Eternal, to look into ourselves.* I believe, and I am still quite certain of it, that I discovered this capacity in myself; I had long had an inkling of it. Now the whole of idealist philosophy stood before me in modified form. What's a sleepless night compared to that!'
Rudolf Steiner begins communicating with leading thinkers of the day, who send him books in return, which he reads eagerly.

July: 'I am not one of those who dives into the day like an animal in human form. I pursue a quite specific goal, an idealistic aim—knowledge of the truth! This cannot be done offhandedly. It requires the greatest striving in the world, free of all egotism, and equally of all resignation.'

August: Steiner puts down on paper for the first time thoughts for a 'Philosophy of Freedom'. 'The striving for the absolute: this human yearning is freedom.' He also seeks to outline a 'peasant philosophy', describing what the worldview of a 'peasant'—one who lives close to the earth and the old ways—really is.

1881–1882:   Felix Koguzki, the herb gatherer, reveals himself to be the envoy of another, higher initiatory personality, who instructs Rudolf Steiner to penetrate Fichte's philosophy and to master modern scientific thinking as a preparation for right entry into the spirit. This 'Master' also teaches him the double (evolutionary and involutionary) nature of time.

1882: Through the offices of Karl Julius Schröer, Rudolf Steiner is asked by Joseph Kürschner to edit Goethe's scientific works for the *Deutsche National-Literatur* edition. He writes 'A Possible Critique of Atomistic Concepts' and sends it to Friedrich Theodor Vischer.

1883: Rudolf Steiner completes his college studies and begins work on the Goethe project.

1884: First volume of Goethe's *Scientific Writings* (CW 1) appears (March). He lectures on Goethe and Lessing, and Goethe's approach to science. In July, he enters the household of Ladislaus and Pauline Specht as tutor to the four Specht boys. He will live there until 1890. At this time, he meets Josef Breuer (1842–1925), the co-author with Sigmund Freud of *Studies in Hysteria,* who is the Specht family doctor.

1885: While continuing to edit Goethe's writings, Rudolf Steiner reads deeply in contemporary philosophy (Eduard von Hartmann, Johannes Volkelt, and Richard Wahle, among others).

1886: May: Rudolf Steiner sends Kürschner the manuscript of *Outlines of Goethe's Theory of Knowledge* (CW 2), which appears in October, and which he sends out widely. He also meets the poet Marie Eugenie Delle Grazie and writes 'Nature and Our Ideals' for her. He attends her salon, where he meets many priests, theologians, and philosophers, who will become his friends. Meanwhile, the director of the Goethe Archive in Weimar requests his collaboration with the *Sophien* edition of Goethe's works, particularly the writings on colour.

1887: At the beginning of the year, Rudolf Steiner is very sick. As the year progresses and his health improves, he becomes increasingly 'a man of letters', lecturing, writing essays, and taking part in Austrian cultural life. In August–September, the second volume of Goethe's *Scientific Writings* appears.

1888: January–July: Rudolf Steiner assumes editorship of the 'German Weekly' *(Deutsche Wochenschrift)*. He begins lecturing more intensively, giving, for example, a lecture titled 'Goethe as Father of a New Aesthetics'. He meets and becomes soul friends with Friedrich Eckstein (1861–1939), a vegetarian, philosopher of symbolism, alchemist, and musician, who will introduce him to various spiritual currents (including Theosophy) and with whom he will meditate and interpret esoteric and alchemical texts.

1889: Rudolf Steiner first reads Nietzsche *(Beyond Good and Evil)*. He encounters Theosophy again and learns of Madame Blavatsky in the theosophical circle around Marie Lang (1858–1934). Here he also meets well-known figures of Austrian life, as well as esoteric figures like the occultist Franz Hartmann and Karl Leinigen-Billigen (translator of C.G. Harrison's *The Transcendental Universe*). During this period, Steiner first reads A.P. Sinnett's *Esoteric Buddhism* and Mabel Collins's *Light on the Path*. He also begins travelling, visiting Budapest, Weimar, and Berlin (where he meets philosopher Eduard von Hartmann).

1890: Rudolf Steiner finishes Volume 3 of Goethe's scientific writings. He begins his doctoral dissertation, which will become *Truth and Science* (CW 3). He also meets the poet and feminist Rosa Mayreder (1858–1938), with whom he can exchange his most intimate thoughts. In September, Rudolf Steiner moves to Weimar to work in the Goethe-Schiller Archive.

1891: Volume 3 of the Kürschner edition of Goethe appears. Meanwhile, Rudolf Steiner edits Goethe's studies in mineralogy and scientific writings for the *Sophien* edition. He meets Ludwig Laistner of the Cotta Publishing Company, who asks for a book on the basic question of metaphysics. From this will result, ultimately, *The Philosophy of Freedom* (CW 4), which will be published not by Cotta but by Emil Felber. In October, Rudolf Steiner takes the oral exam for a doctorate in philosophy, mathematics, and mechanics at Rostock University, receiving his doctorate on the twenty-sixth. In November, he gives his first lecture on Goethe's 'Fairy Tale' in Vienna.

1892: Rudolf Steiner continues work at the Goethe-Schiller Archive and on his *Philosophy of Freedom*. *Truth and Science,* his doctoral dissertation, is published. Steiner undertakes to write Introductions to books on Schopenhauer and Jean Paul for Cotta. At year's end, he finds lodging with Anna Eunike, née Schulz (1853–1911), a widow with four daughters and a son. He also develops a friendship with Otto Erich Hartleben (1864–1905) with whom he shares literary interests.

1893: Rudolf Steiner begins his habit of producing many reviews and articles. In March, he gives a lecture titled 'Hypnotism, with Reference to Spiritism'. In September, volume 4 of the Kürschner edition is completed. In November, *The Philosophy of Freedom* appears. This year, too, he meets John Henry Mackay (1864–1933), the anarchist, and Max Stirner, a scholar and biographer.

1894: Rudolf Steiner meets Elisabeth Fürster Nietzsche, the philosopher's sister, and begins to read Nietzsche in earnest, beginning with the as yet unpublished *Antichrist*. He also meets Ernst Haeckel (1834–1919). In the fall, he begins to write *Nietzsche, A Fighter against His Time* (CW 5).

1895: May, *Nietzsche, A Fighter against His Time* appears.

1896: January 22: Rudolf Steiner sees Friedrich Nietzsche for the first and only time. Moves between the Nietzsche and the Goethe-Schiller

Archives, where he completes his work before year's end. He falls out with Elisabeth Förster Nietzsche, thus ending his association with the Nietzsche Archive.

1897: Rudolf Steiner finishes the manuscript of *Goethe's Worldview* (CW 6). He moves to Berlin with Anna Eunike and begins editorship of the *Magazin für Literatur*. From now on, Steiner will write countless reviews, literary and philosophical articles, and so on. He begins lecturing at the 'Free Literary Society'. In September, he attends the Zionist Congress in Basel. He sides with Dreyfus in the Dreyfus affair.

1898: Rudolf Steiner is very active as an editor in the political, artistic, and theatrical life of Berlin. He becomes friendly with John Henry Mackay and poet Ludwig Jacobowski (1868–1900). He joins Jacobowski's circle of writers, artists, and scientists—'The Coming Ones' (*Die Kommenden*)—and contributes lectures to the group until 1903. He also lectures at the 'League for College Pedagogy'. He writes an article for Goethe's sesquicentennial, 'Goethe's Secret Revelation', on the 'Fairy Tale of the Green Snake and the Beautiful Lily'.

1898–99: 'This was a trying time for my soul as I looked at Christianity. . . . I was able to progress only by contemplating, by means of spiritual perception, the evolution of Christianity. . . . Conscious knowledge of real Christianity began to dawn in me around the turn of the century. This seed continued to develop. My soul trial occurred shortly before the beginning of the twentieth century. It was decisive for my soul's development that I stood spiritually before the Mystery of Golgotha in a deep and solemn celebration of knowledge.'

1899: Rudolf Steiner begins teaching and giving lectures and lecture cycles at the Workers' College, founded by Wilhelm Liebknecht (1826–1900). He will continue to do so until 1904. Writes: *Literature and Spiritual Life in the Nineteenth Century; Individualism in Philosophy; Haeckel and His Opponents; Poetry in the Present;* and begins what will become (fifteen years later) *The Riddles of Philosophy* (CW 18). He also meets many artists and writers, including Käthe Kollwitz, Stefan Zweig, and Rainer Maria Rilke. On October 31, he marries Anna Eunike.

1900: 'I thought that the turn of the century must bring humanity a new light. It seemed to me that the separation of human thinking and willing from the spirit had peaked. A turn or reversal of direction in human evolution seemed to me a necessity.' Rudolf Steiner finishes *World and Life Views in the Nineteenth Century* (the second part of what will become *The Riddles of Philosophy*) and dedicates it to

Ernst Haeckel. It is published in March. He continues lecturing at *Die Kommenden,* whose leadership he assumes after the death of Jacobowski. Also, he gives the Gutenberg Jubilee lecture before 7,000 typesetters and printers. In September, Rudolf Steiner is invited by Count and Countess Brockdorff to lecture in the Theosophical Library. His first lecture is on Nietzsche. His second lecture is titled 'Goethe's Secret Revelation.' October 6, he begins a lecture cycle on the mystics that will become *Mystics after Modernism* (CW 7). November–December: 'Marie von Sivers appears in the audience. . . .' Also in November, Steiner gives his first lecture at the Giordano Bruno Bund (where he will continue to lecture until May, 1905). He speaks on Bruno and modern Rome, focusing on the importance of the philosophy of Thomas Aquinas as monism.

1901: In continual financial straits, Rudolf Steiner's early friends Moritz Zitter and Rosa Mayreder help support him. In October, he begins the lecture cycle *Christianity as Mystical Fact* (CW 8) at the Theosophical Library. In November, he gives his first 'theosophical lecture' on Goethe's 'Fairy Tale' in Hamburg at the invitation of Wilhelm Hubbe-Schleiden. He also attends a gathering to celebrate the founding of the Theosophical Society at Count and Countess Brockdorff's. He gives a lecture cycle, 'From Buddha to Christ,' for the circle of the *Kommenden.* November 17, Marie von Sivers asks Rudolf Steiner if Theosophy needs a Western–Christian spiritual movement (to complement Theosophy's Eastern emphasis). 'The question was posed. Now, following spiritual laws, I could begin to give an answer. . . .' In December, Rudolf Steiner writes his first article for a theosophical publication. At year's end, the Brockdorffs and possibly Wilhelm Hubbe-Schleiden ask Rudolf Steiner to join the Theosophical Society and undertake the leadership of the German section. Rudolf Steiner agrees, on the condition that Marie von Sivers (then in Italy) work with him.

1902: Beginning in January, Rudolf Steiner attends the opening of the Workers' School in Spandau with Rosa Luxemberg (1870–1919). January 17, Rudolf Steiner joins the Theosophical Society. In April, he is asked to become general secretary of the German Section of the Theosophical Society, and works on preparations for its founding. In July, he visits London for a theosophical congress. He meets Bertram Keightly, G.R.S. Mead, A.P. Sinnett, and Annie Besant, among others. In September, *Christianity as Mystical Fact* appears. In October, Rudolf Steiner gives his first public lecture on Theosophy ('Monism and Theosophy') to about three hundred people at the Giordano Bruno Bund. On October 19–21, the

German Section of the Theosophical Society has its first meeting; Rudolf Steiner is the general secretary, and Annie Besant attends. Steiner lectures on practical karma studies. On October 23, Annie Besant inducts Rudolf Steiner into the Esoteric School of the Theosophical Society. On October 25, Steiner begins a weekly series of lectures: 'The Field of Theosophy'. During this year, Rudolf Steiner also first meets Ita Wegman (1876–1943), who will become his close collaborator in his final years.

1903:   Rudolf Steiner holds about 300 lectures and seminars. In May, the first issue of the periodical *Luzifer* appears. In June, Rudolf Steiner visits London for the first meeting of the Federation of the European Sections of the Theosophical Society, where he meets Colonel Olcott. He begins to write *Theosophy* (CW 9).

1904:   Rudolf Steiner continues lecturing at the Workers' College and elsewhere (about 90 lectures), while lecturing intensively all over Germany among theosophists (about 140 lectures). In February, he meets Carl Unger (1878–1929), who will become a member of the board of the Anthroposophical Society (1913). In March, he meets Michael Bauer (1871–1929), a Christian mystic, who will also be on the board. In May, *Theosophy* appears, with the dedication: 'To the spirit of Giordano Bruno'. Rudolf Steiner and Marie von Sivers visit London for meetings with Annie Besant. June: Rudolf Steiner and Marie von Sivers attend the meeting of the Federation of European Sections of the Theosophical Society in Amsterdam. In July, Steiner begins the articles in *Luzifer-Gnosis* that will become *How to Know Higher Worlds* (CW 10) and *Cosmic Memory* (CW 11). In September, Annie Besant visits Germany. In December, Steiner lectures on Freemasonry. He mentions the High Grade Masonry derived from John Yarker and represented by Theodore Reuss and Karl Kellner as a blank slate 'into which a good image could be placed'.

1905:   This year, Steiner ends his non-theosophical lecturing activity. Supported by Marie von Sivers, his theosophical lecturing—both in public and in the Theosophical Society—increases significantly: 'The German Theosophical Movement is of exceptional importance.' Steiner recommends reading, among others, Fichte, Jacob Boehme, and Angelus Silesius. He begins to introduce Christian themes into Theosophy. He also begins to work with doctors (Felix Peipers and Ludwig Noll). In July, he is in London for the Federation of European Sections, where he attends a lecture by Annie Besant: 'I have seldom seen Mrs Besant speak in so inward and heartfelt a manner... Through Mrs Besant I have found the way to H.P. Blavatsky.' September to October, he gives a course of 31 lectures for a small group of esoteric students. In October, the annual meeting of the German Section of the Theosophical Society, which still remains very small, takes place. Rudolf Steiner reports membership has risen from 121 to 377 members. In November, seeking to establish esoteric 'continuity', Rudolf Steiner and Marie von Sivers participate in a 'Memphis-Misraim' Masonic ceremony. They pay 45 marks for membership. 'Yesterday, you saw how little remains of former esoteric institutions.' 'We are dealing only with a "framework" … for the present, nothing lies behind it. The occult powers have completely withdrawn.'

1906:   Expansion of theosophical work. Rudolf Steiner gives about 245 lectures, only 44 of which take place in Berlin. Cycles are given in Paris, Leipzig, Stuttgart, and Munich. Esoteric work also intensifies. Rudolf Steiner begins writing *An Outline of Esoteric Science* (CW 13). In January, Rudolf Steiner receives permission (a patent) from the Great Orient of the Scottish A & A Thirty-Three Degree Rite of the Order of the Ancient Freemasons of the Memphis-Misraim Rite to direct a chapter under the name 'Mystica Aeterna.' This will become the 'Cognitive-Ritual Section' (also called 'Misraim Service') of the Esoteric School. (See: *Freemasonry and Ritual Work: The Misraim Service,* CW 265.) During this time, Steiner also meets Albert Schweitzer. In May, he is in Paris, where he visits Édouard Schuré. Many Russians attend his lectures (including Konstantin Balmont, Dimitri Mereszkovski, Zinaida Hippius, and Maximilian Woloshin). He attends the General Meeting of the European Federation of the Theosophical Society, at which Col Olcott is present for the last time. He spends the year's end in Venice and Rome, where he writes and works on his translation of H.P. Blavatsky's *Key to Theosophy.*

1907:   Further expansion of the German Theosophical Movement according to the Rosicrucian directive to 'introduce spirit into the world'—in education, in social questions, in art, and in science. In February, Col Olcott dies in Adyar. Before he dies, Olcott indicates that 'the Masters' wish Annie Besant to succeed him: much politicking ensues. Rudolf Steiner supports Besant's candidacy. April–May: preparations for the Congress of the Federation of European Sections of the Theosophical Society—the great, watershed Whitsun 'Munich Congress,' attended by Annie Besant and others. Steiner decides to separate Eastern and Western (Christian–Rosicrucian) esoteric schools. He takes his esoteric school out of the Theosophical Society (Besant and Rudolf Steiner are 'in harmony' on this). Steiner makes his first lecture tours to Austria and

Hungary. That summer, he is in Italy. In September, he visits Édouard Schuré, who will write the Introduction to the French edition of *Christianity as Mystical Fact* in Barr, Alsace. Rudolf Steiner writes the autobiographical statement known as the 'Barr Document.' In *Luzifer-Gnosis*, 'The Education of the Child' appears.

1908: The movement grows (membership: 1,150). Lecturing expands. Steiner makes his first extended lecture tour to Holland and Scandinavia, as well as visits to Naples and Sicily. Themes: St John's Gospel, the Apocalypse, Egypt, science, philosophy, and logic. *Luzifer-Gnosis* ceases publication. In Berlin, Marie von Sivers (with Johanna Mücke (1864–1949) forms the *Philosophisch-Theosophisch* (after 1915 *Philosophisch-Anthroposophisch) Verlag* to publish Steiner's work. Steiner gives lecture cycles titled *The Gospel of St John* (CW 103) and *The Apocalypse* (104).

1909: *An Outline of Esoteric Science* appears. Lecturing and travel continues. Rudolf Steiner's spiritual research expands to include the polarity of Lucifer and Ahriman; the work of great individualities in history; the Maitreya Buddha and the Bodhisattvas; spiritual economy (CW 109); the work of the spiritual hierarchies in heaven and on earth (CW 110). He also deepens and intensifies his research into the Gospels, giving lectures on the Gospel of St Luke (CW 114) with the first mention of two Jesus children. Meets and becomes friends with Christian Morgenstern (1871–1914). In April, he lays the foundation stone for the Malsch model—the building that will lead to the first Goetheanum. In May, the International Congress of the Federation of European Sections of the Theosophical Society takes place in Budapest. Rudolf Steiner receives the Subba Row medal for *How to Know Higher Worlds*. During this time, Charles W. Leadbeater discovers Jiddu Krishnamurti (1895–1986) and proclaims him the future 'world teacher,' the bearer of the Maitreya Buddha and the 'reappearing Christ.' In October, Steiner delivers seminal lectures on 'anthroposophy,' which he will try, unsuccessfully, to rework over the next years into the unfinished work, *Anthroposophy (A Fragment)* (CW 45).

1910: New themes: *The Reappearance of Christ in the Etheric* (CW 118); *The Fifth Gospel; The Mission of Folk Souls* (CW 121); *Occult History* (CW 126); the evolving development of etheric cognitive capacities. Rudolf Steiner continues his Gospel research with *The Gospel of St Matthew* (CW 123). In January, his father dies. In April, he takes a month-long trip to Italy, including Rome, Monte Cassino, and Sicily. He also visits Scandinavia again. July–August, he writes the first Mystery Drama, *The Portal of Initiation* (CW 14). In November, he gives 'psychosophy' lectures. In December, he submits 'On the

	Psychological Foundations and Epistemological Framework of Theosophy' to the International Philosophical Congress in Bologna.
1911:	The crisis in the Theosophical Society deepens. In January, 'The Order of the Rising Sun,' which will soon become 'The Order of the Star in the East,' is founded for the coming world teacher, Krishnamurti. At the same time, Marie von Sivers, Rudolf Steiner's co-worker, falls ill. Fewer lectures are given, but important new ground is broken. In Prague, in March, Steiner meets Franz Kafka (1883–1924) and Hugo Bergmann (1883–1975). In April, he delivers his paper to the Philosophical Congress. He writes the second Mystery Drama, *The Soul's Probation* (CW 14). Also, while Marie von Sivers is convalescing, Rudolf Steiner begins work on *Calendar 1912/1913*, which will contain the 'Calendar of the Soul' meditations. On March 19, Anna (Eunike) Steiner dies. In September, Rudolf Steiner visits Einsiedeln, birthplace of Paracelsus. In December, Friedrich Rittelmeyer, future founder of The Christian Community, meets Rudolf Steiner. The *Johannes-Bauverein,* the 'building committee,' which would lead to the first Goetheanum (first planned for Munich), is also founded, and a preliminary committee for the founding of an independent association is created that, in the following year, will become the Anthroposophical Society. Important lecture cycles include *Occult Physiology* (CW 128); *Wonders of the World* (CW 129); *From Jesus to Christ* (CW 131). Other themes: esoteric Christianity; Christian Rosenkreutz; the spiritual guidance of humanity; the sense world and the world of the spirit.
1912:	Despite the ongoing, now increasing crisis in the Theosophical Society, much is accomplished: *Calendar 1912/1913* is published; eurythmy is created; both the third Mystery Drama, *The Guardian of the Threshold* (CW 14) and *A Way of Self-Knowledge* (CW 16) are written. New (or renewed) themes included life between death and rebirth and karma and reincarnation. Other lecture cycles: *Spiritual Beings in the Heavenly Bodies and in the Kingdoms of Nature* (CW 136); *The Human Being in the Light of Occultism, Theosophy, and Philosophy* (CW 137); *The Gospel of St Mark* (CW 139); and *The Bhagavad Gita and the Epistles of Paul* (CW 142). On May 8, Rudolf Steiner celebrates White Lotus Day, H.P. Blavatsky's death day, which he had faithfully observed for the past decade, for the last time. In August, Rudolf Steiner suggests the 'independent association' be called the 'Anthroposophical Society.' In September, the first eurythmy course takes place. In October, Rudolf Steiner declines recognition of a Theosophical Society lodge dedicated to the Star of the East and decides to expel all Theosophical Society members belonging to the order.

Also, with Marie von Sivers, he first visits Dornach, near Basel, Switzerland, and they stand on the hill where the Goetheanum will be built. In November, a Theosophical Society lodge is opened by direct mandate from Adyar (Annie Besant). In December, a meeting of the German section occurs at which it is decided that belonging to the Order of the Star of the East is incompatible with membership in the Theosophical Society. December 28: informal founding of the Anthroposophical Society in Berlin.

1913:   Expulsion of the German section from the Theosophical Society. February 2–3: Foundation meeting of the Anthroposophical Society. Board members include: Marie von Sivers, Michael Bauer, and Carl Unger. September 20: Laying of the foundation stone for the *Johannes Bau* (Goetheanum) in Dornach. Building begins immediately. The fourth Mystery Drama, *The Soul's Awakening* (CW 14), is completed. Also: *The Threshold of the Spiritual World* (CW 147). Lecture cycles include: *The Bhagavad Gita and the Epistles of Paul* and *The Esoteric Meaning of the Bhagavad Gita* (CW 146), which the Russian philosopher Nikolai Berdyaev attends; *The Mysteries of the East and of Christianity* (CW 144); *The Effects of Esoteric Development* (CW 145); and *The Fifth Gospel* (CW 148). In May, Rudolf Steiner is in London and Paris, where anthroposophical work continues.

1914:   Building continues on the *Johannes Bau* (Goetheanum) in Dornach, with artists and co-workers from seventeen nations. The general assembly of the Anthroposophical Society takes place. In May, Rudolf Steiner visits Paris, as well as Chartres Cathedral. June 28: assassination in Sarajevo ('Now the catastrophe has happened!'). August 1: War is declared. Rudolf Steiner returns to Germany from Dornach—he will travel back and forth. He writes the last chapter of *The Riddles of Philosophy*. Lecture cycles include: *Human and Cosmic Thought* (CW 151); *Inner Being of Humanity between Death and a New Birth* (CW 153); *Occult Reading and Occult Hearing* (CW 156). December 24: marriage of Rudolf Steiner and Marie von Sivers.

1915:   Building continues. Life after death becomes a major theme, also art. Writes: *Thoughts during a Time of War* (CW 24). Lectures include: *The Secret of Death* (CW 159); *The Uniting of Humanity through the Christ Impulse* (CW 165).

1916:   Rudolf Steiner begins work with Edith Maryon (1872–1924) on the sculpture 'The Representative of Humanity' ('The Group'—Christ, Lucifer, and Ahriman). He also works with the alchemist Alexander von Bernus on the quarterly *Das Reich*. He writes *The Riddle of Humanity* (CW 20). Lectures include: *Necessity and Freedom in World History and Human Action* (CW 166); *Past and Present in the*

Human Spirit (CW 167); *The Karma of Vocation* (CW 172); *The Karma of Untruthfulness* (CW 173).

1917:   Russian Revolution. The U.S. enters the war. Building continues. Rudolf Steiner delineates the idea of the 'threefold nature of the human being' (in a public lecture March 15) and the 'threefold nature of the social organism' (hammered out in May–June with the help of Otto von Lerchenfeld and Ludwig Polzer-Hoditz in the form of two documents titled *Memoranda,* which were distributed in high places). August–September: Rudolf Steiner writes *The Riddles of the Soul* (CW 20). Also: commentary on 'The Chymical Wedding of Christian Rosenkreutz' for Alexander Bernus (Das *Reich*). Lectures include: *The Karma of Materialism* (CW 176); *The Spiritual Background of the Outer World: The Fall of the Spirits of Darkness* (CW 177).

1918:   March 18: peace treaty of Brest-Litovsk—'Now everything will truly enter chaos! What is needed is cultural renewal.' June: Rudolf Steiner visits Karlstein (Grail) Castle outside Prague. Lecture cycle: *From Symptom to Reality in Modern History* (CW 185). In mid-November, Emil Molt, of the Waldorf-Astoria Cigarette Company, has the idea of founding a school for his workers' children.

1919:   Focus on the threefold social organism: tireless travel, countless lectures, meetings, and publications. At the same time, a new public stage of Anthroposophy emerges as cultural renewal begins. The coming years will see initiatives in pedagogy, medicine, pharmacology, and agriculture. January 27: threefold meeting: 'We must first of all, with the money we have, found free schools that can bring people what they need.' February: first public eurythmy performance in Zurich. Also: 'Appeal to the German People' (CW 24), circulated March 6 as a newspaper insert. In April, *Towards Social Renewal* (CW 23) appears—'perhaps the most widely read of all books on politics appearing since the war'. Rudolf Steiner is asked to undertake the 'direction and leadership' of the school founded by the Waldorf-Astoria Company. Rudolf Steiner begins to talk about the 'renewal' of education. May 30: a building is selected and purchased for the future Waldorf School. August–September, Rudolf Steiner gives a lecture course for Waldorf teachers, *The Foundations of Human Experience (Study of Man)* (CW 293). September 7: Opening of the first Waldorf School. December (into January): first science course, the *Light Course* (CW 320).

1920:   The Waldorf School flourishes. New threefold initiatives. Founding of limited companies *Der Kommende Tag* and *Futurum A.G.* to infuse spiritual values into the economic realm. Rudolf Steiner also focuses on the sciences. Lectures: *Introducing Anthroposophical*

Medicine (CW 312); *The Warmth Course* (CW 321); *The Boundaries of Natural Science* (CW 322); *The Redemption of Thinking* (CW 74). February: Johannes Werner Klein—later a co-founder of The Christian Community—asks Rudolf Steiner about the possibility of a 'religious renewal,' a 'Johannine church.' In March, Rudolf Steiner gives the first course for doctors and medical students. In April, a divinity student asks Rudolf Steiner a second time about the possibility of religious renewal. September 27–October 16: anthroposophical 'university course.' December: lectures titled *The Search for the New Isis* (CW 202).

1921:   Rudolf Steiner continues his intensive work on cultural renewal, including the uphill battle for the threefold social order. 'University' arts, scientific, theological, and medical courses include: *The Astronomy Course* (CW 323); *Observation, Mathematics, and Scientific Experiment* (CW 324); the *Second Medical Course* (CW 313); *Colour*. In June and September–October, Rudolf Steiner also gives the first two 'priests' courses' (CW 342 and 343). The 'youth movement' gains momentum. Magazines are founded: *Die Drei* (January), and—under the editorship of Albert Steffen (1884–1963)—the weekly, *Das Goetheanum* (August). In February–March, Rudolf Steiner takes his first trip outside Germany since the war (Holland). On April 7, Steiner receives a letter regarding 'religious renewal,' and May 22–23, he agrees to address the question in a practical way. In June, the Klinical-Therapeutic Institute opens in Arlesheim under the direction of Dr Ita Wegman. In August, the Chemical-Pharmaceutical Laboratory opens in Arlesheim (Oskar Schmiedel and Ita Wegman are directors). The Clinical Therapeutic Institute is inaugurated in Stuttgart (Dr Ludwig Noll is director); also the Research Laboratory in Dornach (Ehrenfried Pfeiffer and Gunther Wachsmuth are directors). In November–December, Rudolf Steiner visits Norway.

1922:   The first half of the year involves very active public lecturing (thousands attend); in the second half, Rudolf Steiner begins to withdraw and turn toward the Society—'The Society is asleep.' It is 'too weak' to do what is asked of it. The businesses—*Der Kommende Tag* and *Futurum A.G.*—fail. In January, with the help of an agent, Steiner undertakes a twelve-city German lecture tour, accompanied by eurythmy performances. In two weeks he speaks to more than 2,000 people. In April, he gives a 'university course' in The Hague. He also visits England. In June, he is in Vienna for the East–West Congress. In August–September, he is back in England for the Oxford Conference on Education. Returning to Dornach, he gives the lectures *Philosophy, Cosmology, and*

Religion (CW 215), and gives the third priests' course (CW 344). On September 16, The Christian Community is founded. In October–November, Steiner is in Holland and England. He also speaks to the youth: *The Youth Course* (CW 217). In December, Steiner gives lectures titled *The Origins of Natural Science* (CW 326), and *Humanity and the World of Stars: The Spiritual Communion of Humanity* (CW 219). December 31: Fire at the Goetheanum, which is destroyed.

1923: Despite the fire, Rudolf Steiner continues his work unabated. A very hard year. Internal dispersion, dissension, and apathy abound. There is conflict—between old and new visions—within the Society. A wake-up call is needed, and Rudolf Steiner responds with renewed lecturing vitality. His focus: the spiritual context of human life; initiation science; the course of the year; and community building. As a foundation for an artistic school, he creates a series of pastel sketches. Lecture cycles: *The Anthroposophical Movement; Initiation Science* (CW 227) (in Wales at the Penmaenmawr Summer School); *The Four Seasons and the Archangels* (CW 229); *Harmony of the Creative Word* (CW 230); *The Supersensible Human* (CW 231), given in Holland for the founding of the Dutch Society. On November 10, in response to the failed Hitler-Ludendorff putsch in Munich, Steiner closes his Berlin residence and moves the *Philosophisch-Anthroposophisch Verlag* (Press) to Dornach. On December 9, Steiner begins the serialization of his *Autobiography: The Course of My Life* (CW 28) in *Das Goetheanum*. It will continue to appear weekly, without a break, until his death. Late December–early January: Rudolf Steiner re-founds the Anthroposophical Society (about 12,000 members internationally) and takes over its leadership. The new board members are: Marie Steiner, Ita Wegman, Albert Steffen, Elisabeth Vreede, and Gunther Wachsmuth. (See *The Christmas Meeting for the Founding of the General Anthroposophical Society*, CW 260.) Accompanying lectures: *Mystery Knowledge and Mystery Centres* (CW 232); *World History in the Light of Anthroposophy* (CW 233). December 25: the Foundation Stone is laid (in the hearts of members) in the form of the 'Foundation Stone Meditation.'

1924: January 1: having founded the Anthroposophical Society and taken over its leadership, Rudolf Steiner has the task of 'reforming' it. The process begins with a weekly newssheet ('What's Happening in the Anthroposophical Society') in which Rudolf Steiner's 'Letters to Members' and 'Anthroposophical Leading Thoughts' appear (CW 26). The next step is the creation of a new esoteric class, the 'first class' of the 'University of Spiritual Science' (which was to have been followed, had Rudolf Steiner lived longer, by two more advanced classes). Then comes a new language for

Anthroposophy—practical, phenomenological, and direct; and Rudolf Steiner creates the model for the second Goetheanum. He begins the series of extensive 'karma' lectures (CW 235–40); and finally, responding to needs, he creates two new initiatives: biodynamic agriculture and curative education. After the middle of the year, rumours begin to circulate regarding Steiner's health. Lectures: January–February, *Anthroposophy* (CW 234); February: *Tone Eurythmy* (CW 278); June: *The Agriculture Course* (CW 327); June–July: *Speech Eurythmy* (CW 279); *Curative Education* (CW 317); August: (England, 'Second International Summer School'), *Initiation Consciousness: True and False Paths in Spiritual Investigation* (CW 243); September: *Pastoral Medicine* (CW 318). On September 26, for the first time, Rudolf Steiner cancels a lecture. On September 28, he gives his last lecture. On September 29, he withdraws to his studio in the carpenter's shop; now he is definitively ill. Cared for by Ita Wegman, he continues working, however, and writing the weekly instalments of his *Autobiography* and *Letters to the Members/Leading Thoughts* (CW 26).

1925:   Rudolf Steiner, while continuing to work, continues to weaken. He finishes *Extending Practical Medicine* (CW 27) with Ita Wegman. On March 30, around ten in the morning, Rudolf Steiner dies.

Steiner

A NOTE FROM RUDOLF STEINER PRESS

We are an independent publisher and registered charity (non-profit organisation) dedicated to making available the work of Rudolf Steiner in English translation. We care a great deal about the content of our books and have hundreds of titles available – as printed books, ebooks and in audio formats.

As a publisher devoted to anthroposophy…

- We continually commission translations of previously unpublished works by Rudolf Steiner and invest in re-translating, editing and improving our editions.

- We are committed to making anthroposophy available to all by publishing introductory books as well as contemporary research.

- Our new print editions and ebooks are carefully checked and proofread for accuracy, and converted into all formats for all platforms.

- Our translations are officially authorised by Rudolf Steiner's estate in Dornach, Switzerland, to whom we pay royalties on sales, thus assisting their critical work.

So, look out for Rudolf Steiner Press as a mark of quality and support us today by buying our books, or contact us should you wish to sponsor specific titles or to support the charity with a gift or legacy.

office@rudolfsteinerpress.com
Join our e-mailing list at www.rudolfsteinerpress.com

RUDOLF STEINER PRESS